Deposit Required: $14.95

Civil
Service
Exams

Civil
Service
Exams

NEW YORK

Library of Congress Cataloging-in-Publication Data:
Civil service exams.
      p. cm.
  ISBN: 978-1-57685-592-8
  1. Civil service—United States—Examinations. 2. Civil service—United States.
I. LearningExpress (Organization)
  JK716.C466 2007
  352.6'5—dc22

                                  2007008904

Printed in the United States of America

9 8 7 6 5 4 3 2 1

ISBN: 978-1-57685-592-8

The images on pages 199, 233, and 235 are © Corbis.

For information on LearningExpress, other LearningExpress products, or bulk sales,
please write to us at:

  LearningExpress
  55 Broadway
  8th Floor
  New York, NY 10006

Or visit us at:
  www.learnatest.com

Contents

Civil Service Exams

The Three Levels of Civil Service

1 ▶ Civil Service

▶ What Is Civil Service?

The term *civil service* refers to any job in the service of government, with the exception of uniformed military positions. Civil servants teach in public schools, staff libraries, maintain public buildings, collect taxes, enforce laws, fight fires, and perform thousands and thousands of other essential functions.

Today, most civil service jobs are filled competitively, either through a combined process of examination and job application or through a systematic vetting system in which each candidate's qualifications are weighted in order to evaluate (and, in many cases, assign a numerical score to) his or her suitability to the job. This wasn't always the case, however. In the early days of our nation, civil service jobs were regarded as prizes to be awarded to political supporters. Civil service employment ran under a *spoils system*, so called to reflect the old axiom "to the victor belong the spoils." As you might expect, civil service was not especially efficient during this period. For one thing, even the most capable appointees rarely stayed at their jobs long enough to master them. Each election cycle brought with it an army of new, and inexperienced, political appointees. Others were simply incompetent. Fortunately, the government was relatively small, so the fact that it was being run by the president's political pals rather than the most qualified candidates did not do too much damage to the nation.

All that changed in 1883, with the passage of the Pendleton Civil Service Act. Political activists had begun campaigning for reform in the 1870s, arguing that the rapid growth of government during the period mandated the creation of a professional civil service. The problems with the situation were greatly magnified by the 1881 assassination of newly elected president John Garfield by Charles Guiteau, a Garfield supporter angered by the new administration's failure to reward him with a comfortable government job. Support for reform grew, and in 1883, the Pendleton Act passed, reclassifying many patronage positions as competitive civil service jobs. Thereafter, applicants were required to take exams and otherwise prove their worthiness to assume government positions. Many jobs were no longer contingent upon who was in power; the office-holder remained a civil servant regardless of whether Democrats or Republicans held the White House. A Civil Service Commission was established to oversee the system and ensure its fairness.

► The Private Sector versus the Public Sector

Civil service jobs are **public sector** jobs; they are funded publicly through tax revenues and other sources of government income (e.g., lotteries, license fees, bonds). Public sector employers work from a budget provided by the government, which they must meet; because public sector concerns may not turn a profit, they cannot simply increase prices and fees to generate more revenue. Civil service jobs are typically organized hierarchically by grade. The pay for a civil service job at a particular grade is determined by a matrix that takes into account the officeholder's position, years of service, and other relevant details. Many aspects of the job—including job description, work hours, pay, and benefits—are fixed by law. A civil servant's employer is the government for which he or she works (federal, state, or local) or a publicly owned corporation (e.g., the Corporation for Public Broadcasting).

The **private sector** employs many more workers than does the public sector (although the federal government is the single largest employer in the United States). The private sector is competitive; Wal-Mart, for example, competes with Target and other discount retailers. In this way, the private sector differs from the public sector; you will not find two competing government agencies trying to provide you with the same service. You will, however, find many of the same jobs in the public sector that you find in the private sector. Again, though, there is a difference. In the private sector, wages and salaries, benefits, hours, and other aspects of the job are typically open to negotiation; they are not fixed by law (if you belong to a union, however, some or all of these may be fixed by your union contract). The private sector includes privately and publicly owned companies, nonpublic universities and hospitals, nonprofit and nongovernmental organizations, and anything else not operated by the government.

► The Three Levels of Civil Service

Americans talk about the government as if it were one unified entity, but, in fact, Americans live under several sometimes overlapping, sometimes independent governments. First, there's the national, or federal, government in Washington, D.C.; its chief executive is the president of the United States. It provides for the nation's defense, regulates interstate commerce, polices interstate crimes, polices our coastlines, manages Social Security, Medicaid, and Medicare, and performs a host of other duties. Second is the state's government; its chief executive is the governor. State governments police and prosecute crimes, maintain roads (sometimes with financial assistance from the federal government), develop educational standards for public schools, operate state lotteries, administer various licenses (e.g., driver's licenses, hunting and fishing licenses, etc.), and perform many other jobs. Finally, there is the local government, presided over by a mayor, county executive, or perhaps even a board of commissioners. Local governments also police and prosecute crimes, manage garbage collection, fund and manage public schools, build and maintain sewers and other public works, and perform many other necessary tasks.

In this book, we'll cover the federal system in Chapter 2 and the state and local systems in Chapter 3. Note that because state and local systems vary widely, this book focuses on general principles that apply to most. To learn more specifics about working for your state or local government, visit the appropriate website or drop by a government office and ask for literature on the subject. Contact information for state governments is provided at the end of Chapter 3; nearly all state government websites provide links to local government websites.

▶ Why Get a Job in Civil Service?

There are many compelling reasons to choose a career in the civil service. There are also a few drawbacks; for example, you are unlikely to grow wealthy in civil service. Overall, though, a civil service career is a very good one. Civil servants:

- provide essential services to the public
- enjoy the satisfaction of helping fellow citizens
- earn salaries that range from respectable to comfortable to highly desirable
- typically have opportunities for significant career advancement
- typically receive generous benefits packages
- have fewer worries about being downsized or outsourced than do their counterparts in the private sector
- know that their employer will not go bankrupt, as private employers sometimes do

If you're ready to pursue a career in civil service, read on. This book provides valuable information to guide you through the job search, application, and examination processes.

CHAPTER

2 ▶ Federal Civil Service

Our country operates under a federal system of government defined by the Constitution of the United States of America. Because it is a federal system, some powers and responsibilities belong exclusively to the national government, headquartered in Washington, D.C.; some powers and responsibilities belong to state and local governments; and some powers are shared.

Although this use of the term *federal* refers to the national, state, and local governments (and their complex interrelations), when we talk about federal civil service, we are referring only to civil service jobs for the national government. To make matters more confusing, many of these jobs are not located in Washington, D.C. Postal workers, FBI agents, Social Security administrators, and a wide range of other federal employees do their work in every state of the nation.

This chapter discusses which jobs fall under the category of federal civil service positions. It describes the different categories of federal civil service jobs and tells you how to apply for these positions. We will discuss these subjects as they relate to state and local civil service positions in Chapter 3.

Mine Safety and Health Inspector, U.S. Department of Labor

Mining can be dangerous work, which is why mining companies must adhere to strict safety standards. The Mine Safety and Health Administration (MSHA), a division of the Department of Labor, regularly inspects mines to ensure that each mine meets federal workplace requirements so that each miner can do his or her job in a safe and healthy environment.

The MSHA offers a number of entry-level positions to inspectors of both metal and nonmetal mines. Successful candidates must score well on preemployment math and writing tests, pass drug screening and medical examinations, and submit to a background check. In 2006, starting salaries ranged from $35,000 to $67,000, depending on education and background. Those who stick with the job can eventually rise to the GS-12 level.

Applicants for the position are typically required to attend a screening session, at which they take the aforementioned tests. The tests are graded on site; applicants who earn qualifying scores are required to sit for an interview immediately. Those hired are enrolled in a two-year training program that includes extensive on-the-job training supplemented by nearly five months of formal training at the National Mine Health and Safety Academy in Beckley, West Virginia; those who succeed in the program are typically reclassified as permanent employees.

The responsibilities of a mine inspector include conducting on-site inspections of mines (underground and surface) as well as of mills and quarries. During these inspections, inspectors identify and report potential dangerous and/or unhealthy work conditions; inspect equipment to ensure that it is properly used and well maintained; investigate accidents and instruct mining concerns in accident prevention; participate in rescue and firefighting operations at mines; investigate mines for compliance with all relevant safety and health laws and regulations, and issue citations when violations are detected; and survey miners for complaints about work conditions, following up on such complaints through investigation.

Mine inspection is a potentially rewarding line of work for someone who enjoys working in remote locations. The job requires frequent travel—some inspectors spend up to two weeks per month on the road, although most travel less than that—which could be either a drawback or a benefit, depending on your point of view. Mines, it goes without saying, are not the nicest work environments even under optimal conditions, and this work certainly would not suit someone who desperately craves sunshine or who is susceptible to claustrophobia. Because mines are relatively dangerous places (compared to, say, an office building), the job also entails some inherent risks.

▶ Positive Aspects of Federal Civil Service Jobs

There are many good reasons to work for the U.S. government: Government work offers plenty of opportunities, a good salary and benefits, job security, and more. Federal employment provides:

- **Challenging work.** Civil service positions are important, varied, and necessary to the smooth operation of our government.
- **Pay comparability.** Salaries are based on private sector comparisons. In 2005, the average full-time federal employee earned more than $60,000 per year.
- **Extra pay.** Salaries may be augmented by locality pay and special pay provisions (such as extra pay for law enforcement jobs).
- **Job security.** Federal workers are always in demand, and federal layoffs are rare.
- **Step increases within grade.** Time on the job can lead to step increases that bring higher salaries.
- **Merit promotions.** It is possible to compete for merit increases in salary. Internal promotion allows employees to climb the federal ladder, assuming more responsibility and earning better pay.
- **Health and life insurance.** Insurance costs are shared with the government, which offers a wide range of plans.
- **Retirement.** Workers receive benefits from the Federal Employees Retirement System and Social Security.
- **Holidays and vacation/sick days.** Federal employees receive ten paid holidays every year and accrue between 13 and 26 paid vacation days and 13 paid sick days per year. Family and medical leaves may also be available.
- **Alternative work schedules.** Flexible hours, compressed workweek, telecommuting, part-time work, and job transfers may be options, depending on the job.
- **Appeals and grievances process.** There are outlets for complaint—among them are unions, the Merit Systems Protection Board, the Federal Labor Relations Authority, and the Office of Personnel Management (OPM).
- **Training opportunities.** Government-paid training and tuition reimbursement are available.

If you get a federal job, you'll be in good company: The federal government is the largest single employer in the United States, with just under 2.7 million civilian employees as of January 2006. That figure includes nearly three-quarters of one million postal workers and more than 1.5 million employees of the executive branch (which includes the president's office, the Department of State, the Department of Defense, the Department of Justice, the Department of Education, etc.). You'll find just about every type of job in the federal government that you'd find in the private sector. These jobs range from entry-level custodial and clerical positions all the way up to high-power white-collar jobs.

Every year, hundreds of thousands of positions open up because of employee promotions and retirements. The government frequently grows and creates new positions (as it did when it created a new agency, the Department of Homeland Security, in 2002), but even in times of tight budgets and downsizing, there are always lots of jobs available. The government always needs postal workers to deliver the nation's mail; police officers and firefighters to protect us; and clerks, secretaries, and maintenance personnel to keep the government running. During the last decade, the federal government has typically hired between 200,000 and 300,000 new employees during each non-census year (the number spikes to about one million in census years; the extra hires consist of temporary workers employed to conduct the census).

General Vessel Assistant, National Oceanographic and Atmospheric Administration, Department of Commerce

If you're looking for an opportunity to work on the open sea but aren't quite ready to join the Navy, Coast Guard, or Merchant Marine, the National Oceanographic and Atmospheric Administration (NOAA) may be the place for you. The NOAA operates research ships that conduct survey, sampling, and fishing operations to support its mission of leading in environmental research and preservation.

One of the NOAA's entry-level positions is general vessel assistant (GVA). GVA jobs include ordinary seaman, ordinary fisherman, wiper, and messman. Seamen and fishermen load and unload supplies; they also clean, paint, and maintain fishing gear. Wipers work in the engine room, maintaining the engine by wiping down machines, cleaning oil spills, and assisting in all engine repairs. A messman works under the steward; he or she washes dishes and prepares and cleans the dining area and mess deck. Many GVAs gain valuable experience in scientific research by participating in the operation, handling, and maintenance of scientific equipment on the open seas. All GVAs are employed year-round and work a 40-hour workweek. When docked at their homeport, GVAs help prepare for upcoming voyages or complete the work of recently finished voyages.

A GVA must be a U.S. citizen and must receive clearance via medical and dental exams. A drug test is also mandatory. No written exam is required. GVAs do not need to produce U.S. Coast Guard or Merchant Mariner's documents, as do applicants to more advanced positions on NOAA ships.

At a 2006 starting salary of about $29,000, GVAs won't get rich. However, because they typically spend about 240 days a year at sea, they can often forego rent, a considerable expense. Meals are also covered, and because they are typically at sea, GVAs have relatively few opportunities to spend their pay. Thus, a savvy GVA could actually squirrel away a decent amount of savings. Among other benefits of the job, duty locations include some pretty nice locations, such as Charleston, South Carolina; Honolulu, Hawaii; Norfolk, Virginia; San Diego, California; Seattle, Washington; Woods Hole, Massachusetts; Pascagoula, Mississippi; and various port towns in Alaska. Finally, GVAs accrue experience, through which they may earn promotion to positions with greater responsibility and greater pay. For example, five years' experience qualifies a seaman, angler, or wiper for a job as chief boatswain, a position that paid between $41,000 and $50,000 in 2006.

Opportunities to Work Anywhere

The federal government offers jobs all over the country; you don't have to live in or even near Washington, D.C. to hold a federal civil service job. In fact, fewer than 200,000 of the federal government's workforce work in Washington, D.C. There are actually more civilian federal jobs in California (nearly a quarter-million in 2005) than there are in D.C. There are federal workforces of well more than 100,000 in Florida, Maryland, New York, Pennsylvania, Texas, and Virginia as well. Cities with large federal workforces include Atlanta, Baltimore, Chicago, Denver, Los Angeles/Long Beach, New York City, Philadelphia, San Antonio, and San Diego. But you don't have to live in a big city to find work with the federal government. In many small towns, a large percentage of civilians are federal employees. Look at the blue pages of your local telephone book to see just how many federal employees there are in your area. The federal government also employs nearly 20,000 workers in U.S. territories and another 75,000 in foreign countries.

▶ Minimum Qualifications

All you need for a career with the government is a high school diploma (or GED) and, for most positions, U.S. citizenship. (There are also some part-time positions for high school students; we'll discuss them later.) If you are a male over 18 born after December 31, 1959, you must also have registered with (or be exempt from) the Selective Service. Many kinds of positions are available for people with no education beyond high school and for those with little or no job experience. Beyond the minimum requirements, your education, skills, experience, and location will determine what specific jobs you are eligible for within the federal government.

▶ Types of Employees

Federal employees are classified as **full time**, **part time**, **interns**, and **work-study** employees. Full-time employees fall into four subcategories:

- **Temporary** employees hold positions that last for less than one year. They enjoy no special privileges or benefits, but as temporary employees, they get their foot in the door to government employment. This is a great advantage; temporary workers not only get insider knowledge of job openings, but also, if they do their jobs well, have a terrific advantage over other candidates when it comes time to hire for better jobs.
- **Term** employees work for a specified time, usually in the service of a particular project or study. Term employment can last from one to three years and can, on occasion, extend beyond the three-year limit. Term employees often receive health benefits; they are usually not eligible for pension benefits. Like temporary employees, term hires can find out about job openings early and, if they do their jobs well, have an edge in competing for permanent positions.
- **Career-conditional** employees are typically new federal hires on track to a career position. During their first three years of employment, career-conditional employees serve a probation, during which they are evaluated and after which they become eligible for instatement as full-time permanent employees. This three-year period is critical for those who seek career status. It includes most career benefits, although with various restrictions upon them (disability insurance, for example, is often excluded or limited for career-conditional employees).

■ **Career** employees are those with full-time, full-benefit-level jobs. These jobs are not only the best paying in the federal system, but also among the safest; career employees are rarely affected by downsizing and layoffs.

Part-time employees, **interns**, and **work-study employees** work in a variety of agencies, and the parameters of their positions vary widely. In general, if you are at least 16 years old, you can begin working part time for the government, so long as you are a student in good standing and remain so until you graduate. Many agencies, including the U.S. Postal Service (USPS), also have regular part-time and seasonal positions.

▶ The Series and Grade System of Classification

In the federal government, civilian employees are organized—and paid—according to the kind of work they do (called the *series*) and the level of difficulty (called the *grade*) of their position. Salaries and wages, called *schedules*, are determined by these classifications. Each grade consists of several *steps*, or raises. For example, a Grade 7 Park Ranger (GS-0025, Grade 5) earns a base salary of $25,125 at Step 1, $28,555 at Step 5, and $32,755 at Step 10. If he or she is promoted to Grade 7, he or she earns $31,209 at Step 1, $35,369 at Step 5, and $40,569 at Step 10 (all figures as of 2006). Note that these salaries will likely be adjusted up based upon the location in which the ranger works (see **Federal Pay Schedule** and **Percentage Pay Adjustments by Geographic Locality** tables on page 18).

Because the federal government consists of numerous departments and independent agencies, there are many different job series and pay schedules that apply to federal employees. Still, excluding postal workers, most entry-level employees fall into one of two main series and schedules:

■ The **General Schedule (GS)** applies to most professional, technical, administrative, and clerical positions.
■ The **Wage Grade (WG)** series and schedule apply to most blue-collar workers employed by the federal government.

GS employees account for approximately two-thirds of the government civilian workforce (this figure excludes employees of the USPS); the remaining one-third are WG employees.

General Schedule Jobs

There are 23 different *occupational groups* (general job categories) in the General Schedule, and each group can have up to 50 *job series* (jobs that fall within the general job category). For example, the medical, hospital, dental, and public health occupational group includes such job series as autopsy assistant series, nurse series, podiatrist series, etc. Each of these jobs series can, in turn, include numerous *job titles*. The nurse series, for example, includes nurses in hospitals, nurses in clinics, nurses who specialize in a particular field of medicine, etc.

Here's how the hierarchy of GS categories works.

Occupational Group
↓
Job Series
↓
Job Titles

Employees in different GS series—even those in jobs as diverse as computer scientist and food inspector—will receive the same salary if they are at the

Information Management Officer, Office of the Director of National Intelligence (ODNI)

There can be little doubt that intelligence and homeland security will be among the major growth areas in government in the coming years. They are also areas that should offer some of the most gratifying jobs in government; given the state of the world today, it's hard to imagine that workers in these fields will ever wonder whether their work is important.

The director of national intelligence (DNI) is a heavy hitter in D.C. He or she advises the president, the National Security Council, and the Homeland Security Council on intelligence matters. The DNI also supervises the implementation of the National Intelligence Program. The office of the DNI (ODNI) is one of the government's major hubs of crucial intelligence activity.

Information management officers hold entry-level full-time permanent positions in the ODNI. They assist in the implementation of records- and knowledge-management systems. They also assist in the documentation of the ODNI's operations, policies, decisions, procedures, and functions; creation, storage, and cataloging of records; and the promotion the ODNI through marketing, training, and awareness.

To qualify for this position, a candidate must be a U.S. citizen capable of obtaining top secret security clearance. He or she must have a basic understanding of and interest in the intelligence and defense communities, their missions, and their business practices. A solid understanding of current world events is also required. Communication skills (oral and written) in a variety of formats (one on one, small group, presentation, e-mail, report) and the ability to work well in a team environment are also considered essential, as are project management skills. Desirable additional skills include familiarity with the Federal Records Act and federal record-keeping requirements as they apply to the federal government, intelligence agencies, and the defense community; and familiarity with the Freedom of Information and Protection of Privacy Act and all relevant regulations and procedures.

Applicants who meet the aforementioned minimum required qualifications are further evaluated on the basis of supplemental application materials, including a biographic profile or resume, a narrative statement describing the applicant's knowledge, skills, and abilities as they pertain to the job requirements (specific examples should be included), and performance reviews for the prior two years. In 2006, this position offered a starting salary in the $37,000 to $58,000 range, depending on previous experience and qualifications.

same grade and work in the same location; that's because the grading system says that their jobs are equally difficult and equally important. This is also true for the wage schedule. Note, however, that salaries are adjusted for location, meaning that a clerk in New York City will earn more than a clerk at the same grade level who works in Dayton, Ohio.

General Schedule Occupational Groups

There are 23 different occupational groups in the GS.

0000	Miscellaneous Occupations Group
0100	Social Science, Psychology, and Welfare Group
0200	Human Resources Management Group
0300	General Administrative, Clerical, and Office Services Group
0400	Biological Sciences Group
0500	Accounting and Budget Group
0600	Medical, Hospital, Dental, and Public Health Group
0700	Veterinary Medical Science Group
0800	Engineering and Architecture Group
0900	Legal and Kindred Group
1000	Information and Arts Group
1100	Business and Industry Group
1200	Copyright, Patent, and Trademark Group
1300	Physical Sciences Group
1400	Library and Archives Group
1500	Mathematics and Statistics Group
1600	Equipment, Facilities, and Services Group
1700	Education Group
1800	Investigation Group
1900	Quality Assurance, Inspection, and Grading Group
2000	Supply Group
2100	Transportation Group
2200	Information Technology Group

Many personnel-intensive jobs fall into the GS-300 category; the government employs more than 70,000 clerks and assistants (GS-0303), more than 60,000 administrators (GS-0310), more than 50,000 secretaries (GS-0318), and more than 50,000 computer specialists (GS-0334).

The General Schedule includes 15 grades for its positions. They are designated GS-1 through GS-15, with GS-1 the lowest level and GS-15 the highest. Entry-level jobs typically fall into the GS-1 to GS-7 range. Jobs at the GS-5 level typically require a four-year undergraduate degree or comparable work experience; jobs at the GS-7 level and above typically require either graduate-level education or comparable work experience.

All competitive GS jobs are listed at the USAJOBS website (www.usajobs.gov). Many excepted GS positions are listed there as well, although you should check the websites of individual agencies to make sure you find all listings for such positions.

Wage Grade Employees

Federal wage employees are paid at an hourly rate set through the Federal Wage System (FWS), which was established in 1972 to create a uniform wage system that ensured fair compensation. Under FWS, the Federal Prevailing Rate Advisory Committee, which is comprised of both federal agency and labor union representatives, advises the Director of the Office of Personnel Management on the setting of federal wages.

The fundamental principle of FWS pay is that federal wage earners should earn comparable pay to their peers in the private sector. Wage levels are set by locality to reflect differences in cost of living. Each wage-grade position has five steps. At Step 2, wage earners earn the full prevailing rate paid in the private sector; at Step 5, wage earners typically earn 12% above the prevailing rate.

2500	Wire Communications Equipment Installation and Maintenance Group
2600	Electronic Equipment Installation and Maintenance Group
2800	Electrical Installation and Maintenance Group
3100	Fabric and Leather Work Group
3300	Instrument Work Group
3400	Machine Tool Work Group
3500	General Services and Support Work Group
3600	Structural and Finishing Work Group
3700	Metal Processing Group
3800	Metal Work Group
3900	Motion Picture, Radio, Television, and Sound Equipment Operating Group
4100	Painting and Paperhanging Group

4200	Plumbing and Pipefitting Group
4300	Pliable Materials Work Group
4400	Printing Group
4600	Woodwork Group
4700	General Maintenance and Operations Work Group
4800	General Equipment Maintenance Group
5000	Plant and Animal Work Group
5200	Miscellaneous Occupations Group
5300	Industrial Equipment Maintenance Group
5400	Industrial Equipment Operation Group
5700	Transportation/Mobile Equipment Operation Group
5800	Transportation/Mobile Equipment Maintenance Group
6500	Ammunition, Explosives, and Toxic Materials Work Group
6600	Armament Work Group
6900	Warehousing and Stock Handling Group
7000	Packing and Processing Group
7300	Laundry, Dry Cleaning, and Pressing Group
7400	Food Preparation and Serving Group
7600	Personal Services Group
8200	Fluid Systems Maintenance Group
8600	Engine Overhaul Group
8800	Aircraft Overhaul Group

▶ Salaries and Benefits

As a government employee, you'll earn a respectable income, even at the entry level. Positions that require little or no education or work experience often offer higher pay than comparable jobs in the private sector.

In addition, federal employees with relevant education or experience are far more likely than their private-sector counterparts to be promoted to better, higher-paying positions.

The following table shows 2006 entry-level salaries for a variety of federal positions.

SAMPLE SALARIES: U.S. GOVERNMENT EMPLOYEES		
JOB TITLE	**GRADE**	**SALARY RANGE**
Police Officer	GS06	$33,858
USPS City Mail Carrier	GL06	$31,124 to $40,182
USPS Mail Handler	MH04	$30,810 to $46,114
Tax Examiner, IRS	GS04-GS05	$25,338 to $36,856
Tax Assistance Provider, IRS	GS05	$28,349
Entry-Level Engineer/Scientist, NRC	GG05-GG09	$48,014 to $60,325
Intelligence Specialist, USAF	GG07	$35,116 to $48,679
Meteorological Intern	GS05	$29,690
Economist, Bureau of Labor Statistics	GS05-GS07	$26,669 to $48,152

Federal Pay Schedule and Locality Adjustments

The following table shows the pay schedule for full-time salaried employees by grade and step. A second table shows the amount by which pay is increased for those working in various cities; these increases are provided to offset the expense of living in cities in which rents and mortgages, groceries, automobile insurance, etc. are relatively expensive.

SALARY TABLE 2006-GS INCORPORATING THE 2.10% GENERAL SCHEDULE INCREASE EFFECTIVE JANUARY 2006 ANNUAL RATES BY GRADE AND STEP

GRADE	STEP 1	STEP 2	STEP 3	STEP 4	STEP 5	STEP 6	STEP 7	STEP 8	STEP 9	STEP 10	WITHIN GRADE AMOUNTS
1	$ 16,352	$ 16,898	$ 17,442	$ 17,983	$ 18,527	$ 18,847	$ 19,383	$ 19,925	$ 19,947	$ 20,450	VARIES
2	18,385	18,822	19,431	19,947	20,169	20,762	21,355	21,948	22,541	23,134	VARIES
3	20,060	20,729	21,398	22,067	22,736	23,405	24,074	24,743	25,412	26,081	669
4	22,519	23,270	24,021	24,772	25,523	26,274	27,025	27,776	28,527	29,278	751
5	25,195	26,035	26,875	27,715	28,555	29,395	30,235	31,075	31,915	32,755	840
6	28,085	29,021	29,957	30,893	31,829	32,765	33,701	34,637	35,573	36,509	936
7	31,209	32,249	33,289	34,329	35,369	36,409	37,449	38,489	39,529	40,569	1,040
8	34,563	35,715	36,867	38,019	39,171	40,323	41,475	42,627	43,779	44,931	1,152
9	38,175	39,448	40,721	41,994	43,267	44,540	45,813	47,086	48,359	49,632	1,273
10	42,040	43,441	44,842	46,243	47,644	49,045	50,446	51,847	53,248	54,649	1,401
11	46,189	47,729	49,269	50,809	52,349	53,889	55,429	56,969	58,509	60,049	1,540
12	55,360	57,205	59,050	60,895	62,740	64,585	66,430	68,275	70,120	71,965	1,845
13	65,832	68,026	70,220	72,414	74,608	76,802	78,996	81,190	83,384	85,578	2,194
14	77,793	80,386	82,979	85,572	88,165	90,758	93,351	95,944	98,537	101,130	2,593
15	91,507	94,557	97,607	100,657	103,707	106,757	109,807	112,857	115,907	118,957	3,050

Atlanta	15.1%	Detroit	21%
Boston/Worcester	19.99%	Hartford	21.3%
Buffalo	13.52%	Houston	26.37%
Chicago	21.5%	Huntsville/Decatur	13.35%
Cincinnati	17.08%	Indianapolis	12.85%
Cleveland	15.41%	Los Angeles	23.18%
Columbus	14.85%	Miami/Fort Lauderdale	17.84%
Dallas–Fort Worth	16.39%	Milwaukee	14.74%
Dayton	13.83%	Minneapolis–St. Paul	17.31%
Denver/Boulder	19.49%	New York metro region	22.97%

Philadelphia	18.04%	Sacramento	17.91%
Phoenix	12.65%	San Diego	19.19%
Pittsburgh	13.81%	San Francisco/San Jose	28.68%
Portland	17.16%	Seattle/Tacoma	17.93%
Raleigh-Durham	15.57%	Washington, D.C./Baltimore/No. Virginia	17.50%
Richmond	14.15%	Rest of continental U.S.	12.52%

Benefits

Federal benefits are hard to beat. Benefit packages vary from department to department and from position to position, but most career employees receive the following:

- Ten paid holidays per year
- 13 to 26 days of paid vacation per year
- 13 days of sick leave per year
- Regular cost of living adjustments
- Death and disability insurance
- Group life insurance
- Healthcare (medical and dental benefits)
- Government pension

Special Programs

The federal government offers a number of special programs that can make your job even more lucrative. All employees are eligible for the government's Incentive Rewards Program, which provides prizes and bonuses of up to $500,000 to workers who find innovative ways to reduce government costs and improve efficiency. Other programs include the Federal Employee Education and Assistance Fund (FEEAF), which provides grants and scholarships to federal employees and their dependents. Because this program is funded by employee contributions, it doesn't cost the taxpayers a single penny!

Some agencies have their own programs as well. The USPS, for example, has the Postal Employee's Relief Fund, which provides monetary relief to employees who have been victims of natural disasters.

Information Technology (IT) Specialist, Bureau of the Census

The Constitution of the United States mandates a census every ten years, making the Bureau of the Census one of the oldest agencies of the federal government. Originally little more than a head count, the census has evolved over the centuries into a collection of complex demographic, social, and economic data.

The management of such varied and important data requires sophisticated computer systems; as a result, IT specialists will find a broad range of opportunities at the Census Bureau. Depending on their level of academic advancement and previous work experience, IT specialists can start anywhere between the GS-5 level (2006 starting salary: $36,500 to $47,500) to the GS-11 level (2006 starting salary: $59,000 to $77,000). They can sign on as systems administration specialists, network services specialists, or security specialists. Each track offers room for advancement to GS-12 level (2006 starting salary: $65,600 to $85,000). IT specialists at the Census Bureau plan and coordinate hardware and software installations; manage the bureau's network systems; develop and implement privacy tools; support and improve existing software applications; and plan, develop, and troubleshoot data storage and retrieval systems.

All applicants must be U.S. citizens. GS-5 hires must have a bachelor's degree with a major in a computer-related field, or three years of work experience as a computer assistant, program analyst, or some other position that required the development or adaptation of computer programs, or an acceptable combination of schooling (without achieving a degree) and work experience. GS-7s must have a computer-related bachelor's degree with superior academic achievement or a bachelor's plus one year of computer-related graduate work and/or one year of professional experience as an IT Specialist. GS-9s must have a master's degree in computer science or extensive experience in a VMS, Unix, Novell, or Windows NT environment. GS-11s must have a PhD in computer science or extensive professional experience and expertise in the field. Veterans who received honorable or general discharge receive preferential treatment in hiring.

Like all permanent full-time federal jobs, Census Bureau IT positions provide job security, a solid living wage, and a number of plum benefits, including health insurance with more than 100 optional plans to choose from; basic life insurance plus three types of optional supplemental insurance; long-term care insurance for employees, their parents, spouses, children, parents-in-law, and stepparents; annual and sick leave; health and dependent-care flexible spending accounts; and a three-tiered retirement program.

▶ Federal Hiring System

Competitive Service and Excepted Service

The federal government offers two classes of jobs: **competitive service** and **excepted service.**

Competitive service jobs are supervised by the Office of Personnel Management, which sets qualification requirements and pay rates. Competitive service jobs are subject to acts of Congress that ensure fair and equal treatment in hiring. Hiring is based upon the applicants' knowledge, skills, and abilities (often abbreviated as *KSAs*) with no regard to such external factors as race, religion, gender, etc. Applicants for competitive service positions receive a score based upon their qualifications (which may include level of education, years of experience, test scores, and results of personal interview); this score is used to compare candidates and select those most qualified for the job. Hiring authorities have the power to review as many applicants as they like but must evaluate them solely on the basis of job-related criteria.

Excepted service jobs are not subject to the appointment, pay, and classification rules outlined under Title 5 of the United States Code (they are, however, subject to veterans' preferences). Excepted service agencies (which include the U.S. Postal Service, the Federal Bureau of Investigation, the Central Intelligence Agency, the Federal Reserve System, the Foreign Service, and the General Accounting Office) are free to set their own qualification requirements.

Some agencies offer a mix of competitive and excepted service jobs; certain divisions of the agency (or merely specific jobs within each division) may be designated "excepted" with the rest classified as "competitive."

Types of Candidates

Hiring agencies typically choose candidates from among three groups of candidates:

1. a **competitive list of eligible candidates**, ranked by their qualification score for a specific position

2. a **list of eligible candidates with previous civil service status** who are therefore eligible for noncompetitive hiring within a competitive service; these candidates are selected under agency merit-promotion guidelines and can receive appointment by promotion, reassignment, transfer, or reinstatement

3. a **list of eligible candidates who qualify for special noncompetitive appointment under law or executive order** such as the Veterans Readjustment Appointment (VRA), which allows agencies to hire eligible veterans without competition

Ranking Candidates

All competitive service and many excepted service agencies rate applicants on a scale of 1 to 100 according to specific job-related criteria; these criteria are clearly delineated on the job vacancy announcement. Veterans receive a five- or ten-point bonus (ten points are awarded to those with service-related disabilities, to certain unmarried spouses of deceased veterans, or to mothers of deceased or disabled veterans—more on veterans' preference later in this chapter). In the past, the Office of Personnel Management handled grading. Today, many agencies are empowered to grade their own applicant pools; a number of these agencies subcontract the grading back to OPM.

As you are probably aware, in the private sector, a good interview can make or break your application. In government, it doesn't work quite that way; because the interview comes so much later in the hiring process, it does not hold the potential for catapulting a questionable candidate to "must hire" status. While the interview is still very important, much more important are your application or resume and your performance on exams. If these fail to impress, you'll never get the chance to win your employer over during the interview.

Until recently, the OPM maintained registers and eligibility lists of qualified applicants who had not been placed. This allowed the agency to dip into a reserve of potential employees whenever there was a new job opening; often that meant that the job could be filled by a previous applicant without the government's having to post the job and screen a new wave of candidates. As various federal agencies have been given more freedom to evaluate and grade their own candidates, however, this system has become impractical.

As a result, the register and eligibility list systems have been eliminated. Fortunately, anyone interested in a federal job can go to the USAJOBS website (www.usajobs.com) and complete an online resume that can be submitted to any federal employer. The resume is stored in the USAJOBS system, so there is no need to recomplete it every time you apply for a new job (you may want to tweak your resume, however, to highlight skills required for the open position).

Veterans' Preference

If you've served on active duty in the military, you may be eligible for veterans' preference: an additional five points—or ten points to those with service-related disabilities, to certain unmarried spouses of deceased veterans, or to mothers of deceased or disabled veterans—to your rating in the job selection process. To be eligible, you must have been discharged under honorable conditions or, if you began serving after October 15, 1976, you must have a campaign badge, an expeditionary medal, or a service-related disability.

To claim the five-point preference, you need to attach proof of your eligibility in the form of a copy of your DD-214, Certificate of Release or Discharge from Active Duty, or other eligible form. For the ten-point preference, you must attach SF-15, the Application for Ten-Point Veterans' Preference, and the eligibility proofs it requires. For more information regarding Veterans' Preference, visit the USAJOBS website or visit the Department of Labor's Veterans' Preference Advisor page at www.dol.gov/elaws/vetspref.htm.

Unassembled Exams

If there is no exam, then the application itself is considered the entrance test (and is sometimes referred to as an "unassembled exam"). Rating is based solely upon the application and accompanying materials. Applicants achieving the highest scores are placed on the "best qualified" list and are typically invited to interview.

Assembled Exams and Band Testing

The assembled exam—the legendary *civil service test*—is less and less commonly used as time passes. Today, written tests are not required for most federal civil service jobs. Such tests are most often used for clerical jobs at the GS-2, GS-3, and GS-4 level and for technical aid jobs at the GS-2 and GS-3 levels. Tests are used only rarely for jobs at the GS-5 level and above.

When an exam is administered, the hiring agency either:

- holds an *assembled exam* (so named because all applicants are assembled at the same time and place) for all candidates, OR
- calls only the top-ranked candidates for the exam (this is often referred to as *band testing*).

In the case of an assembled exam, your test results can significantly improve your qualification score, which, in turn, can land you the job. In the case of band testing, you will already need to be relatively highly qualified *before* sitting for the exam, as only the best candidates reach the exam stage.

▶ Job Vacancy Announcements

All jobs filled through competitive application are posted at the USAJOBS website (www.usajobs.gov). Positions classified as "excepted"—meaning that they fall outside the legal requirements imposed on competitive hiring—do not have to be posted at the USAJOBS website, but most are anyway. The FBI, for example, hires through the excepted process only, yet still posts all its opening at USAJOBS. To be safe, you should check for job postings at the websites of individual agencies at which you wish to work if you are interested in one of the agency's excepted positions.

Every job vacancy notice provides an overview of the available position, a detailed description of the duties associated with the position, a list of job requirements, an outline of the hiring process, and a list of benefits. Specific information includes:

- Open and close dates (*filing period* or *application window*)
- Job title
- Job number
- Geographic location
- Number of vacancies
- Hiring office/agency
- Salary range
- Terms (part/full time)
- Benefits
- Job duties
- Job qualifications
- Criteria for evaluation or rating (education, experience, etc.)
- Any supplemental information required of candidate
- Who may apply (*area of consideration* or *limits of consideration*)
- Description of application process
- Whom to call for forms
- To whom to address further questions
- Where to mail/e-mail completed forms
- Application deadline

If an agency wants to offer the position to a limited group of current or former employees, the job announcement will list the specific types of applicants to which the job is open; this is often described as the *area of consideration*. When the job is offered to external candidates, the positions may still be restricted to persons within a certain geographical area. It is important to read job announcements carefully to make sure that you are eligible for consideration.

▶ Finding a Job and Getting It

Applying for a federal position is a three-step process. Those steps are:

1. Creating a USAJOBS Account and Creating a Resume
2. Searching and Applying for Jobs
3. Managing Your Career

Step 1: Creating a USAJOBS Account and Creating a Resume

The easiest way to create a USAJOBS account is via the Internet. Point your browser to the USAJOBS website (www.usajobs.gov) and click the "MY USAJOBS" tab. This will take you to a page from which you can either (1) create an account, or (2) access an already existing account. Click the "Create your account now" button.

The next screen asks you to input:

- your name
- your address
- your username and password (You get to choose both; your username must be unique in the

USAJOBS system. Don't forget to write them down somewhere where you will not lose them, because you will need them every time you access your account.)

- a password question that provides a hint about your password (e.g., "What is your dog's name?" Answer the question correctly and the USAJOBS website will give you your password.)
- your citizenship status
- your Veterans' Preference status

Click "Submit" and presto! Your USAJOBS account has been created. Now you are ready to create a resume. USAJOBS allows you to create and save multiple resumes, so you will be able to tailor your resume to specific job opportunities.

When building your USAJOBS resume(s), follow these tips:

- **Use key words.** Remember that employers will scan your resume for key words that reflect your knowledge, skills, and abilities (KSAs). Think carefully about your word choice. Your goal is to communicate that you have the skills and experiences that the employer is seeking. Read job postings for positions in which you are interested and incorporate key words from the description into your resume. When rewriting your resume for a particular position, add words from that specific job description.
- **Keep your resume brief.** Recruiters receive many applications for every position, and during their first review of resumes, they will scan them briefly, looking for qualities that make a candidate stand out. Highlight those qualities and keep all other information to a minimum; this will increase the chances that the recruiter will see the most important information on that first go-round. USAJOBS says that the hiring manager should be able to find your key credentials within ten to 15 seconds of looking at your resume. If he or she can't, your resume is too long and contains too much information.
- **Highlight numbers that emphasize your achievements.** Specific details are much more powerful than nonspecific statements. Don't just say, "I saved my company money by developing new software." Say, "I created software that saved my company $60,000 during the first year of implementation." Because the latter offers a concrete number, it is much more impressive than the former example.

The USAJOBS website provides step-by-step instructions to guide you through the resume-building process. Resume building consists of entering all types of information, such as work experience, educational background, training, references, and skills, into a web-based form. Click "Save" when you're done and your resume will remain on file at the website until you decide to edit or delete it.

You may also submit a hard copy of your resume if you prefer. If you do, make sure that you include all the information included in an online resume and all the information requested in the job vacancy announcement; if you don't, you will not be considered for the position. Remember that your hard-copy resume, like your online resume, should be brief, focusing only on relevant points.

Following is a list of the information you should include in a hard-copy resume.

- **Job information**
  Job announcement number
  Job title
  Grade(s) for which you are applying
- **Personal information**
  Full name and mailing address, with zip code

Daytime and evening telephone numbers, with area code

Country of citizenship

Veterans' preference, if applicable

- **Education**

  The name, city, state, and zip code, if possible, of your high school, along with the date on which you earned your diploma or GED

  The name, city, state, and zip code, if possible, of any colleges and universities you attended, as well as your major(s) and the type of degree(s) you received. If you did not receive a degree, indicate the total number of credits earned and indicate whether they were quarter or semester credits. Do not send a college transcript unless required to do so by the job vacancy announcement.

- **Work experience**

  Include the following information for all paid and unpaid work experience relating to the job vacancy you would like to fill:

  Job title

  Duties and accomplishments

  Name and address of employer

  Name and phone number of supervisor (indicate whether your current supervisor may be contacted)

  Dates employment began and ended (month and year)

  Number of hours worked per week

  Salary/wages

- **Other qualifications**

  The OPM requests that you provide dates for these accomplishments, but do not send documentation unless specifically requested to do so:

  Any job-related training courses you've taken (include course title and year)

  Job-related skills, such as foreign languages, computer software/hardware proficiency, machine operability, and typing speed

  Current job-related certificates and licenses

Job-related honors, awards, and special accomplishments, such as membership in a professional or honor society, leadership activities, publications, and performance awards

Step 2: Searching and Applying for Jobs

Searching for job openings with the federal government has never been easier, thanks to USAJOBS, the government's "one-stop source for federal jobs and employment information." The site includes many helpful tutorials (at www.usajobs.gov/firsttimers.asp) that will help you get started. Once you've learned how to navigate the site, you'll be ready to search for jobs by region, state, zip code, country, department, and salary range. You may also contact USAJOBS by telephone at 703-724-1850 or, for TDD service, at 978-461-8404.

One of the great features of the USAJOBS website is its search agent function, which allows you to create and save up to ten different collections of job-search parameters. Suppose you were looking for an administrative job. You might be willing to accept a job at one pay level if it were in the area where you currently live, but you might be willing to relocate only for a better-paying job. You could create two search agents, one that searched only for administrative jobs in your area and one that searched for administrative jobs nationally. You can fine-tune your search by job category, occupational series, hiring agency or department, salary range, and pay grade. The USAJOBS website will automatically run all your search agents for you as often as you like (monthly, biweekly, weekly, or daily) and will e-mail you the results.

You can also search for job openings at an individual agency's website, a good strategy if you're interested in working at a particular agency. You should also take a look at the Call to Serve website (www.ourpublicservice.org/workforusa/workforusa.htm); it's run by The Partnership for Public Service, a private organization dedicated to "helping revitalize the federal civil service." Another good site is America's Job Bank (http://www.ajb.dni.us); it was created through a partnership of the Department of Labor and a network of nearly 2,000 state-operated public employment services. The site lists both private and government jobs. The Best Places to Work in the Federal Government website (www.bestplacestowork.org) ranks federal jobs by employee satisfaction levels; that's certainly useful information. No matter where you find your job listing, you will likely have to apply through the USAJOBS website.

The Internet is the best resource for your job search, but it isn't the only one. If you live near an OPM service center or a Federal Executive Board (FEB) office, give them a call; they may have printed versions of job listings. You might also consider subscribing to the *Federal Jobs Digest*, an excellent biweekly newsletter. (You can also visit the Federal Jobs Digest website at www.jobsfed.com; it features a very user-friendly search engine for locating open positions in the federal government). Other books worth considering (besides this one) include Dennis V. Damp's *The Book of U.S. Government Jobs*. It, too, has a website (federaljobs.net) that provides an overview of government work and links to many government agency employment sites.

Once you have found a position that interests you, you will have to decipher the job announcement and complete an application. Take special note of the *filing period* or *application window*, which is the specific time period during which applications will be accepted. Be sure you are aware of the filing period; otherwise, you may miss the deadline. Once the filing period ends, you will not be able to apply for the position.

After you submit your resume, what happens next depends on the type of position for which you are applying. Some civil service jobs require that you take a written exam (most federal jobs do not have this requirement, by the way). Others require different qualifying procedures before you can be employed.

Written Exams

When you apply for a competitive position that requires an assembled exam, you will receive a test scheduling card. This is particularly important for positions with the USPS as well as for law enforcement, firefighting, and clerical and secretarial positions. These entry-level jobs require a written test, and because there is often an oversupply of applicants, you'll need to make a reservation to take the exam. Fill out and return the test scheduling card and you'll be notified of exactly when and where you need to be to take the exam. Be aware that sometimes certain areas have such high demand for certain jobs, including clerical workers, that these exams can be taken on a walk-in basis without reservation. Contact your area Federal Job Information Center in the Office of Personnel Management for more details.

For most entry-level positions that require exams, the tests start out by measuring your basic reading, writing, and (sometimes) math skills. The hiring agency is generally more interested in your ability to be trained than in the knowledge you already have about the job. Sample exams testing these basic skills, as well as chapters that teach you how to improve your performance in reading, grammar, vocabulary, spelling, math, and civil service skills, such as coding and memory, are included in this book.

Depending on the position you seek, the exams may also assess your common sense and logic or your memory. There are also different kinds of questions that test specific work-related skills. For instance, postal workers are required to memorize and check addresses; clerical workers are tested on aspects of filing, such as alphabetization. The exams usually present scenarios that would arise in a typical job situation and are almost always multiple choice.

In general, you can retake tests if you fail, and you can always retake a test during a subsequent testing period or for a subsequent job posting in order to improve your score. Improving your score will, of course, improve your job ranking.

Physical Performance Tests

The majority of civilian government jobs don't require any special physical ability, but there are several important exceptions. At the USPS, for example, many jobs require physical strength and stamina, so the USPS requires all applicants to be able to lift 70 pounds in order to be considered.

Firefighters and law enforcement employees, among others, *do* need special physical capacities and skills, and they must pass a series of physical tests before they can be hired. These physical ability tests may include timed runs, obstacle courses, ladder climbs, weight lifting, weight pulling, sit-ups, and push-ups.

Interviews

Interviews for government positions almost always come *after* your agency has determined that you are otherwise qualified for the job. These interviews often serve more as a final checkpoint in the hiring process than as a first step, as in the private sector. Most interviewers will go into detail about the type of work the job entails, the benefits of the position, and the procedures of the agency. They will also probably ask questions that will help them ascertain how motivated, cooperative, intelligent, and logical you are, as well as what kind of work habits, goals, and personal values you have.

The first question almost any interview will ask is "tell me a little bit about yourself." Prepare for this question; it is your chance to create a positive tone for the rest of the interview. Describe where you are from, tell about your education and experience, and state how your skills will help the hiring agency. Maintain a positive attitude throughout the interview; you are acting as a salesperson, and the product you are selling is yourself. Believe in your product or your customer never will. Dress appropriately, and remember that too formal is better than too casual. After the interview, don't forget to send a thank-you letter. This will communicate that you are a thoughtful person and will indicate to the agency that you are very interested in the job.

You can also give yourself an edge in the interview by showing some knowledge of the agency and its business. During the application process, seek out others in the position you desire. Find out what their work is like and what qualities are valued. If you know something about the position and the agency, you'll demonstrate your interest and motivation, two characteristics employers value highly.

You'll also be more likely to succeed if you're able to explain, comfortably, any gaps in your education or experience. Tell the truth; you'll be respected if you can admit to past failures and faults, especially if you can explain how you overcame, or plan to overcome, them.

Finally, you should be able to discuss your short- and long-term career goals. Clearly, if your goals are in line with the goals of the department, you're in a better position to be hired. Here again, your research—talking to people already working with the department—and your overall awareness of the business of the agency will help.

Other Requirements

Before you're hired, Uncle Sam wants to make sure you're government material. That's why you will be asked to fill out a Declaration for Federal Employment (OF-306). This form is used to determine your suitability for working for the federal government and to authorize a background investigation. You must answer personal questions on subjects like loan defaults, felonies, and misdemeanors. Please note: Answering yes to questions does not disqualify you, but your answers will certainly be taken into consideration during the selection process.

You must also certify that all of the information you've provided is accurate and correct to the best of your knowledge. Know that your application will be checked. If investigators find out that you have falsified information on your application or resume, you may suffer any or all of three possible consequences: You won't be hired; you'll be fired (if you are applying for promotion within the federal government); or you may be fined or jailed.

Many positions—especially those that deal directly with public safety, such as those in the police and firefighter series, as well as those that require security clearance—require an employee who not only meets all qualifications criteria and excels in all stages of the hiring process, but also meets certain citizenship standards. That's why before employees are hired for these jobs, they may be subject to one or more of the following:

- a background investigation
- a drug screening test
- a medical examination
- a psychological evaluation or a personality test

These checks may significantly lengthen the hiring process, but they're important to ensure the well-being of all the citizens who interact with these employees. Security concerns are, of course, heightened in this post–9/11 world, so expect such checks to increase in number and duration for the foreseeable future, rather than decrease.

Step 3: Managing Your Career

Once you've created a USAJOBS account and created a resume, you'll be able to use the website's Manage Your Career options to, well, manage your career. Your options include:

- **The Career Interest Guide:** This guide includes a questionnaire designed to gauge your interest level in various types of federal work. When you have completed the questionnaire, your results— suggesting career areas in which you would be most happy—are displayed immediately. It also contains a function that allows you to search available jobs by the following career-interest areas: business detail, humanitarian, leading/influencing, mechanical, plants and animals, protective, scientific, and other. These categories correspond to the results of the career-interest questionnaire.
- **Job Interest Matching:** This function allows you to explore three broad career areas: clerical and technical; professional and administrative; and supervisory, managerial, and executive. In each area, you are asked to read a list of possible tasks and identify those that appeal to you. Your results will produce a list of jobs that match your interests.
- **Specific Job Exploration:** This function allows you to explore jobs by their specific general series number. Input a number to see the job description and a list of minimum qualifications for the job.
- **Match Federal Jobs to Private Sector Jobs:** This function allows you to see what jobs in the private sector correspond to various federal job categories.

► The U.S. Postal Office Uses an Entirely Different Hiring Process

The U.S. Postal Service (USPS)—which, with nearly 800,000 employees, is the nation's second largest employer (Wal-Mart is the first with about 1.2 million)—has its own unique hiring process. New appointments at the USPS enter as either casual (temporary) or part-time flexible (career); either track can lead to full-time career employment, but be aware that competition for such positions can be fierce. Nearly all entry-level positions require applicants to pass an examination that tests address checking, forms completion, coding, and memory; it also includes a personal inventory. To learn more about the USPS and its hiring practices, check out LearningExpress's *Postal Worker Exam.*

► Contact Information

The Office of Personnel Management (OPM) maintains nine regional service centers. Although their primary mission is to serve federal agencies, these offices can also provide information about available jobs and assistance with specific application queries.

OPM Service Centers

Atlanta Services Branch

75 Spring Street SW, Suite 1000

Atlanta, GA 30303

Fax: 404-730-9738

E-mail: atlanta@opm.gov

Chicago Services Branch

230 South Dearborn Street, DPN 30-3

Chicago, IL 60604

Fax: 312-353-6211

E-mail: chicago@opm.gov

Denver Services Section

12345 Alameda Parkway

P.O. Box 25167

Denver, CO 80225

Fax: 303-236-8580

E-mail: denver@opm.gov

Kansas City Services Section

601 East 12th Street, Room 131

Kansas City, MO 64106

Fax: 816-426-5104

E-mail: kansascity@opm.gov

Norfolk Services Section

200 Granby Street, Room 500

Norfolk, VA 23510-1886

Fax: 757-441-6280

E-mail: norfolk@opm.gov

Philadelphia Services Branch

600 Arch Street, Room 3400

Philadelphia, PA 19106

Fax: 215-861-3030

E-mail: philadelphia@opm.gov

Raleigh Services Branch

4407 Bland Road, Suite 200

Raleigh, NC 27609-6296

Fax: 919-790-2824

E-mail: raleigh@opm.gov

San Antonio Services Section

8610 Broadway, Room 305

San Antonio, TX 78217

Fax: 210-805-2429

E-mail: sanantonio@opm.gov

San Francisco Services Branch

120 Howard Street, Room 735

San Francisco, CA 94105

Fax: 415-281-7095

E-mail: sanfrancisco@opm.gov

Washington, D.C. Services Branch

1900 E Street NW, Room 2469

Washington, D.C. 20415

Fax: 202-606-1768

E-mail: washington@opm.gov

Federal Executive Boards (FEBs) coordinate federal activities outside of Washington, D.C.; because these activities comprise 88% of the federal workforce, that's a pretty big job! Your local FEB can provide you with an exhaustive list of federal agencies within its area, along with contact information. If you're hoping not to relocate, a visit to your local FEB will provide you with a thorough list of your potential job options. The following is a list of all 28 FEBs.

Albuquerque–Santa Fe, NM

Gordon Eden, Jr., Co-Chairperson

Felipe J. Jimenez, Co-Chairperson

John Kwait, Executive Director

Federal Executive Board

P.O. Box 156

Albuquerque, NM 87103-1056

Phone: 505-248-6415

Fax: 505-248-6414

Web: www.newmexico.feb.gov

E-mail: john_kwait@fws.gov

Atlanta, GA

Donald Arnette, Chairperson

Gwendolyn Campbell, Executive Director

Federal Executive Board

Richard B. Russell Federal Building

75 Spring Street SW, Room 1140

Atlanta, GA 30303

Phone: 404-331-4400

Fax: 404-331-4270

Web: www.atlanta.feb.gov

E-mail: gwenne.campbell@gsa.gov

Baltimore, MD

Felicita Sola-Carter, Chairperson

Richard Howell, Executive Director

Federal Executive Board

Fallon Federal Building

31 Hopkins Plaza, Room 820A

Baltimore, MD 21201

Phone: 410-962-4047

Fax: 410-962-6198

E-mail: baltimore.feb@verizon.net

Boston, MA

Diane LeBlanc, Chairperson

Kim Ainsworth, Executive Director

Federal Executive Board

10 Causeway Street, Room 178

Boston, MA 02222

Phone: 617-565-6769

Fax: 617-565-8178

Web: www.boston.feb.gov

E-mail: kim.ainsworth@gsa.gov

Buffalo, NY

Philip C. Dissek, Chairperson
Paul Kendzierski, Executive Director
Federal Executive Board
130 South Elmwood Avenue, Suite 416
Buffalo, NY 14202
Phone: 716-551-5655
Fax: 716-551-3007
Web: www.buffalo.feb.gov
E-mail: director@buffalofeb.org

Chicago, IL

Henry Valiulis, Chairperson
Jan Stinson, Executive Director
Federal Executive Board
230 South Dearborn Street, Room 3816
Chicago, IL 60604
Phone: 312-353-6790
Fax: 312-353-3058
Web: www.chicagoinfo.gov/chicagofeb
E-mail: jan.stinson@gsa.gov

Cincinnati, OH

Susan Hansen, Chairperson
Vacant, Executive Director
Greater Cincinnati Federal Executive Board
1116 JWP Federal Office Building
550 Main Street
Cincinnati, OH 45202-3215
Phone: 513-684-2102
Fax: 513-684-2103
Web: www.cincinnati.feb.gov
E-mail: tina@gcfeb.com

Cleveland, OH

Douglas Shelby, Chairperson
Michael Goin, Executive Director
Federal Executive Board
A. J. Celebrezze Federal Building
1240 East Ninth Street, Room 355
Cleveland, OH 44199-2002
Phone: 216-433-6633
Fax: 216-433-9463
Web: www.cleveland.feb.gov
E-mail: michael.w.goin@nasa.gov

Dallas–Ft. Worth, TX

A. Cynthia Leon, Chairperson
Gladean Butler, Executive Director
Federal Executive Board
525 South Griffin Street, Suite 870-LB102
Dallas, TX 75202
Phone: 214-767-5370
Fax: 214-767-5380
E-mail: gbutler@dfwfeb.com

Denver, CO

Darlene Barnes, Chairperson
Lawrence Grandison, Jr., Executive Director
Federal Executive Board
6760 East Irvington Place
Denver, CO 80279-8000
Phone: 303-676-7009
Fax: 303-676-6666
Web: www.denver.feb.gov
E-mail: larry.grandison@dfas.mil

Detroit, MI

Michael Jansen, Chairperson

Michelle Rhodes, Executive Director

Federal Executive Board

477 Michigan Avenue, Room M10

Detroit, MI 48226

Phone: 313-226-3534

Fax: 313-226-2155

Web: www.detriot.feb.gov

E-mail: rhodesm@tacom.army.mil

Honolulu Pacific, HI

Edward Kubo, Jr., Chairperson

Gloria Uyehara, Executive Director

Federal Executive Board

300 Ala Moana Boulevard, Room 8-125

Box 50268

Honolulu, HI 96850

Phone: 808-541-2638

Fax: 808-541-3429

Web: www.honolulu-pacific.feb.gov

E-mail: guyehara@hpfeb.org

Houston, TX

James Marchand, Chairperson

Mike Mason, Executive Director

Federal Executive Board

1919 Smith Street, Suite 632

Houston, TX 77002

Phone: 713-209-4524

Fax: 713-209-3465

Web: www.houston.feb.gov

E-mail: michael.mason@cebridge.net

Kansas City, MO

Steven Tanner, Chairperson

Cindy Hillman, Executive Director

Federal Executive Board

1500 East Bannister Road, Suite 1176

Kansas City, MO 64131-3009

Phone: 816-823-5100

Fax: 816-823-5104

Web: http://kcfeb.gsa.gov

E-mail: feb.mail@gsa.gov

Los Angeles, CA

Theresa Camiling, Chairperson

Kathrene Hansen, Executive Director

Federal Executive Board

501 West Ocean, Suite 3200

Long Beach, CA 90802

Phone: 562-980-3445

Fax: 562-980-3448

Web: www.losangeles.feb.gov

E-mail: kathrene.hansen@dhs.gov

Miami, FL

Francisco Maldonado, Chairperson

Jaqueline Arroyo, Executive Director

Federal Executive Board

4780 SW 64th Avenue, Suite 104

Davie, FL 33314

Phone: 954-846-8248

Fax: 954-846-9260

Web: www.southflorida.feb.gov

E-mail: jarroyo@doc.gov

St. Paul, MN

Kenneth Kasprisin, Chairperson
Ray Morris, Executive Director
Federal Executive Board
1 Federal Drive, Room 510
St. Paul, MN 55111-4008
Phone: 612-713-7201
Fax: 612-713-7203
Web: www.doi.gov/febtc
E-mail: ray_morris@os.doi.gov

Newark, NJ

Maryanne Gerbauckas, Chairperson
Angela A. Zaccardi, Executive Director
Federal Executive Board
970 Broad Street, Room 1434-B
Newark, NJ 07102
Phone: 973-645-6217
Fax: 973-645-6218
Web: www.newark.feb.gov
E-mail: angela.zaccardi@gsa.gov

New Orleans, LA

Rowland Christian, Chairperson
Kathy Barré, Executive Director
Federal Executive Board
P.O. Box 53206
New Orleans, LA 70153-3206
Phone: 504-426-0106
Fax: 504-426-8212
Web: http://sig.nfc.usda.gov/feb
E-mail: kathy.barre@usda.gov

New York, NY

Clifford Kirsch, Chairperson
Cynthia Gable, Executive Director
Federal Executive Board
26 Federal Plaza, Room 3016
New York, NY 10278
Phone: 212-264-1890
Fax: 212-264-1172
Web: www.newyorkcity.feb.gov
E-mail: cynthia.gable@gsa.gov

Oklahoma City, OK

Michael W. Roach, Chairperson
LeAnn Jenkins, Executive Director
Federal Executive Board
215 Dean A. McGee Avenue, Suite 320
Oklahoma City, OK 73102
Phone: 405-231-4167
Fax: 405-231-4165
Web: www.oklahoma.feb.gov
E-mail: leannjenkins@gsa.gov

Portland, OR

Anne Badgley, Chairperson
Ron Johnson, Executive Director
Federal Executive Board
1220 SW Third Avenue, Suite 1776
Portland, OR 97204-2823
Phone: 503-326-2060
Fax: 503-326-2070
E-mail: rjohnson@pcez.com

Philadelphia, PA

Margaret Mannion, Chairperson

Jack Ratcliffe, Executive Director

Federal Executive Board

William J. Green, Jr., Federal Building

600 Arch Street, Room 4320

Philadelphia, PA 19106

Phone: 215-861-3665

Fax: 215-861-3667

E-mail: jack.ratcliffe@gsa.gov

Pittsburgh, PA

Cheryl Campbell, Chairperson

George Buck, Executive Director

Federal Executive Board

1000 Liberty Avenue, Room 1301

Pittsburgh, PA 15222

Phone: 412-395-6223

Fax: 412-395-6221

Web: www.pittsburgh.feb.gov

E-mail: george.buck@opm.gov

St. Louis, MO

Keith Bentley, Chairperson

Susanne Valdez, Executive Director

Federal Executive Board

1222 Spruce, Room 2.202c

St. Louis, MO 63103

Phone: 314-539-6312

Fax: 314-539-6314

Web: www.stlouis.feb.gov

E-mail: susanne.valdez@gsa.gov

San Antonio, TX

Eric Stephens, Chairperson

Rebecca Froboese, Executive Director

Federal Executive Board

7411 John Smith, Suite 1210

San Antonio, TX 78229

Phone: 210-616-8153

Fax: 210-616-8155

Web: www.sanantonio.feb.gov

E-mail: rebecca.froboese@med.va.gov

San Francisco, CA

Larry Eckerman, Chairperson

Dianna Louie, Executive Director

Federal Executive Board

1301 Clay Street, Room 1240N

Oakland, CA 94612-5209

Phone: 510-637-6103

Fax: 510-637-6253

E-mail: dianna.louie@gsa.gov

Seattle, WA

John McKay, Chairperson

Anne Tiernan, Executive Director

Federal Executive Board

Jackson Federal Building, Room 2942

915 Second Avenue

Seattle, WA 98174-1010

Phone: 206-220-6171

Fax: 206-220-6132

E-mail: seattlefeb@gsa.gov

3 ▶ Civil Service at the State and Local Level

Y ou don't have to work for Uncle Sam to work for the government. Hundreds of thousands of people work for state and local governments in jobs that parallel just about every occupation in the private sector, from the receptionist at the public library to the maintenance crews who fill in potholes to the police officers who direct traffic and chase criminals across interstates. There's a lot of work that needs to be done to maintain a state, county, city, or town, and many of these opportunities are available to people with little special training or expertise.

If you prefer working without a supervisor looking over your shoulder and you don't mind the stresses involved in dealing with traffic and sometimes demanding customers, driving a bus may be the right job for you. It's also a great opportunity for someone looking for part-time civil service work, because most entry-level bus drivers begin as part-timers, picking up shifts nobody else wants and gradually working their way up the ladder to more and better shifts.

There are two basic groups of bus drivers on the public payroll: school bus drivers and transit bus drivers. School bus drivers begin and typically remain part-time workers, because their jobs generally can be completed in two two-hour shifts, one in the morning and one in the afternoon. Many school bus drivers perform other jobs within the school system, handling maintenance or janitorial duties at one of the schools they serve. Others pick up occasional jobs driving to and from field trips, sporting events, and other school-related activities. A good school bus driver must have the patience to deal with children and possess good policing skills in order to ensure that students travel safely.

Transit bus drivers generally work more hours and are better paid than their school bus driving peers. They typically have more responsibilities as well; besides transporting passengers safely to their destinations, transit bus drivers must also sell tickets, collect money, prepare trip reports, answer passengers' questions about routes and schedules, and, in some locations, maintain their buses. All bus drivers must drive carefully under challenging weather and traffic conditions, mindful that they neither fall behind nor get ahead of schedule.

State and local law establishes the qualifications for bus driving jobs. In some areas, bus drivers must be at least 24 years of age; other areas set a lower minimum. Bus drivers must have good vision and hearing (with or without correction), must be in good physical condition, and must have normal use of their arms and legs. Many localities require bus drivers to pass a background and/or drug test; such tests are more common for school bus drivers. Bus drivers must hold a special driver's license, the acquisition of which requires passing written and skills tests.

Bus drivers typically earn between $10 and $20 per hour, although wages outside both extremes are not uncommon. Nearly one-third of all bus drivers in the United States work part time. More than two-thirds drive school buses.

▶ Positive Aspects of State and Municipal Civil Service Jobs

The following sections review the many advantages to civil service employment at the state and local level.

Good Prospects
According to the Bureau of Labor Statistics' publication *Occupational Outlook Handbook (2006–07)*, new jobs should be continually created at the state and local level into the foreseeable future. There are two primary reasons for this: First, state populations are increasing, requiring an increase in the size of the government that serves the people. Second, the federal government has shifted some responsibilities from the national to the state and local level. It should be noted, on the other hand, that state and local budgets are typically pretty tight, a factor that dampens job growth somewhat. Some governments have sought to outsource certain

Types of State and Local Government Jobs

While specific job titles may vary considerably, state and local government jobs generally fall into one of the following categories:

- Accounting/financial management
- Agriculture/conservation
- Clerical/administrative
- Education/information services
- Engineering/architecture
- Legal/licensing
- Medical/health services
- Public safety/law enforcement
- Skilled trades/maintenance
- Social services

functions, a process that also reduces the number of state and local jobs.

The biggest employment sectors at the state and local level appear in the professional and service occupations; these account for more than half of all such government jobs. Information technology remains an area of strong growth. Look also for the dramatic growth in the areas of social services, health services, and protective services, with a focus on service to the elderly, children, and the mentally impaired.

One way to learn about what type of positions are available in a specific state is to visit the state's website. For a long time, each state's website used the same formula, *www.state.__.us*, with the state's two-letter abbreviation in the place of the blank. Thus, the website for the state of Utah was *www.state.ut.us*. Although most states have changed their web addresses to something more concise, they have maintained a link to their new pages from their old addresses. Therefore, if you type in *www.state.ut.us*, you will be automatically forwarded to the new Utah website, *www.utah.gov*.

Diverse Opportunities and Job Security

State and local governments provide many of the services that we take for granted in our communities. Public education (not only elementary schools and secondary schools, but also community colleges and universities), parks, hospitals, libraries, prisons, transportation, sanitation, public utilities, fire and police departments, and courts all fall under the jurisdiction of state and local government. Government agencies and departments provide us with all these essential services, ensuring that even during tough economic times, state and local government jobs will still be available. And in most cases, state and local government career employees, like their counterparts in the federal civil service, are well protected from layoffs.

And remember, you don't have to be a teacher to work in a school, a doctor to work in a hospital, or a lawyer to work in a courthouse. All these agencies need a wide variety of personnel to fulfill their mission: clerical support staff, maintenance workers, skilled workers such as carpenters and plumbers, security guards, and so on.

To give you a better idea of exactly what kind of jobs are out there, here is a list of available entry-level jobs found on a random day at the websites of one state and one municipal government:

- Auditor
- Bus operator
- Computer network administrator
- Corrections officer
- Dental assistant
- Financial analyst
- Food services employee
- Housekeeper
- Instructor, Technical college
- Laboratory technician
- Mechanic
- Nurse
- Occupational therapist
- Pharmacy technician
- Police officer
- Program assistant, Division of Family Services
- Recycling collector
- Sanitation worker
- Secretary
- Security personnel
- Social services provider
- Tree trimmer
- Vehicle operator
- Watershed inspector

Good Starting Salaries

Starting salaries range greatly from job to job, state to state, and locality to locality. The following table shows the median average salary for a range of state and municipal positions in 2004, the last year for which the government collected such figures. As you can see, the pay is pretty good.

MEDIAN ANNUAL SALARY FOR SELECTED EXECUTIVE AND MANAGERIAL OCCUPATIONS IN LOCAL GOVERNMENT 2004	
OCCUPATION	SALARY
City manager	$88,695
Assistant chief administrative officer	$80,232
Information services director	$75,582
Engineer	$75,556
Chief financial officer	$74,867
Economic development director	$70,668
Public works director	$70,135
Fire chief	$70,000
Human resources director	$70,000
Chief law enforcement official	$69,837
Human services director	$64,832

Parks and recreation director	$62,988
Health officer	$61,536
Purchasing director	$59,013
Chief librarian	$56,270
Treasurer	$52,053
Clerk	$46,779

Source: *Bureau of Labor Statistics, Occupational Outlook Handbook 2006–07*

Generous Benefits

Like salaries, exact benefits vary widely among governments, but most state and local government employees can expect a reasonable benefits package that includes:

- health insurance
- life insurance
- disability insurance
- paid vacation and holidays
- sick leave
- educational incentives
- pension plan

▶ Minimum Qualifications for State and Local Civil Service

Qualifications for state and local jobs vary widely depending on the kind of job. Some jobs require nothing more than a high school diploma or GED, and a few don't even require that much. Whatever type of job you're looking for, be sure to check the specific job qualifications on the job announcement before you apply.

State and local governments, like the federal government, rank applicants according to specific, clear criteria. If you don't meet the minimum qualifications,

you will not be considered. Your interview for a state or local job typically won't come until several steps into the selections process, so you cannot get around not having minimum qualifications by winning an employer over in an interview.

If you are a veteran, you may be entitled to special treatment in the hiring process at both the state and local level. This is especially true when the selection process entails a clearly defined ranking system. Veterans applying for firefighter or police officer positions, for example, often have five or ten points added to their scores. For more details, you should contact your state or local personnel department.

▶ The Hiring Process at the State and Local Level

There is no uniform process for finding and securing a civil service job at the state or local level, but the following steps provide a pretty good rundown of what you can expect in most places.

Finding a Job Opening

All state governments and nearly all local governments have decided to take advantage of the Internet by making it their primary portal for job searches and job applications. These days, all you need do is find the

Tax Collector

Taxes are collected at the federal, state, and local levels, and everywhere that taxes are collected there will be those who try to avoid paying their fair share. That's when tax examiners and tax collectors spring to action.

Examiners, as their name suggests, examine tax forms for irregularities. When they find them, they notify the taxpayer (individual or business) about the discrepancy. If the response is unsatisfactory, a collector is assigned to the case. Collectors are the muscle in the tax-collecting business; they go after folks who either cannot or will not pay their tax bills. Tax collection is a year-round business; state and local collectors are responsible for collecting not only delinquent income taxes but also taxes that are paid continually, such as sales tax, cigarette tax, and gasoline tax. Work conditions are generally pleasant, with much of the work completed from a comfortable office during a 40-hour workweek, with occasional trips to courthouses, halls of records, and the businesses and homes of delinquent taxpayers.

State tax collectors have a number of options in performing their duties. In many cases, a simple phone call is all that is necessary to get a violator to comply. In other instances, the collector may have to institute legal proceedings that may include the garnishment of wages or the seizure of property. As you might imagine, this is not work for the faint of heart. Confronting delinquent taxpayers, whether at home, in their offices, or at the courthouse, is stressful work that occasionally results in hostile encounters.

Entry-level tax collectors often serve an apprenticeship of up to two years, during which a mentor provides on-the-job training. Ambitious collectors never stop training; they stay abreast of the latest developments in tax laws and collection methods through workshops, conferences, and academic courses. Those who succeed in the field can rise to management level, which affords them greater decision-making authority. Tax collection will never go away, because there will always be taxes and there will always be citizens who cannot or do not pay them. Even so, jobs in this field are quite competitive. This situation is exacerbated by the fact that some state and local governments are starting to outsource their tax collection business. Increased automation within tax departments has facilitated personnel reductions, further stiffening competition for new job openings.

appropriate website that lists the jobs you desire in the area you prefer, point and click, and just like that, you are ready to apply for work.

All states now allow you to complete an application and submit it online; some states, in fact, *only* process applications submitted in this manner. If you do not have online access, your local library should be able to provide it for you. Your regional state government office should also have Internet portals available to the public to facilitate job applications.

Local governments are, of course, more varied in their practices. Some allow for online applications. Others list jobs online but require you to submit a hard-copy application (by mail, fax, or in person). A few don't even list jobs online; instead, you must visit a government office to study job postings and submit your application.

At both the state and local levels, don't forget to visit the websites of specific agencies for which you wish to work as well as the main website that lists all job opportunities. In theory, all job postings should appear at the central site, but websites are operated by human beings and human beings make mistakes or fall behind in their work and don't post a job notice in a timely manner, or . . . well, you get the point. Better safe

Social Worker, Department of Corrections

Not everyone who works in a prison is a guard or warden (that's just the way it is in the movies!). Prisons need maintenance workers, kitchen staff, and a full support staff that includes medical personnel and social workers.

Social workers fulfill a number of important roles in helping prisons operate. They assess prisoners on the basis of their potential for rehabilitation and for the potential risks they pose to the prison community. They provide direct counseling to prisoners and to their families, and they place prisoners in counseling, educational, religious, and self-help programs, including substance abuse treatment programs, where appropriate. They help design practical, meaningful release programs for inmates whose sentences will soon expire, and they work with parole officers before, during, and after release to manage each parolee's readjustment to society. The job involves a lot of record keeping and a substantial amount of interaction with prison officials and the courts, but it primarily focuses on efforts to redirect inmates to productive, lawful lives outside of prison.

Social workers must hold a license, a process that typically requires the applicant to hold at least a bachelor's degree in a social work-related field. Some jobs require an advanced degree. Required skills include familiarity with social work methodology, strong interviewing techniques, strong interpersonal skills, an understanding of the dynamics of human relations, problem identification and resolution skills, familiarity with the criminal justice system and victims' issues, strong investigative skills, case planning skills, and effective communication skills (oral and written). Like all prison employees, a prison social worker must pass a criminal background check prior to employment.

Social work is not a lucrative field, but the pay is not bad either. Starting salaries range from around $30,000 to more than $40,000 and typically include state benefits packages, which are usually quite good. This job should be especially attractive to individuals interested in working in the field of substance abuse. Many prison systems, recognizing that substance abuse contributes heavily to in-prison problems as well as to failures in the rehabilitation process, are increasingly requiring inmates to undergo substance abuse therapy upon arrival and/or as a condition of release. As a result, the number of opportunities in this particular field are growing rapidly.

than sorry; that's why you should visit specific agencies' websites to double-check for job opportunities.

Each job description will provide specific details about the nature of the job, the required qualifications for the job, and the procedure for applying. Follow the directions carefully! A mistake may result in your being disqualified from consideration. Also, make sure to submit all materials by the stated deadline. Deadlines are typically written in stone; miss one and you are out of the running for the job.

What happens after you submit your application depends on the nature of the job. For many jobs, you will be required to take a written exam. Other jobs include a number of other screening processes, which are described in the following sections.

Written Exams

Many state and local government jobs have a written exam as part of the selection process. The type of test will vary greatly from job to job and from location to location, but most exams will include at least some basic reading, writing, and (sometimes) math skills. You can hone your skills in these areas by taking the practice exams in this book and by studying the review material provided here.

Beyond these basic skills, here are some of the areas most often tested for specific occupations:

- **Clerical/office support:** sorting items alphabetically and numerically, proofreading to catch discrepancies in a series of numbers and letters, coding, typing or word processing speed and accuracy, and/or stenography
- **Corrections officer:** memory and observation, logic (placing events in a logical order), using judgment and common sense in a given situation, coding, understanding and applying written rules and procedures
- **Firefighter:** following directions, judgment and reasoning (for example, what you think is the most important thing to do in a certain situation), reading and understanding maps and floor plans, memory and observation. Some municipalities and counties will provide you with a study guide that they'll expect you to study before the exam, so both your understanding and your ability to remember the materials will be tested.
- **Police officer:** memory and observation, map reading, using common sense and good judgment in a given situation

Many other jobs may not include a written test but will require various levels of certification, degrees, or job experience. Whether you have to go through other steps in the selection process depends on what kind of job you seek. Entry-level applicants for almost any public safety job—law enforcement, including corrections, or firefighting, for example—will have to pass through most if not all of these steps: one or more interviews, a physical ability test, a background investigation, a psychological investigation, and a medical evaluation. Clerical workers, on the other hand, may have only an interview—or perhaps not even that;

their written exam scores and applications may be enough to land them their jobs.

Physical Ability Test

People who are applying for almost any physically demanding job, including police officer, firefighter, or sanitation worker, can count on having to pass a physical ability test. These tests vary widely from job to job and from location to location. In some cases, you will be tested on the number of push-ups and sit-ups you can do in a specified period of time, how quickly you can run a mile, and/or how much weight you can bench-press. Other tests of physical fitness may also be administered.

Other tests may be more closely job-related. You may be asked to complete some sort of obstacle course in order to be considered for a police or firefighting job. Sanitation workers may be required to drag a heavy object and then lift and toss it as though they were throwing it onto a collection truck, and then carry several other objects a specified distance. Firefighters might have to crawl through a tunnel, climb stairs, drag a hose, drag a dummy, raise and climb a ladder, and/or jump over a wall—all while wearing full protective gear.

Whatever the parameters of the test, physical tests are usually timed, requiring you to complete a given exercise or program in a given length of time. In some cases, the test is pass/fail; if you come in under the time, you pass, and if you don't, you fail. In other cases, you are ranked based on your time; the better your time, the better your ranking and the better your chances of being hired.

If your job requires a physical ability test, you'll need to be in tip-top shape before you attempt the test. It's important that you do well on your first try, especially if the score weighs into your ranking. A few cities will allow you to retake the physical test if you fail, but most will not allow you to retake an exam until the cur-

Few jobs are as exciting, as dangerous, or as essential as firefighting. Each year firefighters save thousands of lives and prevent many billions of dollars worth of property damage, often while working under extremely perilous conditions. Because nearly two-thirds of the nation's fire departments provide medical services, many firefighters are also trained and engaged in emergency medical service. Firefighters are frequently the first responders to all types of civil disruption, from automobile accidents to forest fires to chemical spills to medical emergencies.

Firefighters must be prepared to work long, irregular hours; some departments require 24-hour shifts, and anything less than a ten-hour shift is rare. Forty-eight-hour workweeks are more the norm than is the traditional 40-hour workweek. The pay isn't commensurate with the value of the work. Firefighters may start earning in the $30,000 range. Higher-ups are more fairly compensated; a captain can earn a base salary between $49,000 and $59,000 annually, while a fire chief can earn a base salary of up to $90,000. For all firefighters, opportunities for overtime are often available. Most firefighters also enjoy generous benefits packages that provide plenty of vacation and sick leave, medical and life insurance, pension plans, and tuition reimbursement.

Despite the challenges and the risks involved, firefighting jobs are tough to land. The field is highly competitive, with many applicants for each open position. Candidates for the job must pass a written test; tests of strength, coordination, agility, and stamina; a background investigation that may include a polygraph test; a medical examination that includes a drug screening test; and a board-conducted interview. The completion of a firefighting-related curriculum at a community college may improve one's chances of employment but is rarely mandatory. Some departments require entering firefighters to arrive with EMT-basic training. Others provide this training as part of their entry-level training programs. Apprenticeship programs of up to four years' duration are available in some locations.

An effective firefighter must be able to function as part of a team under stressful conditions. Alertness, courage, endurance, self-discipline, and a commitment to public service are all essential. The best firefighters continually study to improve their skills and knowledge, learning about new techniques, new medical technology, the latest programs in public education, and the latest research on the detection and prevention of arson. Promotion, like hiring, is often contingent at least in part on performance on written examinations.

rent application period ends and the following application period begins.

Interviews

In the private sector, an initial interview is often one of the first steps in the process of getting hired. You submit your application or resume, and then the company calls you in for an interview to see whether you're the type of person they want. In the public sector, an interview—when there is one—is likely to come later in the process. On the basis of your application and any supporting materials (including your exam score when an exam is required), the agency has already decided that you're the type of person that they want. The interview is to make sure. You'll probably face most of the standard interview questions: who you are, what your experience is and how it has prepared you for this job, where you want to be in six months or five years. Although the interview doesn't give you a chance to make up for a spotty application or bad test scores—

you won't be called if you have those—it does give you a chance to convince the interviewer that you have good verbal communication skills and poise.

People applying for public safety jobs, including police officer, corrections officer, or firefighter, are likely to face a different type of interview than are people applying for office-based jobs. They may also be required to submit to several interviews, perhaps one with a chief or deputy chief, another with a board that includes officers, officials from outside the hiring department, and civilians. In most cases, the primary goal in this type of interview is to assess your communication skills, your interpersonal skills, and your judgment. You'll probably be asked why you want a job in public safety and what qualities you have that will make you good at the job. You will probably also be asked to speak about your background: your upbringing, your education, and any relevant life experiences. You may be presented with hypothetical situations that are job related; these will be designed to measure your ethical and moral standards, not your knowledge of the job. For example, you may be asked what you would do if you caught a fellow officer stealing during an investigation.

Background Information

Many government employers conduct at least a cursory background check of most or all potential employees. For most jobs, the investigation does little more than confirm the facts on your application, checking to make sure that you did indeed attend that fancy university and work for that prestigious company you listed on your resume.

Law enforcement agents and firefighters are subjected to much more rigorous background checks. You might not even be aware that you're being investigated, but if the background investigator—often a federal agent or a detective in the police department—uncovers any discrepancies in your application or other information you've submitted, you can be sure that you will be questioned about them. Therefore, it is critical that you be open and honest throughout all stages of the application and selection process.

Psychological Evaluation

People applying for public safety jobs are also subject to a psychological evaluation. These are stressful jobs, so hiring departments want to make sure that candidates have the emotional stability to handle the pressure. After all, the lives of the employee, his or her fellow officers, and citizens could be at stake. The psychological examination for police officers is generally more extensive than for firefighters and correctional officers. You'll be tested to determine that you won't be hampered by serious emotional disturbances, nervous disorders, or drug and/or alcohol dependence. Sometimes the psychological evaluation consists of one or more written tests. Sometimes an interview with a psychiatrist is also included.

Medical Evaluation

To work for the state, city, or county, you may be asked to submit a letter from your physician certifying that you are in generally good physical health, particularly if your job involves physical stress. You may also have to submit to a drug test.

Candidates for public safety positions usually have to be examined by a doctor of the department's choosing. The medical exam is like a regular physical. Your blood pressure, height, weight, and other vital data will be recorded. Your eyes and ears will probably be checked, and you may have a blood and/or urine test, which may or may not also serve as a drug test. But that's about all. If you've made it this far in the hiring process, you'll probably have a job offer waiting for you once you receive the doctor's okay.

▶ Preparing for the Hiring Process

The best way to prepare for the ordeal that getting hired entails is to talk to people already in the position you desire. They are best able to tell you about the demands of the job and what you can expect both during the hiring process and on the job. You can learn what qualities are most valued by those departments and what techniques successful candidates have used to prepare for exams and interviews.

You can use the practice exams in this book to help you get ready for the parts of your test that include reading, writing, math, and civil service skills. LearningExpress also publishes more specific guides on the tests and selection process for many civil service jobs. Check out the titles we publish at our website, www.learnatest.com.

▶ Contacts for Government Jobs at the State Level

ALABAMA

Jackie B. Graham, Director
Paul Thomas, Deputy Director
State of Alabama Personnel Department
300 Folsom Administrative Building
64 North Union Street
Montgomery, AL 36130-4100
Phone: 334-242-3389
Web: www.personnel.state.al.us

ALASKA

Mailing Address:
Department of Administration
Division of Personnel
P.O. Box 110201
Juneau, AK 99811-0201

Street Address:
State Office Building
333 Willoughby Avenue, Tenth Floor
Juneau, AK 99801-1770

Phone: 800-587-0430 (statewide toll-free number); 907-465-4095 (Juneau and out-of-state callers)
Fax: 907-465-2576
Web: http://dop.state.ak.us (Click "Workplace Alaska" link.)

ARIZONA

Web: http://azstatejobs.gov (Apply via the Internet and follow up by contacting the Human Resources Department of the agency to which you are applying.)

ARKANSAS

Mailing Address:

P.O. Box 3278

Little Rock, AR 72203

Street Address:

Office of Personnel Management

DFA Building

1509 West Seventh Street, Suite 201

Little Rock, AR 72201

Phone: 501-682-1823

Fax: 501-682-5104

Web: www.ark.org/arstatejobs/index.php

E-mail: opmhelp@dfa.state.ar.us

CALIFORNIA

California State Personnel Board

801 Capitol Mall

Sacramento, CA 95814

Phone: 213-620-6450 (Los Angeles); 916-445-0538 (Sacramento); 619-237-6163 (San Diego); 415-557-7871 (San Francisco); 916-651-8782 (TTD)

Web: http://spb.ca.gov/employment

COLORADO

Department of Personnel and Administration

1600 Broadway, Suite 1030

Denver, CO 80202

Phone: 303-866-6566

Fax: 303-866-3034

Web: www.gssa.state.co.us (Click "Colorado State Government Classified Jobs System" link.)

E-mail: dpacomments@state.co.us

CONNECTICUT

Department of Administrative Services

Web: www.das.state.ct.us/exam/default.asp

Anne Gnazzo, Commissioner

165 Capitol Avenue, Room 491

Hartford, CT 06106

Phone: 860-713-5100

Fax: 860-713-7481

E-mail: anne.gnazzo@ct.gov

Brenda Sisco, Deputy Commissioner

165 Capitol Avenue, Room 491

Hartford, CT 06106

Phone: 860-713-5100

Fax: 860-713-7480

E-mail: brenda.sisco@ct.gov

Pamela L. Libby, Ph.D., Director, Human Resource Management

165 Capitol Avenue, Room 411

Hartford, CT 06106

Phone: 860-713-5204

Fax: 860-622-2965

E-mail: pamela.libby@po.state.ct.us

DELAWARE

24-Hour Job Line: 302-739-7750 (in Delaware); 800-345-1789 (out of state)

Web: www.delawarestatejobs.com/postings/index.asp

Carvel State Office Building
New Castle County
820 North French Street
Wilmington, DE 19801
Phone: 302-577-8277
Fax: 302-577-3957

Haslet Armory
Kent County
122 William Penn Street
Dover, DE 19901
Phone: 302-739-5458
Fax: 302-739-2327

Del Tech Owens Campus
Sussex County
P.O. Box 610
Georgetown, DE 19947
Phone: 302-856-5966
Fax: 302-856-5969

FLORIDA

Phone: 877-562-7287; 866-221-0268 (TTY)
Web: http://peoplefirst.myflorida.com

GEORGIA

Civil Service Testing Center
Georgia Merit System Office
Floyd Veterans Memorial Building
Twin Towers (West)
2 Martin Luther King Jr. Drive SE
Atlanta, GA 30334-5100
Phone: 404-656-2728
Web: http://thejobsite.org (Contact individual agency's human resources department to inquire about posted positions. Contact information is available online at http://thejobsite.org/mapsdirections/hr-offices.asp.)

HAWAII

Department of Human Resources Development
Leiopapa a Kamehameha Building
235 South Beretania Street
Honolulu, HI 96813-2437
Phone: 808-587-1100
Fax: 808-587-1106
Web: www.hawaii.gov/hrd

Employee Staffing Division of Human Resources Department:
Examinations—Phone: 808-587-0994; Fax: 808-587-0909
State Recruiting Office—Phone: 808-587-0936; Fax: 808-587-1003

IDAHO

Mailing Address:
Division of Human Resources
P.O. Box 83720
Boise, ID 83720-0066

Street Address:
700 West State Street
Boise, ID 83702-5868
(There is an application drop box outside the
Division of Human Resources office.)

Phone: 208-334-2263 (local); 800-554-5627
(toll-free); 800-542-5738 (TDD)
Fax: 208-334-3182
Web: http://dhr.idaho.gov

ILLINOIS

Illinois Department of Central Management
Services
Web: www.state.il.us/cms/1_employ

CMS Assessment Centers:
(Examining/employment applications are
available at any other Illinois Employment and
Training Center (IETC) operated by the
Illinois Department of Employment Security.)

James R. Thompson Center
100 West Randolph Street, Suite 3-300
Chicago, IL 60601
Phone: 312-793-3565; 312-814-4458 (TTY)

Capital City Center
130 West Mason Street, Second Floor
Springfield, IL 62702
Phone: 217-557-6885; 217-785-3979 (TTY)

State Regional Office Building
2125 South First Street, Main Level
Champaign, IL 61820
Phone: 217-278-3435
Illinois Relay Center: 800-526-0844

State Regional Office Building
2309 West Main Street, Main Level
Marion, IL 62959
Phone: 618-993-7005
Illinois Relay Center: 800-526-0844

E. J. "Zeke" Giorgi Center
200 South Wyman Street, Lower Level
Rockford, IL 61101
Phone: 815-987-7004
Illinois Relay Center: 800-526-0844

Department of Central Management Services
Examining and Counseling Division Office
Stratton Office Building, Room 500
Springfield, IL 62706
Phone: 217-782-7100; 217-785-3979 (TTY)

INDIANA

Indiana State Personnel Department
402 West Washington Street, Room W161
Indianapolis, IN 46204
Phone: 317-232-3080; 800-232-4555 (TDD)
Web: www.in.gov/jobs
(All applications must be submitted online; the
state does not accept applications submitted
by mail or fax.)

IOWA

Department of Administrative Services,
Human Resources Enterprise
Hoover State Office Building
1305 East Walnut Street
Des Moines, IA 50319
Phone: 515-281-3087
Fax: 515-242-6450 (general); 515-281-7970
(applications); 515-281-5102 (benefits)
Office Hours: 8:00 A.M.–4:30 P.M.,
Monday–Friday
Web: http://das.hre.iowa.gov/state_jobs.html
E-mail: dashre.info@iowa.gov

KANSAS

Division of Personnel Services
Phone: 785-296-4278
Web: http://da.state.ks.us/ps/aaa/recruitment
E-mail: psweb@da.state.ks.us
(Apply online or by mail and then follow up
with a call to the human resources
department of the agency to which you are
applying.)

KENTUCKY

Kentucky Personnel Cabinet
200 Fair Oaks Lane, Fifth Floor
Frankfort, KY 40601
Phone: 866-PAL-LINE (866-725-5463) (toll-
free); 502-564-8339 (in Frankfort); 502-564-
8030 (applications, counseling, or testing);
502-564-6922 (registering)
Web: http://personnel.ky.gov/employment

LOUISIANA

Mailing Address:
Louisiana Department of State Civil Service
P.O. Box 94111, Capitol Station
Baton Rouge, LA 70804-9111

Street Address:
Louisiana Department of State Civil Service
1201 North Third Street, Suite 3-280
Baton Rouge, LA 70802

Baton Rouge Testing Center
5825 Florida Boulevard
Baton Rouge, LA 70806

Phone: 225-342-8536
Web: www.dscs.state.la.us/asp/csjobsearch/
search/jobs.htm

MAINE

Department of Administrative and Financial
    Services
Bureau of Human Resources
Burton M. Cross Building, Fourth Floor
#4 State House Station
Augusta, ME 04333-0004
Office Hours: 8:00 A.M.–5:00 P.M.,
    Monday–Friday
Phone: 207-624-7761; 888-577-6690 (TTY)
Fax: 207-287-4414
Web: www.maine.gov/statejobs

MARYLAND

Maryland Department of Budget and
    Management
45 Calvert Street
Annapolis, MD 21401
Phone: 800-705-3493
Web: www.dbm.maryland.gov (Click "State
    Jobs" link. Find job listings online and then
    submit application to hiring agency.)
E-mail: marylandgov@dbm.state.md.us

MASSACHUSETTS

Commonwealth of Massachusetts Human
    Resources Division
Executive Office for Administration and
    Finance
One Ashburton Place, Room 301
Boston, MA 02108
Hours: 8:45 A.M.–5:00 P.M., Monday–Friday,
    except holidays
Phone: 617-727-3555; 800-392-6178 (toll-free)
Web: www.mass.gov

MICHIGAN

Web: www.michigan.gov

Lansing Office:
Capitol Commons Center
400 South Pine Street
Lansing, MI 48913
Phone: 517-373-3048; 800-788-1766 (toll-free);
    517-335-0191 (TDD)
Fax: 517-373-7690

Detroit Office:
Cadillac Place
3042 West Grand Boulevard, Suite 4-400,
    Fourth Floor
Detroit, MI 48202
Phone: 313-456-4400; 313-456-4409 (TDD)
Fax: 313-456-4411

MINNESOTA

Department of Employee Relations Job
    Information Line
Phone: 651-296-2616 (in Minneapolis); 800-
    657-3974 (toll-free)
Web: www.doer.state.mn.us/employment.htm
E-mail: job.info@state.mn.us

MISSISSIPPI

State Personnel Board
Robert G. Clark, Jr. Building
301 North Lamar, Suite 203
Jackson, MS 39201
Phone: 601-359-1406
Fax: 601-359-2729
Web: www.spbrez.ms.gov/appltest/
    starteapp.html

MISSOURI

Mailing Address:
Division of Personnel
Office of Administration
P.O. Box 388
Jefferson City, MO 65102

Street Address:
Division of Personnel
Office of Administration
Harry S. Truman Building
301 West High Street, Room 430
Jefferson City, MO 65102

Phone: 573-751-4162
Fax: 573-751-8641
Web: www.state.mo.us/mo/stjobs.htm
E-mail:persmail@mail.mo.gov

MONTANA

Mailing Address:
Human Resource Office
P.O. Box 200108
Helena, MT 59620-0127

Street Address:
Human Resource Office
Sam W. Mitchell Building, Room 102
125 North Roberts Street
Helena, MT 59601-4558

Phone: 406-444-3871
Fax: 406-444-0703
Web: http://mt.gov/statejobs/statejobs.asp

NEBRASKA

DAS State Personnel
301 Centennial Mall South, Mall Level
Lincoln, NE 68509
Phone: 402-471-2075
Fax: 402-471-3754
Web: www.das.state.ne.us/personnel/
 nejobs/per.htm

NEVADA

Department of Personnel
209 East Musser Street
Carson City, NV 89701-4267

Carson City Training Center
2527 North Carson Street, Suite 275
Carson City, NV 89706-0147

Las Vegas Training Center
555 East Washington Avenue
Las Vegas, NV 89101-1083

Phone: 775-684-0160 (Carson City); 702-486-
 2920 (Las Vegas); 800-992-0900 ext. 0160 (in
 Nevada)
Web: http://dop.nv.gov/fshome.html

NEW HAMPSHIRE

Human Resources Director
State of New Hampshire Division of Personnel
25 Capitol Street
Concord, NH 03301-6313
Phone: 603-271-3262; 800-735-2964 (TDD)
Fax: 603-271-1422
Web: www.nh.gov/hr/employmentlisting.html

NEW JERSEY

Street Address:

Department of Personnel

44 South Clinton Avenue

Trenton, NJ 08625

Mailing Address:

Department of Personnel

P.O. Box 310

Trenton, NJ 08625

Phone: 609-292-4144

Web: www.state.nj.us/personnel/
jobs/index.htm

NEW MEXICO

New Mexico State Personnel Office

2600 Cerrillos Road

Santa Fe, NM 87505

Web: www.state.nm.us/spo (Click on the "Jobs"
link.)

NEW YORK

New York State Department of Civil Service

Alfred E. Smith State Office Building

80 South Swan Street

Albany, NY 12239

Office Hours: 8:30 A.M.–5 P.M., Monday–Friday

Phone: 518-457-2487 (in Albany); 877-NYS-
JOBS (877-697-5627) (toll-free)

Web: www.cs.state.ny.us/jobseeker/public

E-mail: pio@cs.state.ny.us

NORTH CAROLINA

Office of State Personnel

Web: www.osp.state.nc.us/jobs

Mailing Address:

1331 Mail Service Center

Raleigh, NC 27699-1331

Street Address:

Administration Building, Third Floor

116 West Jones Street

Raleigh, NC 27603-1300

Phone: 919-807-4800

Fax: 919-733-0653

Personnel Development Center

101 West Peace Street

Raleigh, NC 27603-1127

Phone: 919-733-2474

Temporary Solutions

620 North West Street, Suite 102

Raleigh, NC 27603-5938

Phone: 919-733-7927

NORTH DAKOTA

Human Resources Management Services

600 East Boulevard Avenue, Department 113

Bismarck, ND 58505-0120

Phone: 701-328-3293

Fax: 701-328-1475

Web: www.nd.gov/hrms

E-mail: hrms@state.nd.us

OHIO

Labor Market and Recruitment Office
100 East Broad Street, 15th Floor
Columbus, OH 43215-3607
Phone: 614-466-7795
Fax: 614-644-5360
E-mail: oleap@das.state.oh.us

Civil Service Testing and State Job Information
   Office
30 East Broad Street, 28th Floor
Columbus, OH 43215-3414
Phone: 614-466-8044
Fax: 614-232-1612
E-mail: oleap@das.state.oh.us
Web: www.stateofohiojobs.com/
   applicant/index.asp

OKLAHOMA

Office of Personnel Management
Jim Thorpe Building
2101 North Lincoln Boulevard
Oklahoma City, OK 73105
Office Hours: 8 A.M.–5 P.M., Monday–Friday
Phone: 405-521-2177
Fax: 405-524-6942
Web: www.ok.gov/opm/opm_html/
   current_job_announcements.htm
E-mail: opm-mail@opm.state.ok.us

OREGON

Department of Administrative Services
155 Cottage Street NE, U-30
Salem, OR 97301-3967
Office Hours: 8 A.M.–5 P.M., Monday–Friday
Phone: 503-378-8344
Web: www.oregonjobs.org
E-mail: statejobs.info@state.or.us

PENNSYLVANIA

State Civil Service Commission
Web: www.scsc.state.pa.us/scsc/site/default.asp

Harrisburg Office:
320 Market Street
Strawberry Square Complex, Second Floor
P.O. Box 569
Harrisburg, PA 17108-0569
Phone: 717-783-3058; 717-772-2685 (TDD)

Philadelphia Office:
10 South 11th Street, Second Floor
Philadelphia, PA 19107-3618
Phone: 215-560-2253; 215-560-4367 (TDD)

Pittsburgh Office:
300 Liberty Avenue
State Office Building, Room 1503
Pittsburgh, PA 15222-1210
Phone: 412-565-7666; 412-565-2484 (TDD)

RHODE ISLAND

Cheryl A. Burrell, Human Resources Program
   Administrator
Department of Administration, Human
   Resources Outreach and Diversity Office
One Capitol Hill
Providence, RI 02908-5860
Phone: 401-222-6397
Fax: 401-222-6391
Web: www.dlt.ri.gov/webdev/jobsri/
   statejobs.htm
E-mail: cburrell@hr.ri.gov

SOUTH CAROLINA

Office of Human Resources

State Career Center

1401 Senate Street

Columbia, SC 29201

Phone: 803-734-9080

Web: www.ohr.sc.gov/ohr/applicant/ohr
jobs.phtm

E-mail: appohr@ohr.state.sc.us

SOUTH DAKOTA

Bureau of Personnel

Web: www.state.sd.us/bop/jobs/jobs_home.htm

E-mail: bopinfo@state.sd.us

Central Office

Capitol Building

500 East Capitol Avenue

Pierre, SD 57501-5070

Phone: 605-773-3148

Fax: 605-773-4344

Training

Foss Building

523 East Capitol Avenue

Pierre, SD 57501-3182

Phone: 605-773-3461

Fax: 605-773-5389

Human Resources

Capitol Building

500 East Capitol Avenue

Pierre, SD 57501-5070

Phone: 605-773-6363

Fax: 605-773-6947

TENNESSEE

Tennessee Department of Personnel

Applicant Services

James K. Polk Building

505 Deaderick Street, Second Floor

Nashville, TN 37243-0635

Phone: 615-741-4841

Web: www.tennesseeanytime.org/
employment.html

TEXAS

Texas Workforce Commission

101 East 15th Street

Austin, TX 78778-0001

Phone: 800-832-2829

Web: https://wit.twc.state.tx.us

E-mail: laborinfo@twc.state.tx.us

UTAH

Utah Department of Human Resource
Management

State Office Building, Suite 2120

Salt Lake City, UT 84114-1531

Phone: 801-538-3025; 801-538-3696 (TDD)

Fax: 801-538-3081

Web: www.dhrm.utah.gov

E-mail: hronline@utah.gov

Utah Department of Workforce Services

P.O. Box 45249

Salt Lake City, UT 84145-0249

Phone: 801-526-WORK (801-526-9675)

Fax: 801-526-9211

Web: https://statejobs.utah.gov

E-mail: dwscontactus@utah.gov

VERMONT

Commissioner, Department of Human
 Resources
 110 State Street, Drawer 20
Montpelier, VT 05620-3001
Phone: 802-828-3491
Fax: 802-828-3409

Director, Recruitment Services/Workforce
 Planning and Development
Cyprian Learning Center
Osgood Building
103 South Main Street
Waterbury, VT 05671-2801
Phone: 802-241-1261
Fax: 802-241-1119

Help Desk: 7:45 A.M.–4:30 P.M., Monday–Friday
Phone: 802-828-0407; 800-253-0191 (TTY)
Web: www.vermontpersonnel.org/
 jobapplicant/index.php
E-mail: recruit@per.state.vt.us

VIRGINIA

Department of Human Resource Management
101 North 14th Street, 12th Floor
Richmond, VA 23219
Phone: 804-225-2131
Fax: 804-371-7401
Web: http://jobs.virginia.gov

WASHINGTON

Department of Personnel
600 South Franklin Street SE
Olympia, WA 98501-1314
Phone: 360-664-1960; 360-664-6211 (TTY)
Web: http://careers.wa.gov
E-mail: information@dop.wa.gov

WEST VIRGINIA

West Virginia Division of Personnel
Charleston Capitol Complex
1900 Kanawha Boulevard East
Building 6, Room 420
Charleston, WV 25305-0139
Phone: 304-558-3950 (job opportunity
 announcements: ext. 503); 304-558-1237
 (TDD)
Fax: 304-558-1399
Web: www.state.wv.us/admin/personnel/jobs

WISCONSIN

Mailing Address:

Office of State Employment Relations

P.O. Box 7855

Madison, WI 53707-7855

Street Address:

Office of State Employment Relations

101 East Wilson Street, Fourth Floor

Madison, WI 53702

Phone: 608-266-1731

Fax: 608-267-1020

Web: www.wiscjobs.state.wi.us/
    public/index.asp

E-mail: oserdir@oser.state.wi.us

WYOMING

State of Wyoming Human Resources Division

Emerson Building

2001 Capitol Avenue

Cheyenne, WY 82002-0060

Phone: 307-777-7188

Fax: 307-777-6562

Web: http://personnel.state.wy.us/
    stjobs/index.htm

E-mail: stjobs@state.wy.us

SECTION

II ▶ Skill Review

Math Skills for Civil Service Exams

ot all civil service exams test your math knowledge, but many do. Knowledge of basic arithmetic, as well as the complex reasoning necessary for algebra, are important qualifications for almost any profession. You have to be able to add up dollar figures, evaluate budgets, compute percentages, and perform similar mathematical tasks in many civil service jobs. Many jobs require someone able to read and interpret data presented in the form of tables and graphs. So even if your exam doesn't include math, you'll probably find that the material in this chapter will help you on the job.

The math portion of the test covers subjects you probably studied in grade school and high school. While every test is different, most emphasize arithmetic skills and word-problem solving.

▶ Strategies for Multiple-Choice Tests

Have you ever wondered why some people are naturally good test takers, while others never seem to reach their potential under test conditions? Good test takers are those who intuitively understand what strategies work best on a multiple-choice test. If you're not one of those people, don't worry: You can learn these strategies. They are not complicated or elaborate, and they will help you greatly improve your test scores. Here they are:

- **Perform all work on paper.** Don't try to solve problems in your head. It is too easy to make a careless mistake that way. And, if you do make a mistake, you will be much less likely to find and correct it because you won't be able to review your work. That's why you should write everything out. Solve equations on paper and draw diagrams whenever necessary. You will not only make fewer careless mistakes, but also be able to recheck your work at the end of the test, time permitting.

- **Skip questions that you find difficult or time consuming.** Remember that you need only to pass this test; you do not need a perfect score. Therefore, you do not have to answer every question. If you can't answer a question, just skip it and move on. There will be other questions ahead that you will be able to answer, and you want to make sure to get to them. Also, because your final score will be based on the number of questions you answer correctly, you do not want to work on time-consuming questions until you have answered every question that you can answer quickly. Circle questions that you skip to make them easier to locate if and when you return to them.

- **Break questions down into component parts.** Don't try to ingest the problem whole. Look at each piece of information to determine its significance in solving the problem. Later in this chapter, we'll discuss techniques you can use to translate word problems into equations. Breaking down questions into component parts helps with this translation technique.

- **Reread the question before you record your final answer.** Some of the incorrect answer choices on multiple-choice tests represent partial answers; these are answers that represent only *some* of the calculations necessary to answer the question. For example, if the question asks you to add two numbers and multiply the sum by a third number, the sum of the two numbers may be one of the incorrect answers. Choosing a partial answer is one of the most common careless errors people make on mathematics multiple-choice exams.

- **Use approximate values whenever you can.** Take a look at the answer choices: Are the values bunched close together, or are they greatly different? If the answer choices are far apart, you can probably approximate to find the correct answer. This is a great time-saver. Suppose a problem asks you to multiply $5.97 and $9.04. It's much easier to multiply $6 and $9, so if the question allows you to approximate, do it! You're also much less likely to make a careless error when you calculate with approximate values. If a question asks you to multiply $5.97 and $9.04, look at the answer choices. If only one answer is near $54 (the product of $6 and $9), you know that you can use approximate values to solve.

- **Before recording your answer, ask yourself if the answer is reasonable.** The most common miscalculation on civil service mathematics exams involves misplacement of a decimal point. Other common errors yield results that are clearly impossible. Use common sense to make sure that your answer is reasonable and that you didn't make a careless error of some type. For example, suppose a question asked you to multiply 10.3 and 1.8. Suppose you calculated the answer 185.4. Check your answer using common sense and approximate values. 10.3 is almost 10 and 1.8 is almost 2, so the correct answer should be somewhere around 20. In this way, you would know that you made a careless error and could correct it.

- **Take advantage of the multiple-choice format of the test.** Multiple-choice tests give you the correct answer. Of course, they bury the answer among three incorrect answers. Even so, the fact that the correct answer already appears in the test means that you do not have to solve every problem from scratch. You can answer some problems by testing the answers. We call this technique "working backward."

► Working Backward

You can answer some questions simply by testing the answer choices against the problem. When you test the correct answer choice against the question, the question will read as a true statement. Each of the incorrect answers will turn the question into a false statement.

Choose an answer choice that will be easy to work with, preferably one that is neither the greatest nor the least value among the answer choices. Then, plug your selection into the text of the problem to see whether it is the correct solution.

Example: Juan ate $\frac{1}{3}$ of the jelly beans in a bag. Maria then ate $\frac{3}{4}$ of the remaining jelly beans in the bag, after which there were 10 remaining jelly beans. How many jelly beans were originally in the bag?

    a. 60   **b.** 90   **c.** 120   **d.** 140

Start by testing 90. If there were 90 jelly beans in the bag originally, then there will be 10 jelly beans remaining in the bag after Juan eats $\frac{1}{3}$ of them and then Maria eats $\frac{3}{4}$ of the remaining jelly beans. $\frac{1}{3}$ of 90 is 30, meaning that Juan ate 30 jelly beans, leaving 60 jelly beans in the bag. Maria then ate $\frac{3}{4}$ of the remaining jelly beans; $\frac{3}{4}$ of 60 is 45, leaving 15 jelly beans in the bag. If 90 were the correct answer, there would have been 10, not 15, jelly beans left in the bag when Maria was done eating. Therefore, 90 is not the correct answer. The correct answer is probably the smaller answer 60. (Do you see how starting with an answer that is neither the least nor the greatest value allows you to eliminate more than one incorrect answer at a time?) Let's test 60 just to be sure.

Juan eats $\frac{1}{3}$ of the 60 jelly beans in the bag. $\frac{1}{3}$ of 60 is 20, meaning that 40 jelly beans remain in the bag. Maria eats $\frac{3}{4}$ of the 40 remaining jelly beans. $\frac{3}{4}$ of 40 is 30, which means that 10 jelly beans remain in the bag. That's true; the problem tells us that 10 jelly beans remain in the bag. 60 is the correct answer; when you plug it into the question, the result is a true statement.

► Word Problems

Many of the math problems on civil service tests are word problems. A word problem can include any kind of math, including simple arithmetic, fractions, decimals, percentages, and even algebra.

The hardest part of any word problem is translating the problem into an equation. Fortunately, there are a few reliable tricks that help you translate English statements into mathematical statements. At other times, a key word in the problem hints at the mathematical operation to be performed. Study the following information to see how to translate word problems into mathematical statements and equations.

Equals   key words: is, are, has, was, were, had

English	Math
Bob is 18 years old.	$B = 18$
There are 7 hats.	$H = 7$
Judi has 5 books.	$J = 5$

Addition   key words: sum, together, more, total, greater, or older than

English	Math
The sum of two numbers is 10.	$x + y = 10$
Karen has $5 more than Sam.	$K = 5 + S$
Judi is 2 years older than Tony.	$J = T + 2$
The total of the three numbers is 25.	$a + b + c = 25$
Joan and Tom together have $16.	$J + T = 16$

Subtraction   key words: difference; less, fewer, or younger than; remain; left over

English	Math
The difference between the two numbers is 17.	$x - y = 17$
Mike has 5 fewer cats than twice the number Jan has.	$M = 2J - 5$
Jay is 2 years younger than Brett.	$J = B - 2$
After Carol ate 3 apples, R apples remained.	$R = C - 3$

Multiplication   key words: product, times, of

English	Math
20% of the students	$\frac{20}{100} \times S$
Half of the boys	$\frac{1}{2} \times b$
The product of two numbers is 12.	$a \times b = 12$ or $ab = 12$

Division   key words: per, evenly

English	Math
15 drops per teaspoon	$\frac{15 \text{ drops}}{\text{tsp}}$
22 miles per gallon	$\frac{22 \text{ miles}}{\text{gal}}$
100 gifts divided evenly among 10 people	$100 \div 10$

▶ Distance Formula: Rate × Time = Distance

Distance formula problems include key words such as *speed*, *plane*, *train*, *boat*, *car*, *walk*, *run*, *climb*, and *swim*. They provide two of the three elements—rate, time, and distance—in the distance formula. Plug those two elements into the formula and solve for the third. Don't forget that rate and time have to be measured in common units. If the rate is measured in miles per hour, the time has to be measured in hours, not minutes or days.

Example: How far did the plane travel in 4 hours if it traveled at an average speed of 300 miles per hour?

$rt = d$
$r = 300$
$t = 3$
$300 \times 4 = d$
$1,200 = d$

The plane traveled 1,200 miles.

Example: Ben walked 20 miles in 4 hours. What was his average speed?

$rt = d$
$t = 4$
$d = 20$
$r \times 4 = 20$
$(r \times 4) \div 4 = 20 \div 4$
$r = 5$

Ben walked at a rate of 5 miles per hour.

Example: Jill drives 12 miles in 15 minutes. How far does she drive in 1 hour?

$rt = d$

Convert all measurements to a common unit. Because the question asks for an answer in terms of hours, convert all time measurements to hours. 15 minutes equals $\frac{15}{60}$ hours. $\frac{15}{60}$ reduces to $\frac{1}{4}$.

$t = \frac{1}{4}$
$d = 12$
$r \times \frac{1}{4} = 12$
$(r \times \frac{1}{4}) \times 4 = 12 \times 4$
$r = 48$

Jill drives 48 miles in 1 hour.

Two Ways to Solve Word Problems

Consider the following problem:

David has a box of doughnuts. He gives $\frac{1}{3}$ of the doughnuts in the box to Wanda, and then gives 2 doughnuts to Andrew, after which 8 doughnuts remain in the box. How many doughnuts were originally in the box?

a. 9 **b.** 12 **c.** 15 **d.** 18

There are two ways to solve this problem. The first is to translate the problem into an equation and solve.

- David has a box of doughnuts.

  Call the box of doughnuts D.

- He gives $\frac{1}{3}$ of the doughnuts in the box to Wanda . . .

  Subtract one-third of the number of doughnuts from the box.
  $D - \frac{1}{3}D$, which equals $\frac{2}{3}D$

- then gives 2 doughnuts to Andrew . . .

  $\frac{2}{3}D - 2$

- after which 8 doughnuts remain in the box.

  $\frac{2}{3}D - 2 = 8$

Now you have an equation you can solve.

$\frac{2}{3}D - 2 = 8$

Add 2 to both sides.

$\frac{2}{3}D - 2 + 2 = 8 + 2$
$\frac{2}{3}D = 10$

Multiply both sides by 3.

$3 \times \frac{2}{3}D = 3 \times 10$
$\frac{3}{1} \times \frac{2}{3}D = 3 \times 10$
$\frac{3 \times 2}{1 \times 3}D = 3 \times 10$
$\frac{6}{3}D = 30$
$2D = 30$

Finally, divide both sides by 2.

$2D \div 2 = 30 \div 2$
$D = 15$

Therefore, there were originally 15 doughnuts in the box.

There is another way to solve the problem, a way that is possible only because this is a multiple-choice question. You can work backward from the answers to see which one is correct. Let's work backward from choice **b**, 12.

- David has a box of doughnuts.

    David has 12 doughnuts.

- He gives $\frac{1}{3}$ of the doughnuts in the box to Wanda . . .

    David gives Wanda $\frac{1}{3}$ of his 12 doughnuts. Thus, he gives her 4 doughnuts and has 8 doughnuts left.

- then gives 2 doughnuts to Andrew . . .

    $8 - 2 = 6$

- after which 8 doughnuts remain in the box.

No, 6 doughnuts remain in the box, which means that 12 is not the correct answer to the question. If 12 had been the correct choice, there would have been 8 doughnuts left in the box instead of 6 when your calculations were finished. There are too few doughnuts left in the box; therefore, the correct choice is greater than 12. Test choices **c**, 15, or **d**, 18, next to determine which is correct. Let's test choice **c**, 15. David gives $\frac{1}{3}$ of his 15 doughnuts to Wanda; he gives her 5, keeping 10. He gives 2 to Andrew, after which 8 doughnuts remain in the box. That's right! The correct answer is **c**, 15.

▶ Fractions and Decimals

Fractions are used to describe the relationship between a part and a whole. The number representing the *part* appears in the top half of the fraction, called the *numerator*. The number representing the *whole* appears in the bottom half of the fraction, called the *denominator*.

Consider the following example.

Example: A pizza is cut into 8 equal slices. You eat 3 of the slices.

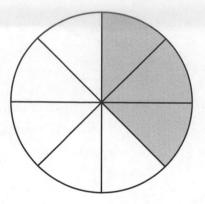

The whole pizza consists of 8 slices, of which you ate a part consisting of 3 slices. In fractional terms, that means you ate $\frac{3}{8}$ of the pizza.

Fractions appear in three different forms.

In a *proper fraction*, the numerator is smaller than the denominator.

$\frac{1}{2}, \frac{6}{11}, \frac{3}{7}, \frac{5}{9}$

In an *improper fraction*, the numerator is equal to or larger than the denominator.

$\frac{7}{3}, \frac{10}{2}, \frac{38}{7}, \frac{125}{2}$

A *mixed number* consists of a whole number and a proper fraction. Improper fractions can be rewritten as mixed numbers.

$3\frac{1}{2}, 7\frac{5}{9}, 21\frac{1}{13}, 4\frac{11}{25}$

To **convert an improper fraction to a mixed number**, use the following procedure:

1. Divide the numerator by the denominator. The result will be a whole number, with or without a remainder.
2. Write the whole number.
3. If there is a remainder, write a fraction with the remainder in the numerator and the original denominator as the denominator.

Example: Convert $\frac{17}{5}$ to a mixed number.
$17 \div 5 = 3$ with a remainder of 2
$\frac{17}{5} = 3\frac{2}{5}$

You should convert improper fractions to mixed numbers whenever you are asked to add or subtract improper fractions. Mixed numbers are easier to add and subtract than are improper fractions.

To **convert a mixed number to an improper fraction**, use the following procedure:

1. Multiply the whole number in the mixed number by the denominator of the fraction.
2. Add the result to the numerator of the fraction.

> **Example:** Convert $5\frac{1}{6}$ to an improper fraction.
> $5 \times 6 = 30$
> $30 + 1 = 31$
> $5\frac{1}{6} = 3\frac{1}{6}$

You should convert mixed numbers to improper fractions whenever you are asked to multiply or divide mixed numbers. Improper fractions are easier to multiply and divide than are mixed numbers.

Reducing Fractions

When the numerator and the denominator of a fraction are divisible by the same number, we say that the fraction can be *reduced*. When you reduce a fraction, you rewrite it with smaller numbers in the numerator and the denominator without changing the value of the fraction. When a fraction cannot be reduced further, we say that it has been written in *lowest terms* or in its *simplest form*.

Reduce a fraction by dividing both the numerator and denominator by a single value that divides evenly into both of them.

> **Example:** Reduce $\frac{5}{10}$.
> Both 5 and 10 are divisible by 5.
> $\frac{5 \div 5}{10 \div 5} = \frac{1}{2}$

A fraction is reduced to simplest terms when you divide it by the largest value that will divide evenly into the numerator and denominator. Sometimes you won't be able to think of the largest number that divides evenly into the numerator and denominator. That's okay; just divide both by whatever number you can think of that divides evenly into both, and then study your result to see whether you can think of another number that divides evenly.

> **Example:** Reduce $\frac{33}{132}$.

Both 33 and 132 are divisible by 33, but that's not so easy to see. It's much easier to see that both are divisible by 3. (Here's a neat trick: To determine whether a number is divisible by 3, add all its digits. If the sum of the digits is divisible by 3, the number itself is divisible by 3. We know that 132 is divisible by 3 because $1 + 3 + 2 = 6$, and 6 is divisible by 3. This trick works for 9, too!) So, divide by 3 first.

$$\frac{33 \div 3}{132 \div 3} = \frac{11}{44}$$

Now it's much easier to see that 11 and 44 are both divisible by 11. Reduce again.

$$\frac{11 \div 11}{44 \div 11} = \frac{1}{4}$$

$\frac{33}{132}$ reduces to $\frac{1}{4}$.

Raising Fractions to Higher Terms

When you reduce a fraction, you rewrite it so that the numerator and denominator are smaller. Raising a fraction to a higher term reverses the process; it allows you to rewrite a fraction with a larger numerator and denominator. You often need to raise one or more fractions to higher terms in order to add or subtract them.

> **Example:** Raise $\frac{2}{3}$ to higher terms with 24 in the denominator.

1. Divide 24 by the denominator, 3.
2. Multiply the numerator by the quotient, 8 (because $24 \div 3 = 8$).
3. Write the product in the numerator of a fraction with 24 in the denominator.
   $2 \times 8 = 16$, so write the fraction $\frac{16}{24}$.
4. Check your work by multiplying both the numerator and the denominator of the original fraction by 8.

$$\frac{2 \times 8}{3 \times 8} = \frac{16}{24}$$

Adding Fractions

It is easy to add fractions that have a common denominator. Simply perform the appropriate calculation on the numerators and write the result over the denominator. Do NOT add the denominators!

> **Example:** $\frac{3}{5} + \frac{1}{5} = 3 + \frac{1}{5} = \frac{4}{5}$

When adding mixed numbers, add the whole numbers together and then add the fractions together.

> **Example:** $3\frac{1}{9} + 12\frac{4}{9} = 3 + 12 + \frac{1}{9} + \frac{4}{9} = 15 + \frac{1+4}{9} = 15\frac{5}{9}$

If the sum of the fractions is an improper fraction, convert the improper fraction to a mixed number.

> **Examples:** $\frac{4}{7} + \frac{6}{7} = 4 + \frac{6}{7} = \frac{10}{7}$
> $10 \div 7 = 1$ remainder 3, so $\frac{10}{7} = 1\frac{3}{7}$
>
> $2\frac{2}{3} + 4\frac{2}{3} = 2 + 4 + \frac{2}{3} + \frac{2}{3} = 6 + \frac{2+2}{3} = 6\frac{4}{3}$
> $4 \div 3 = 1$ remainder 1, so $\frac{4}{3} = 1\frac{1}{3}$
> $6 + 1\frac{1}{3} = 7\frac{1}{3}$

Don't forget to reduce your answer to lowest terms.

> **Example:** $\frac{4}{9} + \frac{2}{9} = \frac{4+2}{9} = \frac{6}{9}$
> $\frac{6 \div 3}{9 \div 3} = \frac{2}{3}$

You cannot add fractions unless they share a common denominator. If the numbers in the bottom of the fractions are not equal, you must first rewrite one or all of the fractions until the denominators are equal. In order to add fractions, they must share a *common denominator*.

To find a common denominator, look at the denominators of all the fractions in the problem. Do they all divide evenly into the largest denominator? If they do, great! That number is your common denominator. If they don't, run through the multiplication table of the largest denominator until you find a number that all the other denominators divide into evenly.

Example: $\frac{2}{3} + \frac{1}{5} =$

Does 3 divide evenly into 5? No.

So, run through the multiplication table for 5 in your mind: 10, 15, 20, 25, etc. Does 3 divide evenly into 10? No. Does it divide evenly into 15? Yes! So, 15 is your common denominator.

Now, use the technique you learned to raise fractions to higher terms to rewrite $\frac{2}{3}$ and $\frac{1}{5}$ so that each has a denominator of 15.

$$\frac{2 \times 5}{3 \times 5} = \frac{10}{15}$$
$$\frac{1 \times 3}{5 \times 3} = \frac{3}{15}$$
$$\frac{10}{15} + \frac{3}{15} = \frac{10+3}{15} = \frac{13}{15}$$

Adding three fractions is only a little more complicated.

Example: $\frac{1}{4} + \frac{1}{3} + \frac{1}{6} =$

Do 4 and 3 divide evenly into 6? 3 does, but 4 does not. All three fractions must be written over a common denominator, so 6 cannot be the common denominator.

Run through the multiples of 6: 12, 18, 24, etc. Do 4 and 3 divide evenly into 12? Yes, so 12 is your common denominator.

Use the technique for raising fractions to higher terms to rewrite all three fractions with a denominator of 12.

$$\frac{1 \times 3}{4 \times 3} = \frac{3}{12}$$
$$\frac{1 \times 4}{3 \times 4} = \frac{4}{12}$$
$$\frac{1 \times 2}{6 \times 2} = \frac{2}{12}$$
$$\frac{3}{12} + \frac{4}{12} + \frac{2}{12} = \frac{3+4+2}{12} = \frac{9}{12}$$

Don't forget to reduce to lowest terms.

$$\frac{9 \div 3}{12 \div 3} = \frac{3}{4}$$

Subtracting Fractions

Subtracting fractions is a lot like adding fractions. When the fractions share a common denominator, the job is a pretty easy one. Simply subtract the numerators. Do NOT subtract the denominators.

Example: $\frac{7}{8} - \frac{4}{8} = 7 - \frac{4}{8} = \frac{3}{8}$

To subtract mixed numbers, subtract the whole number from the whole number and the fraction from the fraction.

Example: $5\frac{3}{4} - 1\frac{2}{4} = (5-1) + (\frac{3}{4} - \frac{2}{4}) = 4\frac{1}{4}$

Sometimes you will have to perform an extra step. If the fraction in the second mixed number is larger than the fraction in the first mixed number, you will have to borrow in order to rewrite the first number.

Example: $12\frac{1}{5} - 7\frac{3}{5} =$

Can you subtract $\frac{3}{5}$ from $\frac{1}{5}$? No, because $\frac{3}{5}$ is greater than $\frac{1}{5}$. You must rewrite $12\frac{1}{5}$ by borrowing. Because $\frac{5}{5}$ equals 1, you can borrow 1 from the 12 and add $\frac{5}{5}$ to $\frac{1}{5}$. In this way, you can rewrite $12\frac{1}{5}$ as $11\frac{1+5}{5}$, or $11\frac{6}{5}$. Now you can complete the calculation.

$$12\frac{1}{5} - 7\frac{3}{5} =$$
$$11\frac{6}{5} - 7\frac{3}{5} =$$
$$(11-7) + (\frac{6}{5} - \frac{3}{5}) = 4\frac{6-3}{5} = 4\frac{3}{5}$$

To subtract numbers that do not share common denominators, you must first rewrite one or all of the fractions until the denominators are equal. To find a common denominator, look at the denominators of all the fractions in the problem. Do they all divide evenly into the largest denominator? If they do, great! That number is your common denominator. If they don't, run through the multiplication table of the largest denominator until you find a number that all the other denominators divide into evenly.

Example: $\frac{3}{4} - \frac{1}{6} =$

Do the fractions share a common denominator? No. Does 4 divide evenly into 6? No.

So, run through the multiplication table for 6 in your mind: 12, 18, 24, 30, etc. Does 4 divide evenly into 12? Yes! So, 12 is your common denominator.

Now, use the technique you learned to raise fractions to higher terms to rewrite $\frac{3}{4}$ and $\frac{1}{6}$ so that each has a denominator of 12.

$$\frac{3\times3}{4\times3} = \frac{9}{12}$$
$$\frac{1\times2}{6\times2} = \frac{2}{12}$$
$$\frac{9}{12} - \frac{2}{12} = \frac{9-2}{12} = \frac{7}{12}$$

The same holds true for mixed numbers that do not share a common denominator. You must first rewrite the fractions so that their denominators are equal.

Example: $7\frac{1}{6} - 2\frac{4}{5} =$

Do the fractions share a common denominator? No. Does 5 divide evenly into 6? No.

So, run through the multiplication table for 6 in your mind: 12, 18, 24, 30, etc. Does 5 divide evenly into 12? No, nor does it divide evenly into 18 or 24. Your common denominator is 30.

$$\frac{1 \times 5}{6 \times 5} = \frac{5}{30}$$

$$\frac{4 \times 6}{5 \times 6} = \frac{24}{30}$$

$$7\frac{6}{30} - 2\frac{24}{30} =$$

Because you cannot subtract $\frac{24}{30}$ from $\frac{5}{30}$, you must rewrite $7\frac{5}{30}$ by borrowing 1, or $\frac{30}{30}$, from the 7.

$$7\frac{5}{30} =$$

$$6 + 1 + \frac{5}{30} =$$

$$6 + \frac{30}{30} + \frac{5}{30} =$$

$$6 + \frac{30 + 5}{30} = 6\frac{35}{30}$$

$$6\frac{35}{30} - 2\frac{24}{30} =$$

$$(6 - 2) + \frac{35}{30} - \frac{24}{30} =$$

$$4 + \frac{35 - 24}{30} =$$

$$4\frac{11}{30}$$

Multiplying Fractions

Multiplying fractions is actually easier than adding them. All you have to do is multiply the numerators and multiply the denominators.

Examples: $\frac{2}{3} \times \frac{5}{7} = \frac{2 \times 5}{3 \times 7} = \frac{10}{21}$

$\frac{1}{2} \times \frac{3}{5} \times \frac{7}{4} = \frac{1 \times 3 \times 7}{2 \times 5 \times 4} = \frac{21}{40}$

Sometimes you can cancel *before* multiplying. Canceling is a shortcut that lets you multiply smaller numbers. It's just like reducing: You find a number that divides evenly into a top number and bottom number and do the division before you multiply. If you don't cancel, it's no big deal; you'll still be able to reduce after you multiply. Canceling just makes your calculations a little bit easier.

Example: $\frac{5}{6} \times \frac{9}{20}$

1. Both 6 and 9 are divisible by 3, so you can cancel. Divide each by 3. $\frac{5}{\overset{}{\underset{2}{6}}} \times \frac{\overset{3}{9}}{20}$

2. Both 5 and 20 are divisible by 5, so you can cancel. Divide each by 5. $\frac{\overset{1}{5}}{\underset{2}{6}} \times \frac{\overset{3}{9}}{\underset{4}{20}}$

3. Now you can multiply. $\frac{1 \times 3}{2 \times 4} = \frac{3}{8}$

To multiply a fraction by a whole number, first rewrite the whole number as a fraction with a denominator of 1.

Example: $5 \times \frac{2}{3} = \frac{5}{1} \times \frac{2}{3} = \frac{10}{3}$

If the question asks for the answer in the form of a mixed number, use the technique discussed earlier to rewrite $\frac{10}{3}$ as $3\frac{1}{3}$.

To multiply mixed numbers, rewrite the mixed numbers as improper fractions before multiplying.

Example: $4\frac{2}{3} \times 5\frac{1}{2}$

1. Convert $4\frac{2}{3}$ to an improper fraction.

$(4 \times 3) + 2 = 14.\ 4\frac{2}{3} = \frac{14}{3}$

2. Convert $5\frac{1}{2}$ to an improper fraction.

$(5 \times 2) + 1 = 11.\ 5\frac{1}{2} = \frac{11}{2}$

3. Cancel and multiply.

$\frac{\overset{7}{\cancel{14}}}{3} \times \frac{11}{\underset{1}{\cancel{2}}} = \frac{77}{3}$

If the question asks for the answer in the form of a mixed number, use the technique discussed earlier to rewrite $\frac{77}{3}$ as $25\frac{2}{3}$.

You can find the fractional part of a whole by multiplying by the fraction.

Example: 8,400 fans attended a college football game. $\frac{3}{4}$ of the fans rooted for the home team. The rest rooted for the visiting team. How many fans rooted for the home team?

To solve, multiply 8,400 by $\frac{3}{4}$.

$$\frac{8,400}{1} \times \frac{3}{4} =$$

$$\frac{8,400 \times 3}{1 \times 4} =$$

$$\frac{25,200}{4}$$

A fraction is one way of writing a division problem. When you see a fraction with a numerator larger than a denominator, you can divide (that's also how we convert improper fractions to mixed fractions).

$$25,200 \div 4 = 6,100$$

There were 6,100 fans rooting for the home team.

Dividing Fractions

Dividing fractions is like multiplying fractions, but with one extra step. Before multiplying, flip the second fraction so that the numerator and denominator are reversed.

Example: $\frac{1}{2} \div \frac{3}{5}$

1. Flip the second fraction.

$\frac{3}{5} \rightarrow \frac{5}{3}$

2. Change the division sign to a multiplication sign.

3. Calculate to solve.

$\frac{1}{2} \times \frac{5}{3} = \frac{1 \times 5}{2 \times 3} = \frac{5}{6}$

To divide a fraction by a whole number, first change the whole number to a fraction by putting the whole number in the numerator of a fraction with a denominator of 1. Then follow the aforementioned steps.

Example: $\frac{3}{5} \div 2 = \frac{3}{5} \div \frac{2}{1} = \frac{3}{5} \times \frac{1}{2} = \frac{3 \times 1}{5 \times 2} = \frac{3}{10}$

To divide mixed numbers, rewrite them as improper fractions.

Example: $3\frac{1}{5} \div 1\frac{1}{2}$

1. Convert $3\frac{1}{5}$ to an improper fraction. $\qquad (3 \times 5) + 1 = 16.\ 3\frac{1}{5} = \frac{16}{5}$
2. Convert $1\frac{1}{2}$ to an improper fraction. $\qquad (1 \times 2) + 1 = 3.\ 1\frac{1}{2} = \frac{3}{2}$
3. Calculate.

$$\frac{16}{5} \div \frac{3}{2} =$$
$$\frac{16}{5} \times \frac{2}{3} =$$
$$\frac{16 \times 2}{5 \times 3} = \frac{32}{15}$$

If the problem asks for an answer in the form of a mixed number, use the conversion technique to convert $\frac{32}{15}$ to $2\frac{2}{15}$.

Decimals

A decimal is a way to write a fraction without a numerator or denominator. You use decimals every day when you deal with money—$10.35 is a decimal that represents 10 dollars and 35 cents. The period separating the dollars from the cents is called a decimal point. In $10.35, 35 represents a fraction; because 1 cent equals $\frac{1}{100}$ of a dollar, 35 in $10.35 represents $\frac{35}{100}$ of a dollar.

Every decimal digit to the right of the decimal point has a name.

$0.1 = 1$ tenth $= \frac{1}{10}$
$0.02 = 2$ hundredths $= \frac{2}{100}$
$0.003 = 3$ thousandths $= \frac{3}{1,000}$
$0.0004 = 4$ ten thousandths $= \frac{4}{10,000}$

You can add zeros to the right of a decimal without changing its value. 0.1 and 0.10000 are equal. This is helpful when adding, subtracting, and dividing with decimals.

A decimal with numbers on both sides of the decimal point is called a *mixed decimal*. 264.03 is a mixed decimal. A decimal with numbers to the right of the decimal point only is called a decimal. A whole number is understood to have a decimal point to the right; the number 15, for example, could be written 15.0 or 15.00, etc.

To write a fraction as a decimal, divide the numerator by the denominator.

Example: Write $\frac{3}{4}$ as a decimal.

1. Divide the numerator by the denominator.

$3 \div 4$

2. Rewrite the problem as a long division problem. You will have to add a decimal point and some zeros to the right of the number 3.

$$\begin{array}{r} .75 \\ 4)\overline{3.00} \\ \underline{2\ 8} \\ 20 \\ \underline{20} \\ 0 \end{array}$$

3. The quotient is your answer.

$\frac{3}{4}$ equals 0.75.

To change a decimal to a fraction, write the digits of the decimal as the numerator of a fraction and write the decimal's name as the denominator of the fraction. Reduce if possible.

Example: Rewrite 0.018 as a fraction.

1. Write 18 in the numerator of a fraction.

$\frac{18}{?}$

2. Write the name of the fraction in the denominator. 0.018 is *eighteen one-thousandths*, so you should write 1,000 in the denominator of the fraction.

$\frac{18}{1,000}$

3. Reduce. Both 18 and 1,000 are divisible by 2, so $\frac{18}{1,000}$ can be reduced:

$18 \div \frac{2}{1,000} \div 2 = \frac{9}{500}$

It is a good idea to memorize the decimal equivalent of common fractions.

$\frac{1}{5} = 0.2$

$\frac{1}{4} = 0.25$

$\frac{1}{3} = 0.3\overline{3}$

$\frac{2}{5} = 0.4$

$\frac{1}{2} = 0.5$

$\frac{3}{5} = 0.6$

$\frac{2}{3} = 0.6\overline{6}$

$\frac{3}{4} = 0.75$

The bar over the 3 and 6 in the decimal equivalents of $\frac{1}{3}$ and $\frac{2}{3}$ indicate that the decimal repeats infinitely. Decimals are not the most precise way to represent fractions whose denominators are not factors of a power of 10 (powers of 10 include 10; 100; 1,000; 10,000, etc.).

Comparing Decimals

Because decimals are easier to compare when they have the same number of digits after the decimal point, you should tack additional zeros onto the end of shorter decimals until the decimals you want to compare are of equal length. Then all you have to do is compare the numbers as though the decimal points weren't even there.

Example: Compare 0.08 and 0.1.

1. Tack one zero onto the end of 0.1 so that both decimals extend two places to the right of the decimal point. The result is the decimal 0.10.
2. Compare 0.08 and 0.10 as though the decimal points weren't there. Which is greater, 8 or 10? 10 is, so 0.1 is greater than 0.08.

▶ Percentages

The word *percent* comes from the Latin words meaning "for every one hundred." A percent expresses the relationship between a part and a whole in terms of 100. When we say that 10% of the customers at a grocery store pay with cash, we are saying that 10 out of every 100 customers pay with cash. You encounter percentages every day. Sales tax, interest, discounts, and tips on meals are just a few of the percent calculations people make on a daily basis.

Changing a Percent to a Fraction and Vice Versa

A percent can easily be written as a fraction. Simply take the percent and put it in the numerator of the fraction. Then, write 100 in the denominator. That's all there is to it.

Example: Convert 75% to a fraction.

1. Write a fraction with 75 in the numerator. $\frac{75}{?}$
2. Write 100 in the denominator. $\frac{75}{100}$
3. Reduce if possible. $\frac{75 \div 25}{100 \div 25} = \frac{3}{4}$

To write a fraction as a percent, multiply the fraction by $\frac{100}{1}$.

Example: Convert $\frac{1}{4}$ to a percent.
$$\frac{1}{4} \times \frac{100}{1} = \frac{1 \times 100}{4} = \frac{100}{4} = 25$$
$\frac{1}{4}$ equals 25%.

There is another way to convert a fraction to a percent: Divide the numerator by the denominator, and then move the decimal point two places to the right in your quotient.

$$4\overline{)1.00} \quad \begin{array}{c} .25 \end{array} \qquad .25 = 25\%$$

It's a good idea to memorize the fraction equivalents of these common percents.

$10\% = \frac{1}{10}$

$20\% = \frac{1}{5}$

$25\% = \frac{1}{4}$

$30\% = \frac{3}{10}$

$33\frac{1}{3}\% = \frac{1}{3}$

$40\% = \frac{2}{5}$

$50\% = \frac{1}{2}$

$60\% = \frac{3}{5}$

$66\frac{2}{3}\% = \frac{2}{3}$

$80\% = \frac{4}{5}$

$100\% = 1$

Changing a Decimal to a Percent and Vice Versa

To change a decimal to a percent, move the decimal point two places to the right and tack on a percent sign (%). If there aren't enough places to move the decimal point two places to the right, add a zero to the right before moving the decimal.

Example: Write 0.247 as a percent.

1. Move the decimal two places to the right.	24.7
2. Add a percent sign.	24.7%

Example: Write 0.6 as a percent.

1. Because there aren't enough places to move the decimal two places to the right, add a zero to the far right of the decimal.	0.60
2. Move the decimal two places to the right.	60
3. Add a percent sign.	60%

To change a percent to a decimal, reverse the process. Delete the percent sign, and then move the decimal two places to the left. If there aren't enough places to move the decimal point two places to the left, add a zero to the left before moving the decimal.

Example: Write 28% as a decimal.

1. Delete the percent sign.	28
2. Move the decimal two places to the left.	0.28

28% equals 0.28.

Example: Write 4% as a decimal.

1. Delete the percent sign.   4
2. Because there aren't enough places to move the decimal two places to the left, add a zero to the far left of the number.   04
3. Move the decimal two places to the left.   0.04

4% equals 0.04.

Solving Percent Word Problems

Word problems involving percents generally take one of three forms.

- Find the percent of a whole.

  Example: What is 30% of 40?

- Find what percent of one number is another number.

  Example: 12 is what percent of 40?

- Find the whole when the percent is given.

  Example: 12 is 30% of what number?

  Each can be solved using the translation techniques reviewed earlier in the chapter. Just remember that:

what	=	x, y, Λ (i.e., a variable)
what percent	=	$\frac{x}{100}$
is	=	equals (=)
of	=	multiplied by ($\times$)

Let's see how to use the translation technique to solve each of the examples.

Example: What is 30% of 40?

Translate:

What	=	x
is	=	=
30%	—	$\frac{30}{100}$
of	=	$\times$
40	=	40

"What is 30% of 40" translates to $x = \frac{30}{100} \times 40$.

Now let's solve:

$x = \frac{30}{100} \times 40$

$x = \frac{30}{100} \times \frac{40}{1}$

$x = 30 \times \frac{40}{100} \times 1$

$x = \frac{1,200}{100}$

$x = 1,200 \div 100$

$x = 12$

Example: 12 is what percent of 40?

Translate:

12	=	12
is	=	=
what %	=	$\frac{x}{100}$
of	=	×
40	=	40

"12 is what percent of 40" translates to $12 = \frac{x}{100} \times 40$.

Now let's solve:

$12 = \frac{x}{100} \times 40$

$12 = \frac{x}{100} \times \frac{40}{1}$

$12 = \frac{40x}{100}$

$12 \times 100 = \frac{40x}{100} \times \frac{100}{1}$

$1,200 = 40x$

$1,200 \div 40 = 40x \div 40$

$30 = x$

12 is 30% of 40.

Example: 12 is 30% of what number?

Translate:

12	=	12
is	=	=
30%	=	$\frac{30}{100}$
of	=	×
what number	=	y

"12 is 30% of what number" translates to $12 = \frac{30}{100} \times y$.

Now let's solve:

$12 = \frac{30}{100} \times y$

$12 = \frac{30}{100} \times \frac{y}{1}$

$12 = \frac{30y}{100}$

$12 \times 100 = \frac{30y}{100} \times 100$

$1,200 = 30y$

$1,200 \div 30 = 30y \div 30$

$40 = y$

12 is 30% of 40.

The same techniques work for questions that ask about percent increase and percent decrease. Remember that after you calculate the percent, you must add (increase) or subtract (decrease) in order to determine the final result.

Example: A merchant usually sells hats for $20. He decides to have a sale during which he decreases the price of the hats by 25%. What is the price of the hats during the sale?

To answer this question, you must first answer the question "What is 25% of $20?" This is a question you can translate and solve. "What is 25% of $20" translates to:

$x = \frac{25}{100} \times 20$

$x = \frac{25}{100} \times \frac{20}{1}$

$x = 25 \times \frac{20}{100}$

$x = \frac{500}{100}$

$x = 5$

25% of $20 is $5. The merchant plans to decrease the price of the hat by 25%, so he plans to decrease the price by $5. That means the sale price of the hats will be $20 – $5, which equals $15.

A Quick Way to Find 10% of a Number

To find 10% of a number, simply move the decimal point one place to the left. The result equals 10% of the original number.

Example: Find 10% of 570.
Move the decimal point one place to the left.   57.0
10% of 570 is 57.

You can use this method to find multiples of 10% as well. If a question asks you to find 30% of a number, for example, first find 10%, and then multiply the result by 3 to get 30%.

Example: Find 30% of 570.
10% of 570 is 57.
$3 \times 57 = 171$
171 is 30% of 570.

► Data and Statistics

Many civil service exams require you to read tables, charts, and graphs. Questions on these subjects ask you to identify key elements of a table or graph, retrieve data, and draw conclusions based on the data. This section reviews the different types of graphs and explains how to read them. It also discusses several basic concepts of statistics, including arithmetic mean (what most people call "the average" of a set of numbers) and range.

The simplest form of data presentation is a *reading table*. A reading table presents data in rows and columns. The following reading table shows the average weight of five different large animals.

AVERAGE WEIGHT, IN POUNDS, OF SELECT ANIMALS	
ANIMAL	WEIGHT IN POUNDS
Gorilla	200
Cow	1,000
Horse	1,500
Giraffe	2,600
Elephant	10,700

Each *column* of the table contains a type of data: The left column gives the names of the animals, while the right column gives weights. Each *row* of the table presents the data for a particular animal. The first row of the table tells you that an average gorilla weighs 200 pounds. The fourth row tells you that an average giraffe weighs 2,600 pounds.

A reading table is great for presenting data in a straightforward manner. Although some data benefits from graphic representation in a graph or pie chart, some data is perfectly clear in this simple reading table format. Reading tables are best for presenting a limited amount of data; when reading tables get too long, they are difficult to read and information can be hard to find. Anyone who has ever tried to pore over a pages-long Excel spreadsheet knows this too well.

Often the data that appears in a reading table can also be represented in a *bar graph*. A bar graph is great for comparing values; because each number is graphically represented, it is easy to determine quickly which value in a data set is greatest, which value is least, etc. The bar graph that follows shows the number of lunch specials sold at a restaurant during a workweek.

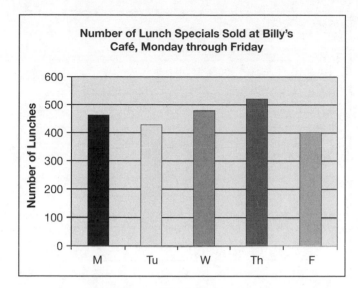

The bar graph makes it easy to determine that Billy's Café sold the most lunch specials on Thursday and that it sold the least on Friday. It makes it very easy to compare each day's sales with each of the other day's sales. It is not always easy to determine the precise value represented by a bar in a bar graph, however. We can tell that Billy's Café sold between 400 and 500 lunch specials on Monday, but it is not so easy to determine exactly how many lunch specials the restaurant sold on that day. Some bar graphs provide data labels to provide the exact value represented by each bar.

A bar graph has an *x-axis* and a *y-axis*. The *x*-axis is the horizontal axis; it usually represents the categories of data shown in the graph. A bar graph of the reading table titled "Average Weight, in Pounds, of Select Animals," for example, would list the names of the animals along the *x*-axis. The *y*-axis is the vertical axis. It usually shows the data scale; it tells you how many things are in each category. A bar graph of the reading table titled "Average Weight, in Pounds, of Select Animals" would have the weights shown on the *y*-axis.

Like a bar graph, a *line graph* represents data graphically, making it easy to compare values. A line graph is usually used to show changes in data over time. The line graph that follows shows changes to the population of Hardintown between 1995 and 2006.

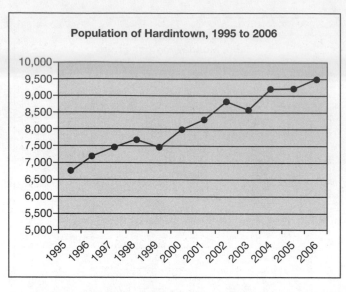

The line makes it easy to see the general trend toward growth in Hardintown's population. It also makes it easy to find the years in which population declined from the previous year (1999 and 2003). To determine the population of the town each year, find the dot corresponding to the year, and then look at the scale on the vertical axis (i.e., the *y*-axis) to find the value to which the dot corresponds. As in a bar graph, it is sometimes difficult to determine the exact value represented. We can tell that the population of Hardintown in 1998 was about 7,600, but we can't really say for sure whether it was 7,600; 7,601; 7,602; etc.

Sometimes a bar graph or a line graph will compare several sets of data. When they do, a *legend* is necessary to tell you how to read the graph. The bar graph that follows compares the responses of Democrats and Republicans to two survey questions.

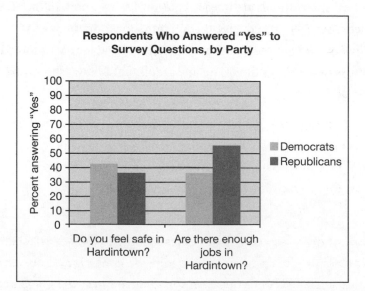

The legend of this bar graph tells you how to interpret the data. Democrats' responses are shown in light gray, while Republicans' responses are shown in dark gray.

A *pie chart* is best for showing how a whole is divided into parts. Each slice of the pie represents one part of the whole. The pie chart that follows shows how the city budget of Hardintown is divided among different expenses.

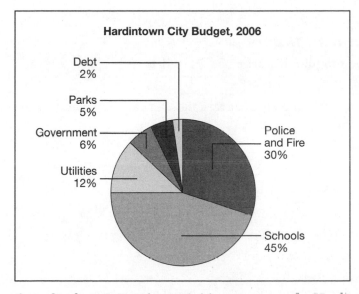

This pie chart shows that schools represent the single biggest expense for Hardintown, claiming 45% of the budget. Police and fire consume 30% of the budget, utilities 12%, etc.

Drawing Conclusions from Graph Data

Some questions will ask you to draw conclusions based on data presented in graphs. These questions do not ask you to draw subtle conclusions reached by reading between the lines or by making a lot of assumptions. On the contrary, the answers to these questions will be indisputably correct, and they will be fairly obvious. The incorrect answers are those that are not supported by the data or that require major assumptions to support the conclusion.

Let's look again at the pie chart titled Hardintown City Budget, 2006. Here's a typical "draw a conclusion" question based on that graph.

Example: Which of the following conclusions is best supported by data in the graph?

a. The people of Hardintown would like to reduce spending on education.

b. Hardintown would have more parks if the city increased its parks budget.

c. Schools and police and fire account for $\frac{3}{4}$ of the city's budget.

d. Hardintown's debt is too large.

You might be tempted to choose choice **a**; education is the single largest item on the city budget, so it is possible that people in Hardintown would like to reduce spending on education. However, it's also possible that the people of Hardintown would like to *increase* education spending. Because the graph provides no data on public opinion in Hardintown, it is impossible to say whether the people there would like to reduce spending on education. Choice **a** cannot be correct; eliminate it.

Choices **b** and **d** can be eliminated the same way. Each is based on an assumption that may or may not be correct. Only choice **c** is indisputably correct; because schools account for 45% of the budget and police and fire account for 30% of the budget, the two together account for 75% of the budget. 75% equals $\frac{3}{4}$, so choice **c** is the best answer.

Range and Arithmetic Mean

Some questions will ask you to find the range of a set of data. Others may ask you to calculate the average, or arithmetic mean, of a data set.

The *range* of a data set is the difference between the least and the greatest value in the set. Consider the following reading table.

JANE'S BOWLING SCORES	
Game 1	188
Game 2	215
Game 3	170

The greatest value in the data set is 215. The least value in the set is 170. The range of the data set is 215 − 170, which equals 45.

The *arithmetic mean* of a data set is what we sometimes refer to as the average of the set. It is calculated by adding all the data in the set and dividing the sum by the number of pieces of data in the set. In the previous table, there are three pieces of data, namely Jane's three bowling scores. The sum of the data is 188 + 215 + 170, which equals 573. To calculate the arithmetic mean, divide 573 by 3.

573 ÷ 3 = 191

The arithmetic mean of Jane's bowling scores is 191.

▶ Strategy Review

Remember to employ these strategies to maximize your score on multiple-choice mathematics tests.

- Perform all work on paper.
- Skip questions that you find difficult or time consuming.
- Break questions down into component parts.
- Reread the question before you record your final answer.
- Use approximate values whenever you can.
- Before recording your answer, ask yourself if the answer is reasonable.

■ Take advantage of the multiple-choice format of the test by working backward whenever you can.

Follow these steps and complete the math review in this chapter; if you do, passing the math portion of your civil service exam should be as easy as 1, 2, 3!

► Review Exercise

1. $\frac{2}{3} \times \frac{3}{4} =$
   a. $\frac{5}{8}$
   b. $\frac{1}{2}$
   c. $\frac{8}{9}$
   d. $\frac{9}{8}$

2. 73% of District X voters approve of the job their congressperson is doing. If there are 410,000 voters in the district, how many approve of the job done by the congressperson?
   a. 5,616
   b. 287,000
   c. 299,300
   d. 320,000

3. Before leaving the fire station, Firefighter Sorensen noted that the mileage gauge on Engine 2 registered $4,357\frac{4}{10}$ miles. When he arrived at the scene of the fire, the mileage gauge registered $4,400\frac{1}{10}$ miles. What was the distance from the fire station to the scene of the fire?
   a. $42\frac{3}{10}$ miles
   b. $42\frac{7}{10}$ miles
   c. $43\frac{7}{10}$ miles
   d. $57\frac{3}{10}$ miles

4. $\frac{1}{4} + \frac{1}{3} =$
   a. $\frac{1}{12}$
   b. $\frac{3}{4}$
   c. $\frac{1}{7}$
   d. $\frac{7}{12}$

5. Reduce $\frac{18}{24}$ to lowest terms.
   a. $\frac{1}{24}$
   b. $\frac{2}{3}$
   c. $\frac{9}{12}$
   d. $\frac{3}{4}$

Study the following graph, and then use it to answer questions 6 to 8.

Number of sick days per year of employment

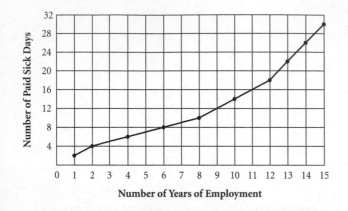

6. What is the range of the data displayed in the graph?
a. 2
b. 28
c. 30
d. 32

7. The average (arithmetic mean) number of paid sick days taken by employees who have been employed for 4, 5, 6, or 7 years is
a. 6.5
b. 7
c. 7.5
d. 9

8. Which of the following conclusions can be drawn from the data in the graph?
a. The more years a person is employed, the more likely he or she is to take paid sick days.
b. The rate of increase in paid sick days is constant from year to year for the first 15 years of a person's employment.
c. The older a person is, the more likely he or she is to take paid sick days.
d. Employees are not allowed to take more than eight sick days per year during their first six years of employment.

9. As he drives away from his home, Jason notes that the gas tank of his car is $\frac{7}{8}$ full. When he returns home later in the day, he notes that his gas tank is $\frac{1}{4}$ full. How much gasoline did Jason use during the day?
a. $\frac{1}{4}$ tank
b. $\frac{3}{8}$ tank
c. $\frac{3}{4}$ tank
d. $\frac{5}{8}$ tank

10. An automobile traveling at an average speed of 75 miles per hour travels for 40 minutes. How far does the automobile travel?
a. 35 miles
b. 40 miles
c. 45 miles
d. 50 miles

11. James spends 5% of each day watching television. How much time does James spend watching television each day?
a. 61 minutes
b. 72 minutes
c. 120 minutes
d. 144 minutes

12. Reduce $\frac{27}{108}$ to lowest terms.

   a. $\frac{1}{4}$

   b. $\frac{3}{11}$

   c. $\frac{1}{3}$

   d. The fraction cannot be reduced.

13. $2\frac{1}{12} \div 2\frac{1}{4} =$

   a. $\frac{25}{27}$

   b. $4\frac{11}{16}$

   c. $\frac{1}{3}$

   d. $\frac{1}{6}$

14. A savings bond yields 3.75% simple interest annually. If the bond is worth $8,000 on January 8, 2006, what is the value of the bond on January 8, 2007?

   a. $8,003.75

   b. $8,300

   c. $8,375

   d. $11,750

15. $1\frac{1}{7} - \frac{2}{3} =$

   a. $\frac{10}{21}$

   b. $\frac{19}{21}$

   c. $\frac{1}{4}$

   d. $\frac{4}{5}$

16. Randy earns an hourly wage of $12 for each of the first 40 hours he works in a week. For any hours he works in excess of 40 hours, Randy earns an hourly wage that is $1\frac{1}{2}$ times his standard wage. If Randy works a 50-hour week, how much does Randy earn?

   a. $600

   b. $480

   c. $660

   d. $900

17. A bus travels a route that runs $3\frac{3}{4}$ miles along Elm Street, and then turns right onto Palmetto Road. It then travels $2\frac{1}{2}$ miles along Palmetto Road before turning left on Main Street. The bus travels $5\frac{3}{4}$ miles along Main Street, completing its route. How many miles long is the bus route?

   a. 10 miles

   b. $11\frac{1}{2}$ miles

   c. 12 miles

   d. 15 miles

Study the following graph, and then use it to answer questions 18 to 20.

AVERAGE PRICE OF GROCERIES, 2006	
ITEM	**AVERAGE PRICE**
ground beef, 1 pound	$2.99
milk, $\frac{1}{2}$ gallon	$2.49
carrots, 5 pounds	$3.27
chicken noodle soup, 1 can	$1.82
oatmeal, 42 ounce box	$3.58

18. The data support which of the following conclusions?

   a. One can of chicken soup is not enough food to constitute a healthy meal.

   b. It is important to drink milk every day.

   c. Carrots are cheaper per pound than ground beef.

   d. Ground beef is too expensive for the quality of meat you receive.

19. What is the range of prices shown in the table?

   a. $1.82

   b. $2.49

   c. $2.99

   d. $1.76

20. The average (arithmetic mean) price of the items shown is

   a. $2.83

   b. $2.99

   c. $3.58

   d. $14.15

▶ Answers

1. b. To multiply fractions, multiply numerator by numerator and denominator by denominator, then reduce if necessary. $\frac{2}{3} \times \frac{3}{4} = \frac{2 \times 3}{3 \times 4}$, which equals $\frac{6}{12}$. Divide both numerator and denominator by 6 to reduce $\frac{6}{12}$ to $\frac{1}{2}$.

2. c. The question asks you to find 73% of 410,000. There are a number of ways to solve this problem. One way is to multiply 410,000 by the fractional equivalent of 73%, which is $\frac{73}{100}$. $\frac{410,000 \times 73}{100} = \frac{29,930,000}{100}$, which reduces to 299,300.

3. b. This question asks you to subtract $4,357\frac{4}{10}$ from $4,400\frac{1}{10}$. To calculate $4,400\frac{1}{10} - 4,357\frac{4}{10}$, you will have to rewrite $4,400\frac{1}{10}$. Borrow 1, or $\frac{10}{10}$, from 4,400 to rewrite $4,400\frac{1}{10}$ as $4,399\frac{11}{10}$. Now calculate. $4,399\frac{11}{10} - 4,357\frac{4}{410} = (4,399 - 4,357) + (\frac{11}{10} - \frac{4}{10})$. The solution is $42\frac{7}{10}$.

4. d. To add fractions, rewrite them over a common denominator. 12 is divisible by 3 and 4, so 12 is a good common denominator for $\frac{1}{3}$ and $\frac{1}{4}$. $\frac{1}{3} \times \frac{4}{4} = \frac{4}{12}$ and $\frac{1}{4} \times \frac{3}{3} = \frac{3}{12}$, so $\frac{1}{3} + \frac{1}{4} = \frac{4}{12} + \frac{3}{12} = \frac{7}{12}$.

5. d. To reduce a fraction to its lowest terms, divide the numerator and the denominator by the largest value that divides evenly into both. 18 and 24 are both divisible by 6. $\frac{18 \div 6}{24 \div 6} = \frac{3}{4}$. If you selected choice **c**, you divided both numerator and denominator by 2. Your answer equals $\frac{18}{24}$, but it does not represent lowest terms for the fraction because both 9 and 12 are divisible by 3.

6. b. The least value shown on the graph is 2, representing the number of sick days for people who have been employed for one year. The greatest value is 30, representing the number of sick days for people who have been employed for 15 years. The range of the data is the difference between the greatest and least value, so the range of this data set is 30 − 2, which equals 28.

7. c. According to the graph, employees who have been employed for 4 years take an average of 6 sick days; for 5 years, 7 sick days; for 6 years, 8 sick days; and for 7 years, 9 sick days. To find the average (arithmetic mean), add the number of sick days and divide by 4, the number of time periods represented. 6 + 7 + 8 + 9 = 30. 30 divided by 4 equals 7.5.

8. a. For each year a person is employed, the average number of sick days taken increases; thus, the statement "The more years a person is employed, the more likely he or she is to take paid sick days" is supported by the data in the graph. The rate of increase shown in the graph is constant between years 2 and 8, but after that, the rate increases; therefore, choice **b** is incorrect. The graph includes no information about age, so choice **c** is not supported by data in the graph. Choice **d** draws a conclusion about company policy; because no information about company policy is provided, this cannot be the correct answer.

9. d. This question asks you to subtract $\frac{1}{4}$ from $\frac{7}{8}$. To add or subtract fractions, you must rewrite them over a common denominator. Because 8 is divisible by 4, 8 would be a good common denominator. $\frac{1}{4} \times \frac{2}{2} = \frac{2}{8}$. $\frac{7}{8} - \frac{2}{8}$ equals $\frac{5}{8}$.

10. d. To solve rate problems, apply the equation $rt = d$, where r equals rate, t equals time, and d equals distance. This problem provides the rate (75 miles per hour) and the time (40 minutes). Before plugging the numbers into the formula, make sure your numbers are in common units. The rate is in miles per *hour*, but the time is measured in *minutes*. That's no good; you have to use all minutes or all hours. Rewrite 40 minutes in terms of hours; 40 minutes equals $\frac{40}{60}$ hours, or $\frac{2}{3}$ hours. Now, plug the values into the formula. $75(\frac{2}{3}) = t$. $\frac{75 \times 2}{3} = \frac{150}{3} = 50$.

11. b. This question asks you to calculate 5% of 24 hours. You can calculate percents easily using the 10% trick. To find 10% of a number, simply move the decimal point one place to the left. Therefore, 10% of 24 is 2.4. The question asks you to find 5% of 24 hours; 5% is half of 10%, so the answer is half of 2.4 hours, or 1.2 hours. Multiply 1.2 by 60 to determine that 1.2 hours equals 72 minutes.

12. a. To reduce a fraction to its lowest terms, divide the numerator and the denominator by the largest value that divides evenly into both. Both 27 and 108 are divisible by 27, so you can reduce $\frac{27}{108}$ to $27 \div \frac{27}{108} \div 27$, which equals $\frac{1}{4}$. If you don't recognize that 108 is divisible by 27 (most people don't), that's okay. Divide by something you do know goes evenly into 27 and 108, such as 3 or 9. Then, look at the result and see whether you can't reduce it again. Eventually you will wind up with the result $\frac{1}{4}$, which is the correct answer to this question.

13. a. To divide mixed numbers, first rewrite them as improper fractions. Rewrite $2\frac{1}{12}$ as $\frac{25}{12}$ and $2\frac{1}{4}$ as $\frac{9}{4}$. Next, multiply the dividend (the first fraction in the equation) by the reciprocal of the divisor (the second fraction in the equation). $\frac{25}{12} \times \frac{4}{9} = \frac{100}{108}$. Divide numerator and denominator by 4 to reduce $\frac{100}{108}$ to $\frac{25}{27}$.

14. b. The problem asks you to calculate 3.75% of $8,000. One way to solve this problem is to multiply $8,000 by 0.0375, the decimal equivalent of 3.75%. The result is $300. Add the $300 (interest) to the $8,000 (principal) to determine the bond's value of $8,300 after one year.

15. a. To add or subtract fractions, you must rewrite them over a common denominator. 21 is divisible by 7 and 3, so rewrite both

fractions with a denominator of 21. Rewrite the mixed number $\frac{11}{7}$ as the improper fraction $\frac{8}{7}$, and then multiply by $\frac{3}{3}$ to get $\frac{24}{21}$. Multiply $\frac{2}{3}$ by $\frac{7}{7}$ to get $\frac{14}{21}$. $\frac{24}{21} - \frac{14}{21}$ equals $\frac{10}{21}$.

16. c. Randy earns $12 per hour for each of the first 40 hours he works. Thus, he earns $480 for his first 40 hours of work. His overtime pay is $1\frac{1}{2}$ times his regular pay of $12. Half of $12 is $6, so Randy's overtime pay is $12 + $6 per hour, or $18 per hour. Randy works 10 hours of overtime, so he earns $18 × 10, which equals $180, in overtime pay. $480 + $180 equals $660, the correct answer.

17. c. This question asks you to add $3\frac{3}{4}$, $2\frac{1}{2}$, and $5\frac{3}{4}$. To do this, first add all the whole numbers: 3 + 2 + 5 equals 10. Next, add the fractions; this requires you to rewrite the fractions over a common denominator. Because 4 is divisible by 2, 4 is an excellent choice for common denominator. $\frac{3}{4} + \frac{2}{4} + \frac{3}{4} = \frac{8}{4}$, which equals 2. 10 + 2 equals 12, the correct answer.

18. c. According to the table, one pound of ground beef costs $2.99 and 5 pounds of carrots cost $3.27. Therefore, one pound of carrots costs $3.27 ÷ 5, or a little more than 65 cents per pound. The data in the table support the conclusion that a pound of carrots costs less than a pound of ground beef.

19. d. The range of the data is the difference between the greatest and least value, so the range of this data set is $3.58 – $1.82, which equals $1.76.

20. a. The average of a data set is the sum of the data divided by the number of pieces of data. In this case, there are 5 pieces of data. Their sum is $2.99 + $2.49 + $3.27 + $1.82 + $3.58, which equals $14.15. $14.15 ÷ 5 equals $2.83.

5 ▶ Written Communication Skills

All civil service exams test written communication skills in some form. Nearly all include a section testing your ability to read and understand extended passages. Many also include questions about grammar, vocabulary, and spelling.

There are good reasons for including these skills on civil service exams. To be an effective civil servant, you must be able to read and comprehend memos, policy statements, procedural instructions, documents, and reports. Similarly, most positions require you to communicate effectively in writing. You can't do that without some mastery of English grammar, vocabulary, and spelling.

The good news is that these exams test basic skills. No one is going to ask you to read a complicated novel and interpret its symbolism. Nor will a civil service test ask you to spell *Australopithecus* or to conjugate verbs in the future subjunctive tense (or even to know what the future subjunctive tense is, for that matter). All you need to do is to read a passage and answer some related questions, which will be pretty straightforward, and to recall some fundamental principles of grammar and spelling.

The chapter that follows reviews the basic skills necessary to pass the written communications portion of a civil service exam.

► Reading Comprehension

You have probably encountered reading comprehension questions before. Many standardized tests, including the SAT and the ACT, include them. A reading comprehension section provides a reading passage, followed by a number of multiple-choice questions about the passage. There is an advantage to this question format:

> You do not need to know anything about the topic of the passage. All the information you need to answer the questions is contained within the passage itself.

The challenge, of course, is knowing where and how to find the information in a reasonable amount of time. The time element adds pressure, which causes some people to make careless mistakes. The test writers understand this and will phrase some incorrect answers in a way that makes them *seem* correct at first glance.

The best way to do well on reading comprehension questions is to be familiar with the types of questions that are typically asked, and to learn the defining characteristics of the correct and incorrect answers to each question type. The most common question types are those that ask you to:

1. describe the **main idea** of the passage
2. identify a **specific fact or detail** in the passage
3. draw an **inference or conclusion** based on information in the passage
4. define a **vocabulary word** that appears in the passage

On the following pages, we'll review each type of question and the characteristics of correct and incorrect answers for each. To do this, you'll first need to read a passage. All the sample questions that follow will be based on this passage.

Practice Passage

In television procedural dramas such as *Law & Order*, criminal defendants invariably stand trial for the crimes they commit. They enter a plea of "not guilty," the evidence against them is heard, and a jury decides their fate. Under the circumstances, the average American can be forgiven for assuming that this is the way our criminal justice system always works, but, in fact, it is hardly representative of the way that most criminal cases are resolved. In the real world, only a relatively small number of such cases ever reach trial. The majority are settled out of court, most often in a plea arrangement, sometimes referred to as a plea bargain or copping a plea.

There are numerous practical reasons that this practice is so <u>prevalent</u>. Prosecutors use plea arrangements to avoid costly trials that tie up prosecutors who could otherwise be working on other cases. Defendants avoid the risk of going to trial, where they might receive a more severe sentence than the prosecutor is willing to offer as part of a plea arrangement. They also elude the negative publicity a trial can bring. The uncertainty of a trial's result, in fact, is something that both prosecutors *and* defendants may wish to avoid; a plea arrangement achieves that end. The court system also benefits, as it can remove plea-bargained cases from its overbooked dockets.

While plea bargains are extremely common in American courts, they are not without their critics. Victims' rights groups believe that many plea arrangements result in overly lenient sentences. Defendants' rights groups argue that the system unfairly favors those defendants who can afford expensive, highly skilled lawyers. In this way, they say, the system actually favors big-time criminals over small-time criminals, quite the opposite of the way the system should work. Then there are those who say that the system subverts the intended function of the courts; they argue that in a truly just system every defendant would face his or her accusers.

Regardless of their drawbacks, plea arrangements are likely to remain a prominent fixture in our courts for the foreseeable future. Without plea arrangements, our courts would soon fall hopelessly behind their caseloads. If the United States wants to move away from a plea-arrangement dependent system, it must figure out a way either to reduce crime drastically or to increase dramatically its judiciary and its prosecutorial and public defense offices.

Main Idea Questions

The main idea of a passage or paragraph of a passage is what it is *mostly* about. When determining whether an answer choice could be the correct answer to a main idea question, ask yourself, "Does this statement apply to the *entire* passage or paragraph?" If your answer is yes, then the answer choice could be the correct answer to the question. If your answer is no and the answer choice applies only to one detail or one small portion of the passage/paragraph, then that answer choice cannot be the correct answer.

Sometimes the answer to a main idea question is stated clearly in the passage, frequently in the first or last sentence. The sentence that expresses the main idea is often described as the *topic sentence*. Other times, the main idea is not stated in a topic sentence but rather is *implied* by the overall content of the passage. In such circumstances, you'll need to deduce the main idea from the passage. In either circumstance, the rule remains the same.

> The correct answer to a main idea question describes the *entire* passage or paragraph. If it describes only one part or one detail, it is not the correct answer.

Just because an answer refers to the entire passage doesn't mean that it is correct. Although such answers are *usually* correct, occasionally an incorrect answer will refer to the entire passage or paragraph. What makes that answer incorrect is that it describes the content of the passage or paragraph inaccurately. Most often, it states a position stronger than the one the writer takes. Suppose, for example, the main idea of a passage is that Frank Sinatra is a great singer. An incorrect answer might state that Frank Sinatra is the greatest singer who ever lived. This answer is close to the author's main idea, but overstates it.

> Make sure that the answer to a main idea question *accurately* describes the content of the passage or paragraph.

Example:

Which statement from the passage best summarizes the main idea of paragraph 3?

    a. While plea bargains are extremely common in American courts, they are not without their critics.

    b. Defendants' rights groups argue that the system unfairly favors those defendants who can afford expensive, highly skilled lawyers.

    c. Without plea arrangements, our courts would soon fall hopelessly behind their caseloads.

    d. Victims' rights groups believe that many plea arrangements result in overly lenient sentences.

Let's consider each answer, applying the rules previously provided.

Choice **a** is the topic sentence of paragraph 3. This is the likely answer, but we should check all the other answers before we choose this one.

Choice **b** is a supporting detail from paragraph 3. It describes one of several groups who criticize plea bargains. It is not the main idea of the paragraph.

Choice **c** is taken from paragraph 4. Although it is possible that the main idea of one paragraph may be expressed by a sentence in another paragraph, it is not likely. Furthermore, this statement does not summarize paragraph 3, so it cannot be the correct answer.

Choice **d**, like choice **b**, is a supporting detail from paragraph 3. It describes one of several groups who criticize plea bargains. It is not the main idea of the paragraph.

The correct answer is choice **a**.

Example:

Which of the following best expresses the main idea of the passage?

    a. Plea arrangements are unfair to poor defendants because they cannot afford to hire good lawyers.

    b. Because plea arrangements are by definition unjust, American courts must find ways to hire more judges and lawyers so that all cases can be tried.

    c. For a number of reasons, plea arrangements play a central role in the American justice system.

    d. Prosecutors use plea arrangements when they are afraid that a jury might find a defendant "not guilty."

Let's consider each answer, applying the rules previously provided.

Choice **a** restates an idea from the third paragraph of the passage. It refers to one detail of the entire passage; it does not describe or summarize the passage as a whole. Therefore, it cannot be the correct answer to a main idea question.

Choice **b** overstates one of the points made in the passage. In paragraph 3, the writer observes that some people find the plea arrangement system unjust. In paragraph 4, he points out that the only way to address this problem is to hire more judges and lawyers. However, the author never states that he subscribes to this opinion. In fact, we never find out what the writer thinks about this subject. The purpose of this passage is to inform us about a subject, not to persuade us to take the author's position on that subject. This answer breaks the second rule. It overstates an idea expressed in the passage, and so it cannot describe the content of the passage accurately.

Choice **c** summarizes the passage well. In the first paragraph, the writer states that "The majority are settled out of court, most often in a plea arrangement . . ." In paragraph 2, he details the "numerous practical reasons that this practice is so prevalent." After discussing some people's objections to the practice in paragraph 3, he reasserts that "plea arrangements are likely to remain a prominent fixture in our courts for the foreseeable future," providing "a number of reasons" why that is so. Choice **c** is almost certainly the correct answer to the question. Even so, you *must* read choice **d** before you can be sure.

Choice **d** paraphrases one of the supporting details of paragraph 2. Like choice **a**, this answer fails to describe or summarize the passage as a whole. It is not the correct answer to this question.

The correct answer is choice **c**.

Detail Questions

Detail questions ask you to identify a specific piece of information from the passage. Detail questions often contain one of the following phrases:

> According to the passage . . .
> The passage states . . .

The correct answer to a detail question will be a direct quote or a paraphrase of information in the passage.

> On a detail question, any answer stating information that does not appear in the passage cannot be the correct answer.

Not all answers that repeat information from the passage are necessarily correct, however. The information must also be relevant to the question being asked. Some incorrect answers will contain irrelevant information from the passage.

> On a detail question, make sure that your answer not only can be found in the passage, but also addresses the question that is being asked.

To answer a detail question, first read the question to determine its subject. Next, determine where in the passage the subject of the question is discussed. Reread that portion of the passage before answering the questions.

Example:
According to the passage, defendants sometimes decide to accept a plea arrangement because they

   a. are in a hurry to begin serving their sentences.
   b. do not want to overburden prosecutors.
   c. do not want to appear in a television procedural drama.
   d. worry that a trial might result in a harsher sentence.

First, determine where in the passage this information is most likely to appear. Paragraph 2 of the passage discusses the reasons that prosecutors, defendants, and courts sometimes prefer plea agreements to trials. This is where the correct answer is most likely to be found. Reread the paragraph before reading the answer choices.

Let's consider each answer, applying the rules previously provided.

The passage never states or implies that defendants "are in a hurry to begin serving their sentences," so choice **a** cannot be correct.

Paragraph 2 mentions that prosecutors sometimes make a plea arrangement to keep their fellow prosecutors from being overburdened with cases. The passage does not suggest that defendants share this goal. Common sense should help you eliminate this answer: Why would defendants care about overburdening prosecutors? Choice **b** cannot be correct.

Television procedural dramas are mentioned in the first paragraph as part of rhetorical device, the purpose of which is to distinguish between the courts as they are portrayed on television and the way they actually function. These TV shows have nothing to do with why defendants sometimes decide to accept a plea arrangement. Paragraph 2 notes that defendants sometimes wish to avoid the negative publicity of a trial; it does not, however, state or suggest that such negative publicity would be the result of the defendant's appearing on a television drama. Again, common sense should help you here. Actors appear on television dramas, not actual courtroom defendants. Choice **c** is not correct.

Choice **d** paraphrases the following sentence from the paragraph 2: "Defendants avoid the risk of going to trial, where they might receive a more severe sentence than the prosecutor is willing to offer as part of a plea arrangement."

The correct answer is choice **d**.

Inference Questions

Inference questions are not all that different from detail questions. Detail questions ask you restate information from the passage, often in the form of a paraphrase. Inference questions ask you to find information in the paragraph, and then use it to draw an inference that is necessarily, or deductively, true. Inference questions often begin with one of the following phrases.

> It can be inferred from the passage . . .
>
> The passage suggests . . .
>
> Which of the following conclusions is best supported . . .

For example, suppose the passage states that all voters in a city are either Democrats or Republicans and that the majority of voters in the city are Democrats. The correct answer to an inference question may state that a minority of voters in a city are Republicans. This is an inference because the passage does not state directly that the minority of voters in the city are Republicans; even so, it is necessarily true Republicans constitute a minority if the majority of voters are Democrats.

> When answering an inference question, do not choose an answer that requires you to make a major assumption or to use outside knowledge. Look for answers that are fully supported by information in the passage.

Example:
It can be inferred from the passage that groups that safeguard the rights of victims worry that the plea arrangement system

a. is biased against poor defendants.
b. allows criminals to go free too soon.
c. overloads the dockets of criminal courts.
d. contributes to an increase in the crime rate.

First, determine where in the passage this information is most likely to appear. Groups that criticize the plea arrangement system are discussed in paragraph 3. That is where the answer to this question is likely to appear.

Let's consider each answer, applying the rules previously provided.

Defendants' rights groups worry that the plea arrangement system is biased against poor defendants. This question asks about victims' rights groups, however, not defendants' rights groups. Choice **a** is not the correct answer to this question.

Choice **b** is a good paraphrase of the following sentence from the passage: "Victims' rights groups believe that many plea arrangements result in overly lenient sentences." Note that this is the only sentence in the entire passage that discusses "groups that safeguard the rights of victims." The correct answer must, therefore, be contained in this sentence. There is a slight inference involved in connecting the sentence to choice **b**. It requires you to infer that "overly lenient sentences"—i.e., sentences that are not long enough—result in sentences that "allow criminals to go free too soon." Notice that the jump from statement to inference is a tiny one, not a huge leap. That's the way correct answers to inference questions are.

Choice **c** refers to a concern expressed by the courts, not by victims' rights groups. Furthermore, that concern is expressed in favor of the system of plea arrangements, not in opposition to it. This cannot be the correct answer.

Choice **d** is an example of a huge inference, one much too big to be the correct answer. One might be tempted to think that because victims' rights groups "believe that many plea arrangements result in overly lenient sentences" that this, therefore, means that they believe these arrangements "contribute to an increase in the crime rate." However, the crime rate is never mentioned in the passage; therefore, there is no basis on which to draw any inferences about it or about how a particular group feels about it. Second, in order for choice **d** to be a correct answer, choice **b** must also be correct, because choice **d** relies on an assumption stated directly in choice **b**. The reverse is not true; choice **b** can be correct without choice **d** also being correct. Therefore, choice **b** is the correct answer, and choice **d** is incorrect.

Vocabulary

Questions designed to test vocabulary are really trying to measure how well you can figure out the meaning of an unfamiliar word from its context. *Context* refers to the words and ideas surrounding a vocabulary word. If the context is clear enough, you should be able to substitute a nonsense word for the one being sought and still be able to find the correct answer, because you will be able to determine meaning strictly from the sense of the sentence. Consider the following sentence:

> The scholarship recipient was quite *exbobulated* when she learned that her award would cover the entire cost of her tuition, room, and board.
> In the sentence, *exbobulated* most likely means
> **a.** disappointed.
> **b.** confused.
> **c.** thrilled.
> **d.** concerned.

The context of the sentence makes clear that the correct answer is choice **c**, thrilled. No one would be disappointed, confused, or concerned to receive such a generous award.

The tested word itself may contain a context clue. Look for familiar prefixes and suffixes. Look to see whether the word shares a common root with some other word you know.

As in all reading comprehension questions, use the answer choices to guide your work. Replace the vocabulary word with each of the answer choices and ask yourself, does the sentence make sense this way? If an answer turns the sentence into nonsense, eliminate the answer choice. It cannot be correct.

> Test each answer choice by rereading the sentence with the answer choice in place of the vocabulary word. Eliminate answers that don't make sense.

Example:

As used in the passage, the word *prevalent* most nearly means

    a. expensive.
    b. popular.
    c. uncertain.
    d. moral.

First, consider the context. Read the sentence in which the word *prevalent* appears ("There are numerous practical reasons that this practice is so prevalent"), and then think about the purpose of the paragraph in which it appears. The sentence mentions "practical reasons," suggesting that the tone of the sentence and paragraph is favorable toward plea arrangements. The paragraph goes on to list reasons that prosecutors, defendants, and courts sometimes favor plea arrangements. Again, the tone is favorable.

Would plea arrangements meet with such favorable responses if they were *expensive* (choice **a**) or *uncertain* (choice **c**)? No, these are negative words, and the tone of this paragraph is positive. Eliminate choices **a** and **c**. The correct answer is either *popular* (choice **b**) or *moral* (choice **d**). The practice of plea arrangements is clearly popular; many cases are settled in plea arrangements, and prosecutors, defendants, and courts all have their reasons for using them. The morality of plea arrangements, however, is not discussed in paragraph 2. It is hinted at later in the passage, in paragraph 3, but for the purposes of this question, we are interested only in paragraph 2.

The correct answer is choice **b**.

Strategies for All Reading Comprehension Questions

You can improve your performance on reading comprehension questions by employing a few simple strategies.

Learn to skim passages for information. Because the passages are relatively short, you will probably have time to read them carefully before answering questions. You don't want to answer questions from memory, though; you want to return to the passage, find the part that addresses the subject of the question, and reread it before choosing your answer. That's where skimming comes in. If you can't figure out where the answer to a question is found, try skimming the passage for a key word or words. For example, if the question is about defendants' rights groups, skim the passage for the words *defendants*, *rights*, and *groups*. Skimming is especially helpful in finding the answers to questions about proper nouns (e.g., people's names, place names) because capital letters are especially easy to skim for.

Take advantage of the multiple-choice format of the test by using process of elimination. Multiple-choice tests give you the correct answer. Of course, they bury the answer among three incorrect choices. Even so, the fact that the correct answer already appears in the test means that you do not have to come up with the choices on your own. A good way to find the correct answer on multiple-choice tests is to look at all the choices and eliminate all those that you know are incorrect. Quite often you will be able to eliminate every choice except the correct one.

When nonnative speakers of English have trouble with reading comprehension tests, it is often because they lack the cultural, linguistic, and historical frame of reference that native speakers enjoy. People who have not lived in or been educated in the United States often don't have the background information that comes from reading American newspapers, magazines, and textbooks.

The second and much more significant problem for nonnative English speakers is the difficulty in recognizing vocabulary and idioms (i.e., expressions such as *chewing the fat*) that assist comprehension. In order to read with good understanding, you need to have an immediate grasp of as many words as possible in the text. Test takers need to be able to recognize vocabulary and idioms immediately so that the ideas those words express are clear.

The Long View

Read newspapers, magazines, and other periodicals that deal with current events and matters of local, state, and national importance. Pay special attention to articles related to the career you want to pursue.

Be alert to new or unfamiliar vocabulary or terms that occur frequently in the popular press. Use a highlighter pen to mark new or unfamiliar words as you read. Compile a list of those words and their definitions. Review your list for 15 minutes each day. Although at first you may find yourself looking up a lot of words, don't be frustrated—as time progresses, you will be looking up fewer and fewer words, and your vocabulary will quickly expand.

During the Test

While you are taking the test, make a picture in your mind of the situation being described in the passage. Remain focused on the main idea; ask yourself, what is it that is most important to the writer? What is the most major point that the writer is trying to make?

Locate and underline the topic sentence of the passage. Remember that it does not necessarily have to be the first sentence of the passage or of any of the paragraphs. If there is no clear main idea sentence, try to summarize the main idea in a few words of your own. Remember, most of the correct answers will reflect the main idea in some way, and none of the correct answers will contradict the main idea.

Skip questions that you find difficult. Remember that you need only to pass this test; you do not need a perfect score. Therefore, you do not have to answer every question. If you can't answer a question, skip it and move on. There will be other questions ahead that you can answer, and you want to make sure to get to them. Also, because your final score will be based on the number of questions you answer correctly, you do not want to work on difficult questions until you have answered every easy question that you can answer quickly. Circle questions that you skip to make them easier to locate if and when you return to them. When you have finished answering all the questions you know you can answer correctly for a particular passage, take one more look at the difficult questions. You may be surprised to find that the question seems much easier now. Often a question seems difficult when your mind gets stuck on one way of thinking. Skipping a question and returning to it later is a good way to get unstuck.

Vocabulary questions have only three answer choices. If you can eliminate one of the answer choices, your chance of guessing correctly among the remaining choices is 50-50. Those are pretty good odds!

► Spelling and Vocabulary

Spelling and vocabulary are tested on many civil service exams. Both are necessary to communicate effectively, and many civil service jobs require strong communication skills.

Vocabulary is seen as a measure of one's ability to express ideas clearly and precisely. For almost any job, you must know the working vocabulary of the profession or have the tools needed to acquire that vocabulary quickly. Spelling is regarded as a measure of a person's accuracy in presenting information. Most civil service jobs require you to write correctly in order to communicate clearly. In addition, accurate spelling and a rich, varied vocabulary both indicate someone who is thoughtful and well educated, desirable qualities in any job candidate.

Vocabulary

Many civil service exams test vocabulary. There are two basic types of questions:

1. Synonyms and antonyms: These questions provide a word and ask you to identify an answer that has the same or opposite meaning.
2. Complete the sentence: These questions provide a sentence with a crucial word missing and ask you to select the best option for the missing word.

All are multiple-choice questions, meaning that you will never have to come up with an answer on your own. All you will need to do is determine which of the answer choices is the best option.

Synonym and Antonym Questions

Two words are *synonyms* if they have the same meaning or nearly the same meaning. *Antonyms* are words that have opposite meanings. Synonym and antonym questions ask you to find an answer choice that has the same or opposite meaning as an underlined word in the question stem. The word is often part of a phrase or sentence so that some context is provided. Sometimes the context is helpful, but at other times, context alone is not enough to help you determine which answer is correct.

Regardless of whether a question asks for a synonym or an antonym and regardless of whether it provides context clues, you should always take advantage of the multiple-choice format of the exam by using process of elimination. Look critically at each answer choice and get rid of those that cannot be the correct answer.

Example:
Select the answer that is closest in meaning to the underlined word.

a <u>substantial</u> novel

a. meaningless
b. weighty
c. alleged

If you know the word *substantial*, you know that it means *considerable* or *significant*. You would probably also realize that *weighty* is closest in meaning and that choice **b** is the correct answer.

If you did not know the word *substantial*, you would still have a chance to answer this question correctly if you recognized that *substantial* is a form of the word *substance*. Substance is something that is solid and dependable. It is not *meaningless*, nor is it *alleged*. It is *weighty*; therefore, choice **b** would be your best guess.

Example:

Find the answer that is most nearly the opposite of the underlined word.

such <u>exorbitant</u> prices

a. expensive
b. mysterious
c. reasonable

Note that the question asks for the opposite, or antonym, of exorbitant. The most common careless mistake on antonym questions involves choosing a synonym instead of the antonym.

Sure enough, choice **a** is a synonym for *exorbitant*. If this were a synonym question, choice **a** would be the correct answer. However, this is an antonym question, so this answer is incorrect.

Choice **b**, *mysterious*, is unlikely to be the correct answer. The opposite of *mysterious* is *straightforward*. Could prices be straightforward? Not really. Choice **b** is unlikely to be correct.

The opposite of *reasonable* is *unreasonable*, and prices certainly can be unreasonable. In fact, that's exactly what *exorbitant* prices are. The correct answer is choice **c**.

Complete the Sentence Questions

Complete the sentence questions provide a sentence with a single word missing. Your job is to figure out which of the answer choices is the missing word.

To answer a complete the sentence question, you must study the context of the missing word. Context is the text surrounding the missing word. You can use context to determine the meaning of an unfamiliar

word provided that the context offers enough hints. If you read that a *pusillanimous* boxer trembled in his corner and refused to fight, you could probably figure out that *pusillanimous* means *cowardly* even if you've never seen the word *pusillanimous* before. The context clues strongly suggest the meaning of the word. You will use context clues in exactly this way to answer complete the sentence questions.

As always, take advantage of the multiple-choice format of the exam by using process of elimination. Look critically at each answer choice and get rid of those that cannot be the correct answer.

Example:

Professor Hardison's _____ was amply demonstrated by the references to ancient scholarly texts throughout his address.

a. erudition
b. discipline
c. indecency

The context clues in the sentence include the phrase "ancient scholarly texts," which indicates that Professor Hardison is a learned man. Which of the words is closest in meaning to *learned*? Choice **a**, *erudition*, means *learned*. Suppose you don't know that, though. What should you do? The first thing you should do is look at the other answer choices without eliminating choice **a**. If you don't know the meaning of an answer, you cannot eliminate it.

Choice **b**, *discipline*, is tempting. A scholar must certainly be *disciplined* to master a field of study. But *disciplined* does not have the same meaning as *learned*; one can be disciplined in many ways without being a highly educated individual. Choice **b** is not likely to be the correct answer.

Choice **c**, *indecency*, should be easy to eliminate. Someone who is *indecent* is cruel or morally deficient.

If your native language is a Romance language (e.g., Spanish, French, or Italian), look for roots of words. Many English words have etymologies that trace back to Romance languages, meaning that a number of English words share roots with words in Spanish, French, and Italian. You may recognize a shared root, and that may be enough to tell you the meaning of the English word.

Also, as you read a word, imagine how it would sound spoken. Some nonnative English speakers find it easier to recognize words they hear than words they read on a page.

Indecency has nothing to do with scholarship, so choice **c** cannot be the correct answer.

At this point, if you did not know the meaning of *erudition*, you would be forced to guess between choices **a** and **b**. Because we've determined that choice **b** is unlikely to be the correct answer, you should guess choice **a**, which is, in fact, the correct answer.

Spelling

Spelling questions provide you with three answer choices. Typically, one is spelled correctly and two are spelled incorrectly. Occasionally a question will offer two correctly spelled answer choices and one incorrectly spelled answer choice; it will ask you to identify the word that is *not* spelled correctly.

The best way to prepare for a spelling test is to review spelling fundamentals so that you will recognize when common spelling rules are violated. Remember, though, that the English language is full of exceptions in spelling. You have to develop a good eye to spot spelling errors.

Even though there are many variant spellings for English words, civil service exams focus primarily on a few areas. Mostly these exams want to ensure that you know and can apply some basic rules, such as:

- *i* before *e* except after *c*, or when the word makes the long *a* sound (i.e., rhymes with *way*).

    Examples: *piece, receive, neighbor*

- *gh* can replace *f* or be silent.

    Examples: *enough, night*

- When you add an ending to a word that ends in a consonant, double the consonant.

    Examples: *forget/forgettable, shop/shopping*

- When you add a suffix to a word that ends in *e*, don't drop the *e*.

    Examples: replace/replacement/replaceable, peace/peaceful/peaceable

- Drop the *e* when you add *-ing*.

    Examples: *hope/hoping, dive/diving*

- The spelling of prefixes and suffixes generally doesn't change.

    Examples: *project, propel, proactive*

- When writing the plural of a word that ends in a consonant and a *y*, drop the *y* and add *ie*.

    Examples: *baby/babies, filly/fillies*

- When writing the plural of a word that ends in a vowel and a *y*, just add *s*.

    Examples: *monkey/monkeys, day/days*

You should also learn common roots and the words in which they are found.

WORD ELEMENT	MEANING	EXAMPLES
ama/amo	love	amateur, amorous
ambi	both	ambivalent, ambidextrous
aud	hear	audition, audible
bell	war	belligerent, bellicose
bene	good	benefactor, benediction
cid/cis	cut	homicide, scissors
cogn/gno	know	cognitive, recognize
curr	run	current
flu/flux	flow	fluid, fluctuate
gress	to go	congress, congregation
in	not, in	ingenious, integral
ject	throw	inject, reject
luc/lux	light	lucid, translucent
neo	new	neophyte, neoconservative
omni	all	omnivorous, omnipotent
pel/puls	push	impulse, propeller
pro	forward	project, produce
pseudo	false	pseudonym, pseudoscientific
rog	ask	interrogate
sub	under	subjugate, subterranean
spec/spic	look, see	spectator, spectacles
super	over	superfluous, supercede
temp	time	contemporary, temporal
un	not, opposite	uncoordinated, uninvited
viv	live	vivid, vivacious

Finally, compile spelling lists. Some test writers will give you a list to study before you take the test. If you receive such a list:

- Divide the list into smaller groups of words. Study them one smaller batch at a time. Make flash cards for the words that give you difficulty.
- Highlight or circle troublesome elements in each word.

- Cross out or discard words that you know for certain. Don't waste time studying words you already know how to study.
- Say the words aloud as you read them. Spell them out in your mind so you can "hear" the spelling.

Following is a sample spelling list. These words are typical of the words that appear on exams. Study this list if the people administering your test do not provide you with a spelling list.

achievement	doubtful	ninety
allege	eligible	noticeable
anxiety	enough	occasionally
appreciate	enthusiasm	occurred
asthma	equipped	offense
arraignment	exception	official
autonomous	fascinate	pamphlet
auxiliary	fatigue	parallel
brief	forfeit	personnel
ballistics	gauge	physician
barricade	grieve	politics
beauty	guilt	possess
beige	guarantee	privilege
business	harass	psychology
bureau	hazard	recommend
calm	height	referral
cashier	incident	recidivism
capacity	indict	salary
cancel	initial	schedule

circuit	innocent	seize
colonel	irreverent	separate
comparatively	jeopardy	specific
courteous	knowledge	statute
criticism	leisure	surveillance
custody	license	suspicious
cyclical	lieutenant	tentative
debt	maintenance	thorough
definitely	mathematics	transferred
descend	mortgage	warrant

▶ Grammar

Grammar questions, like spelling and vocabulary questions, typically have only three answer choices. Thus, grammar questions greatly reward those who use process of elimination. Eliminate one answer choice and you have a 50-50 chance of guessing correctly; eliminate two answer choices and you will have found the correct answer by process of elimination.

Grammar questions typically present three variations of a single sentence and ask you to determine which is written correctly. Each of the incorrect answers will contain at least one identifiable error.

In order to perform well on the grammar section, you must know a few basic grammatical principles. Master them and you will be able to distinguish correctly written sentences from poorly written sentences. The section that follows reviews all the concepts that are tested frequently on civil service exams.

Complete and Incomplete Sentences

The sentence is the basic unit of written language. Written communication typically uses complete sentences (there are a few exceptions, but they are rare), so it is important to know when a sentence is complete and when it is not complete. Incomplete sentences are called *sentence fragments*.

A complete sentence expresses a complete, independent thought. If a group of words can stand alone and have an understandable meaning, that group is a sentence. Consider the following examples.

Fragment: The dog walking down the street.
Sentence: The dog was walking down the street.

Fragment: Exploding from the bat for a home run.
Sentence: The ball exploded from the bat for a home run.

These examples show that a sentence must have a subject and a verb to complete its meaning. The first fragment has a subject (*dog*) but not a verb. Although *walking* looks like a verb, it is not a verb in this fragment; it is an adjective describing *dog*. By adding *was* to *walking*, the sentence transforms it from an adjective to a verb. In the second example, the fragment has neither a subject nor a verb. Again, *exploding* may look like a verb, but it is, in fact, an adjective in this fragment.

When distinguishing between sentences and fragments, be especially aware of answer choices that begin with a subordinating conjunction. What follows is a list of subordinating conjunctions:

after	that
although	though
as	unless
because	until
before	when
if	whenever
once	where
since	wherever
than	while

Answer choices that begin with these words are often sentence fragments. That's because these words indicate that more information is required to complete the thought being expressed.

Example: Unless you want to travel by automobile.

The preceding example is a sentence fragment. It suggests that something will happen *unless you want to travel by automobile*, but it never tells us what that something is. The thought expressed is incomplete. Here are some ways to complete the sentence.

Examples: We will go to the park by bus unless you want to travel by automobile.
Unless you want to travel by automobile, we should take our bikes to the park.

The second example shows that it is possible to write a complete sentence that begins with a subordinating clause. So, do not eliminate answer choices just because they start with subordinating clauses. Be aware, however, that many incorrect answers to complete sentence questions begin with subordinating clauses, and read such answer choices carefully.

Occasionally, a complete sentence question will ask you to identify and eliminate a *run-on sentence* from among the answer choices. A run-on sentence contains more than one *independent clause*, which is a group of words that would form a sentence if they stood alone. The sentences are run-on sentences because the independent clauses are not properly connected. To connect two independent clauses properly, you must use either a conjunction or appropriate punctuation (either a semicolon or a colon). Here is a run-on sentence:

Example: I went to the store I bought some food.

The clauses *I went to the store* and *I bought some food* are both independent, so they must be connected appropriately. A conjunction, such as *and*, *but*, or *or*, is the most common way to connect independent clauses.

Example: I went to the store, *and* I bought some food.

You can also use a preposition to turn one of the independent clauses into as prepositional phrase.

Example: I went to the store, where I bought some food.

To determine whether a sentence is complete and correctly formulated, check to make sure that:

- the sentence has both a subject and a verb
- the sentence is not a run-on sentence

Capitalization

You may encounter questions that test your ability to capitalize correctly. Here is a quick review of the most common capitalization rules:

- Capitalize the first word of a sentence. If the first word is a number, write it as a word.
- Capitalize the first word of a complete quotation, as in:

  Roger said, "I think I'll go to the ball game tonight."

- Don't capitalize the first word of a partial quotation, as in:

  Roger may go to the ball game tonight, but for now he's "still thinking about it."

- Capitalize proper nouns and proper adjectives.

The following table provides examples.

CAPITALIZATION	
CATEGORY	**EXAMPLES (PROPER NOUNS)**
days of the week, months of the year	Friday, Saturday; January, February
holidays, special events	Christmas, Halloween; Two Rivers Festival, Dilly Days
names of individuals	John Henry, Zora Neale Hurston
names of structures, buildings	Lincoln Memorial, Chrysler Building
names of trains, ships, aircraft	Queen Elizabeth, the Orient Express
product names	Corn King hams, Dodge Intrepid
cities and states	Des Moines, Iowa; Juneau, Alaska
streets, highways, roads	Grand Avenue, Interstate 29, Roxboro Road
landmarks, public areas	Continental Divide, Grand Canyon, Glacier National Park
bodies of water	Atlantic Ocean, Mississippi River
ethnic groups, languages, nationalities	Asian American, English, Arab
official titles	Mayor Daley, President Johnson
institutions, organizations, businesses	Dartmouth College, Lions Club, Goya Foods
proper adjectives	English muffin, Polish sausage

To answer capitalization questions, eliminate answers that include capitalization errors.

Example: Select the sentence that is written most correctly.

a. Abraham Adams made an appointment with Mayor Burns to discuss the building plans.
b. Abraham Adams made an appointment with Mayor Burns to discuss the Building Plans.
c. Abraham Adams made an appointment with mayor Burns to discuss the building plans.

To find the correct answer, compare the answer choices. Note that they are mostly the same. Choice **c**, however, is different because it does not capitalize the word *mayor*. In this example, the word *mayor* is used as a person's official title, so it should be capitalized. Eliminate choice **c**. Choices **a** and **b** are different because choice **b** capitalizes the phrase *Building Plans*. This phrase is not a proper noun, however, so it should not be capitalized. Eliminate choice **b**. The correct answer is choice **a**.

Punctuation

The English language uses many punctuation marks, but fortunately civil service exams focus on just a few: periods, commas, apostrophes, and quotation marks. Let's review the rules for using each.

Periods

Use a period:

- at the end of a sentence that is not a question or an exclamation
- after an initial in a name, e.g., Millard T. Fillmore
- after an abbreviation (e.g., Mrs., Dr., etc.), unless the abbreviation is an acronym (e.g., UNICEF, NASA)

When a sentence ends in an abbreviation, use only one period (e.g., We brought food, tents, sleeping bags, etc.).

Commas

Using commas correctly can make the difference between presenting information clearly and obscuring the meaning of a sentence. Study the following chart to see how commas clarify meaning.

COMMAS AND MEANING	
Number of people unknown	My sister Diane John Carey Melissa and I went to the fair.
Four people	My sister Diane, John Carey, Melissa and I went to the fair.
Five people	My sister, Diane, John Carey, Melissa and I went to the fair.
Six people	My sister, Diane, John, Carey, Melissa and I went to the fair.

Here are the rules covering the most common uses of commas.

- Use a comma before *and*, *but*, *or*, *for*, *nor*, and *yet* when they separate two independent clauses.

    Example: The coaches laid out the game plan, and the team executed it to perfection.

- Use a comma to separate items in a series.

    Example: Careful drivers use the IPDE method in which they identify, predict, decide, and execute a plan for safe driving.

- Use a comma to separate two or more adjectives modifying the same noun.

    Example: The hot, black, rich coffee tasted great after an hour in below-zero weather.

- Use a comma after introductory words, phrases, or clauses in a sentence.

    Examples: Usually, the class begins with a short writing assignment.
    Racing down the street, the yellow car ran a stoplight.
    After we found the source of the noise, we relaxed and enjoyed the rest of the evening.

- Use a comma after a name followed by Jr., Sr., or some other abbreviation.

    Example: The class was inspired by the speeches of Martin Luther King, Jr.

- Use a comma to separate items in an address.

    Example: The car stopped at 1433 West G Avenue, Orlando, Florida 36890.

- Use a comma to separate a day and a year, as well as after the year.

    Example: I was born on July 21, 1954, during a thunderstorm.

- Use a comma after the greeting of a friendly letter and after the closing of any letter.

    Example: Dear Uncle Jon,
    Sincerely yours,

- Use a comma to separate contrasting elements in a sentence.

    Example: Your essay needs strong arguments, not strong opinions, to convince me.

- Use commas to set off an appositive (a word or phrase that explains or identifies a noun).

    Example: My cat, a Siamese, is named Ron.

Apostrophes

Apostrophes communicate important information in written language. There are two main rules governing the use of apostrophes:

- Use an apostrophe to show that letters have been omitted from a word to form a contraction.

    Examples: do not = don't; I will = I'll; it is = it's

- Use an apostrophe to show possession.

    Examples: Bob's guitar; Linda's new car

APOSTROPHES TO SHOW POSSESSION		
SINGULAR NOUNS (ADD 'S)	**PLURAL NOUNS ENDING IN S (ADD ')**	**PLURAL NOUNS NOT ENDING IN S (ADD 'S)**
boy's	boys'	men's
lion's	lions'	children's
lady's	ladies'	women's

There's one important exception that you should remember, because it often turns up on tests: The possessive of *it* is *its*, not *it's* as many people mistakenly think. *It's* only means *it is*; *its* means *belonging to it*.

Quotation Marks

Quotation marks are generally used to indicate that someone's exact words are being reproduced. There are other uses for quotation marks (to indicate irony, for example), but for the purposes of this test, you need to know only about their primary use.

Here are the rules for using quotation marks:

- Quotes that are complete sentences are preceded by a comma and begin with a capital letter. End punctuation appears inside the quotes.

   Examples: The reporter asked the governor, "Do you have any plans to increase the education budget this year?"
   The governor said, "I would love to find a way to increase the education budget."

- Quotations that are not complete sentences begin with a lowercase letter and include end punctuation only if they appear at the end of the sentence.

   Examples: The governor added that he would "look into the matter further."
   The governor added that he would "look into the matter further" before reaching a decision.

- Use single quotation marks instead of double quotation marks for a quotation that appears within a quotation.

   Example: The head of the teacher's union told reporters that "The governor told me 'I will do everything I can to increase the education budget,' and I see no reason to doubt her."

Subject-Verb Agreement

For a sentence to be grammatically correct, its subject and verb must agree in number. This means that if the subject is singular, the verb must be singular; if the subject is plural, the verb must also be plural.

Generally speaking, the third person singular form of a verb (i.e., the form used with the words *he* or *she*) ends in the letter *s*.

   Examples: He walks; she sings; Jane dances; Robert cooks

The first and second person forms of a verb (i.e., the forms used with the words *I*, *you*, and *we*) generally do not end in the letter *s*.

   Examples: I relax; you read; we visit

Pronoun Subjects

Pronoun subjects can make things a little tricky, even for expert English speakers. Some pronouns are always singular, others are always plural, and still others can be both singular and plural.

These pronouns are always singular.

anybody

anyone

each

either

everybody

everyone

neither

no one

nobody

one

somebody

someone

The indefinite pronouns *each*, *either*, and *neither* are most often misused. You can avoid a mismatch by mentally adding the word *one* after the pronoun and removing the other words between the pronoun and the verb.

Examples: Each **of the men** wants his own car.
Each **one** wants his own car.

Although these sentences may sound awkward, they are written correctly (they sound awkward because you are used to hearing these pronouns used incorrectly).

Some pronouns are always plural and require a plural verb. They include:

both

few

many

several

Some pronouns can be either singular or plural. The verb they take depends on the words or prepositional phrases that follow them.

all

any

most

some

Examples: All of the milk **is** gone.
All of the students **are** gone.

Subjects joined by the word *and* are called *compound subjects*. They always take a plural verb.

Examples: He and she want to buy a new house.
Roger and George sing nicely together.

Subjects joined by the words *or* or *nor* agree with the noun or pronoun closest to the verb.

Examples: He or she wants to buy a house.
Either the Wilsons or the Johnsons plan to buy the house.

Verb Tense

The tense of a verb tells readers when the action occurs. Present tense verbs tell the reader to imagine that the action is happening right now, as they are reading the words. Past tense verbs tell readers that the action has already happened. Future tense verbs tell readers that the action will happen at a later time. This table shows the three basic verb tenses:

VERB TENSE		
PRESENT TENSE **(TODAY I . . .)**	**PAST TENSE** **(YESTERDAY I . . .)**	**FUTURE TENSE** **(TOMORROW I . . .)**
drive	drove	will drive
think	thought	will think
rise	rose	will rise
catch	caught	will catch

When a sentence describes two or more actions that occur at the same time, both tenses must be described in the same tense. The sentence "Terry opens the door and saw the crowd" contains a confusing and grammatically incorrect verb tense shift. Because both actions occurred at about the same time, both should be described using the same tense. Either "Terry opens the door and sees the crowd" or "Terry opened the door and saw the crowd" are acceptable.

That does not mean that it is impossible to use more than one verb tense in a sentence, however. A sentence that describes actions that occur at different times, for example, must use more than one verb tense. For example, the sentence "The game warden sees the fish that you caught" is correctly formulated. The verb *sees* is in the present tense, because the sentence indicates that the warden is seeing the fish right now. The fish was caught earlier; that's why *caught* is in the past tense, to indicate that it happened before the warden saw the fish.

Pronoun Case

In most cases, a single pronoun in a sentence is easy to use correctly. Most English speakers can identify the errors in the sentences that follow.

Errors: Me went to the movie with he.
My teacher gave she a ride to school.

In the first sentence, *me* should be *I* and *he* should be *him*. In the second sentence, *she* should be *her*. These are errors in pronoun case; they use the subject form of the pronoun when they should use the object form, or vice versa. As previously noted, such errors are relatively easy to spot when the pronoun stands alone. They are more difficult to spot, however, when the pronoun is paired with another pronoun or a noun. Consider the following sentences:

Errors: The director rode with Jerry and I.
Belle and him are going to the arena.

Both of these sentences contain pronoun case errors. Did you find them? The trick to finding these errors is to turn each sentence into two sentences.

Errors: The director rode with Jerry.
The director rode with I.

Belle is going to the arena.
Him is going to the arena.

By isolating each noun or pronoun in its own sentence, you can check pronoun case more easily. This will help you determine that the sentences should read *The director rode with Jerry and me* and *Belle and he are going to the arena.*

Pronoun Agreement

Like subjects and verbs, pronouns must agree in number with the nouns they represent. If a pronoun replaces a singular noun, the pronoun must also be singular. If the pronoun replaces a plural noun, the pronoun must also be plural.

Examples: A doctor should take a break whenever *she* gets tired.
Doctors should take a break whenever *they* get tired.

If a pronoun replaces another pronoun, the same rule applies: They must agree in number.

Examples: One of the girls misplaced *her* purse.
All of the girls misplaced *their* purses.

If two or more nouns or pronouns are joined by *and*, use a plural pronoun to represent them.

Example: Ben and Jerry built an ice cream company that made *them* rich and famous.

If two or more singular nouns or pronouns are joined by *or* or *nor*, use a singular pronoun to represent them.

Example: Matthew or Jacob will loan you *his* calculator.

If a singular and plural noun or pronoun are joined by *or* or *nor*, choose a pronoun that agrees with the one that comes after *or* or *nor*.

Examples: Neither the soldiers nor the sergeant was sure of *his* location.
Neither the sergeant nor the soldiers were sure of *their* location.

Passive Voice

Verbs have an *active voice* and a *passive voice*. A verb is in the active voice when the subject performs the action. A verb is in the passive voice when the subject receives the action.

Active: Roger kicked the ball.
Passive: The ball was kicked by Roger.

In the sentence written in active voice, *Roger* is the subject and he performs the action: He *kicks* the ball. In the sentence written in the passive voice, *the ball* is the subject and it receives the action: It *is kicked*.

The active voice is more precise than the passive voice; it clarifies what has happened and who is responsible. (Note that when the government or a corporation admits to something embarrassing, it uses the passive voice. It says *mistakes were made* in the passive voice rather than *we made mistakes* in the active voice.) Therefore, the active voice is preferred in most instances. There are times when the passive voice is appropriate and clear (e.g., *I was paid reasonably for my work*), but generally answers written in the passive voice are incorrect. When given the choice between two answers—one active, one passive—the active answer is much more likely the correct one.

Remember that regardless of the voice used, voice must remain consistent throughout a sentence. It is almost always incorrect to shift from the active to passive voice, or vice versa, in a sentence.

Incorrect: The swimmer won the race, and a medal was received by her.
Correct: The swimmer won the race and received a medal.

Modifiers

A modifier is a descriptive word, clause, or phrase. Modifiers are like adjectives. They help describe nouns (people, places, things, and concepts) by adding useful information.

A modifier must be clearly attached to the word or words it is describing; if it is not, it creates confusion. It can even result in an unintended (and often comical) meaning to the sentence.

Errors: Nailed to the tree, Cedric saw a "No Hunting" sign.
Waddling down the road, we saw a skunk.

Both *nailed to the tree* and *waddling down the road* are examples of *misplaced modifiers*. They are called misplaced modifiers because their placement makes it difficult to determine which noun they modify. The first sentence incorrectly suggests that it was Cedric and not the sign that was nailed to the tree; the second suggests that the people, rather than the skunk, were waddling down the road.

Here's how to correct the errors:

Corrected: Cedric saw a "No Hunting" sign nailed to a tree.
We saw a skunk waddling down the road.

Sometimes a modifier does not refer to any word or phrase in the sentence; rather, it refers to a concept that is implied but not stated. This is a grammatical error called a *dangling modifier*. Here are some examples:

Errors: After teaching all day, relaxing with a book is always a nice way to spend the evening.
Having received a letter, a reply was necessary.

The modifiers *after teaching all day* and *having received a letter* suggest a person who taught all day or received the letter. No such person is mentioned in the sentence, however; that's why the modifiers are called

dangling modifiers. These modifiers are metaphorically dangling in space, attached to nothing.

Here's how to correct the errors:

Corrected: The teacher feels that, after teaching all day, relaxing with a book is always a nice way to spend the evening.
Having received a letter, Bill realized that a reply was necessary.

Unnecessary Words

Good writing is clear and concise. Extra words take up valuable time and space, and they create opportunities for misunderstanding.

A *redundant* sentence is one that repeats an idea unnecessarily. Here are some examples of redundant sentences.

Examples: They refunded our money back to us.
We can proceed ahead with the plan we made ahead of time.
The car is red in color.

Consider the first example. To *refund* money is to give it back; therefore, it is unnecessary to say that the money was refunded *back to us*. The words *back to us* repeat an idea already expressed by the word *refund* without adding any new information. Similarly, *proceed* means *to go ahead* and a plan must, by definition, be made *ahead of time*; thus, *ahead* and *ahead of time* are redundant in the second example. Because *red* is a color, it is unnecessary and redundant to say the car is *red in color*. Simply write *The car is red*.

Other common examples of redundancy include:

actual experience
cheap price
connected together
consensus of opinion

final end

5 A.M. in the morning

join together

past experience

postponed until later

proven conclusively

the reason is because

unanimous consensus

true facts

A *wordy* sentence contains unnecessary words. When an idea can be expressed more concisely, it should be.

Examples:
Error: Bill is as good as or better than Marty.
Corrected: Bill is at least as good as Marty.

Error: It appears to me that it is starting to rain.
Corrected: It is starting to rain.

Error: It is the purpose of the encyclopedia to provide information on all topics.
Corrected: The encyclopedia's purpose is to provide information on all topics.

▶ Additional Resources

Here are some good ways to build your vocabulary, reading, and grammar skills so that you can do your best on the written communication section of a civil service test.

- If you have Internet access, search for articles related to the career you'd like to pursue. Find bulletin boards related to your career and use them to exchange views with others on the Internet. These strategies will help you expand your knowledge of job-related material that may appear on the test while they help you develop your communication skills.
- Use the library. Many public libraries have sections, sometimes called "Lifelong Learning Centers," that contain materials for adult learners. In these sections, you will find books with exercises for reading and study skills. It's also a good idea to enlarge your base of information by reading related books and articles. Many libraries have computer systems that allow you to access information quickly and easily. Library personnel will show you how to use the computers and microfilm and microfiche machines.
- Begin now to build a broad knowledge of your potential profession. Get in the habit of reading articles in newspapers and magazines on job-related issues. Keep a clipping file of those articles. This will help keep you informed of trends in the profession and familiarize you with relevant vocabulary.
- Consider reading or subscribing to professional journals. They are usually available for a reasonable annual fee. Your public library may have copies you can read for free.
- If you need more help building your reading skills and taking vocabulary tests, consider *Reading Comprehension in 20 Minutes a Day* and *501 Reading Comprehension Questions*, both by LearningExpress. If you need more help with spelling, consult *Vocabulary and Spelling in 20 Minutes a Day* by LearningExpress.
- Nonnative English speakers should consider *English Made Simple* by Arthur Waldhorn and Arthur Ziegler or *Errors in English and Ways to Correct Them* by Harry Shaw. Other good grammar reviews include *501 Grammar and Writing Questions* and *Writing Skills in 20 Minutes a Day*, both by LearningExpress.

► **Review Exercise**

Reading Comprehension
Read the following passage. Then, answer questions 1 to 5.

Although not admissible as evidence in most courts of law, polygraph tests play an important role in modern law enforcement. Commonly referred to as a "lie detector," a polygraph is an electronic instrument that monitors certain involuntary biological reactions. By tracking heart rate, blood pressure, respiratory rate, and sweat secretion on the subject's fingertips, the polygraph detects biological indicators of the type of stress associated with lying.

A polygraph test is typically broken up into four stages. The first is the pretest, during which the subject engages in a casual interview with his or her interrogator. This portion of the exam, during which the matter under investigation is discussed in detail, can take up to an hour to complete. The second stage is the design stage, during which examiners confer to design a series of questions about the matter under investigation; these are the questions to be asked during the actual polygraph exam. After the questions have been formulated, the actual exam is administered.

During the actual exam, the interrogator asks a series of questions, only a few of which have to do with the matter under investigation. The other questions are control questions, general questions designed to get the subject to lie, such as "Have you ever lied to get out of trouble with the police?" Most people will answer no to this question even though most people have, in fact, lied to get out of trouble with the police; this lie provides the examiner with a baseline response with which to compare other

responses, allowing him to determine when the subject is lying. A polygraph exam concludes with a posttest, during which the polygraph operator examines the results and determines whether the subject has lied and, if so, when.

Polygraph test results are not universally accepted. Even champions of the test concede that it cannot indicate whether a person is lying; rather, it detects symptoms and reactions that are indicative of lying in most people. Detractors argue that the test is stress-inducing, causing some people to register a "false positive" (a test result indicating that they are lying even though they are telling the truth), and that this is an uncorrectable flaw in the procedure. For this reason, some people are skeptical that polygraph tests will ever be reliable enough to gain universal acceptance in the courtroom.

1. According to the passage, which of the following occurs during the pretest segment of a polygraph test?
   a. The examiners ask the subject control questions.
   b. The examiners design questions to ask the subject.
   c. The examiners engage the subject in a casual interview.
   d. The subject's heart rate and blood pressure fluctuate.

2. As used in the passage, the word *skeptical* most nearly means
   a. doubtful.
   b. irate.
   c. intolerant.
   d. enthusiastic.

3. Which of the following best summarizes the author's purpose in writing the passage?
  a. to convince readers that polygraph tests are accurate
  b. to inform readers about how polygraph tests work
  c. to praise police forces that rely on polygraph tests
  d. to propose new methods for conducting polygraph tests

4. Critics would most likely argue that the biggest problem with polygraph tests is that
  a. too few polygraph operators are skilled enough to read test results accurately.
  b. the test is susceptible to power surges and power outages.
  c. their flaws cannot be fixed through redesign.
  d. a polygraph test takes too long to complete.

5. According to the passage, lie detectors monitor which of the following biological functions?
  a. brain waves
  b. saliva production
  c. eye movement
  d. breathing rate

Read the following passage. Then, answer questions 6 to 10.

The year 2005 was a watershed for school nutrition. That's because 2005 was the year that 42 state legislatures considered major revisions to policies concerning vending machines and cafeteria offerings in public schools; many passed legislation that imposed sweeping reforms. For many public school students, that meant the end of access to potato chips, candy bars, and high-sugar soft drinks.

This revolution was slow in coming and for a predictable reason: money. Schools are chronically underfunded, and as a result, they are always looking for ways to increase revenue in order to fund such "luxuries" as arts programs, athletic teams, field trips, and extracurricular clubs. Over the years, vending machines stocked with junk food became a reliable source of this much-needed income. Schools were understandably dubious about any new nutrition regulations. They wanted to promote healthy eating, but they also relied on vending machines for cash, and they knew that the most successful vending machines in schools sold junk food.

Then came an avalanche of reports on childhood obesity. The consensus: that anywhere between 10% and 33% of all American children were either overweight or in danger of becoming overweight. This is no small problem: Childhood obesity carries with it a number of potential complications, including high blood pressure, sleep disorders, liver disease, and Type 2 diabetes. Psychological effects can include depression and learning difficulties. Under the circumstances, state legislatures had little choice. When the media began reporting regularly on childhood obesity, citizens began to demand that the government take action.

It's too early to determine what, if any, effect these changes have had on childhood obesity. As for school revenues, reports are mixed. Philadelphia schools report no drop in income since they stopped stocking machines with soda and started stocking them with juice, milk, and water. Chicago schools, on the other hand, report a loss in income. Miami-Dade County public schools actually report a notable increase in income since making the switch. Public health expert Damien Seip notes, "Regardless of the impact on revenue, it's clear to everyone that junk food has got to go from our schools. We simply cannot participate in the fattening of America's youth. It's unconscionable."

6. Which of the following best summarizes the main idea of the passage?
   a. Somewhere between 10% and 33% of American children today are overweight.
   b. In Miami-Dade County, public schools saw an increase in vending machine revenue when they switched from junk food to healthy snacks.
   c. Type 2 diabetes is especially dangerous in young people, as it can lead to lifelong health problems and even premature death.
   d. Increased awareness of childhood obesity has led many states to enact new school food-service regulations.

7. According to the passage, changes to school food policies have so far resulted in
   a. a measurable decrease in obesity among public school students.
   b. an increase in truancy as students leave campus to buy junk food off school premises.
   c. a variety of positive and negative effects on school income from food sales.
   d. a decrease in the incidence of depression among high school students.

8. According to the passage, schools resisted changes to nutrition policies because they
   a. relied on vending machine sales to fund extracurricular activities.
   b. believed the changes didn't go far enough in banning junk food.
   c. felt that such decisions should be made by school boards, not state legislatures.
   d. worried that the changes would require an increase in cafeteria staff, which the schools could not afford.

9. The writer most likely puts the word *luxuries* in quotes to indicate that he is
   a. repeating what someone else said.
   b. using the word ironically.
   c. uncertain about the meaning of the word.
   d. introducing an unfamiliar technical term.

10. As used in the passage, the word *dubious* most nearly means
   a. uncertain.
   b. opposed.
   c. excited.
   d. misinformed.

Spelling and Vocabulary

Select the best answer choice for each question.

11. Chester's _____ table manners drove me to leave the dinner early.
   a. apaling
   b. apalling
   c. appalling

12. Shaniqua bought a snow globe as a _____ of her skiing vacation.
   a. momento
   b. memento
   c. mimento

13. Find the word that is closest in meaning to the underlined word below.

a person of remarkable <u>composure</u>
   a. calm
   b. skill
   c. humor

14. Find the word that is closest in meaning to the underlined word below.

a <u>potent</u> drug
a. ineffective
b. powerful
c. illegal

15. Find the word that best completes the sentence below.

Engineers speak in a technical _____ I simply cannot understand.
a. dialect
b. jargon
c. vigilance

Grammar

Select the best answer choice for each question.

16. Select the sentence that is written most correctly.
a. The Henderson family plans to visit the Grand Canyon some time in february.
b. the Henderson Family plans to visit the Grand canyon some time in February.
c. The Henderson family plans to visit the Grand Canyon some time in February.

17. Select the sentence that is written most correctly.
a. Neither of the salespeople seems to know how much this item costs.
b. Neither of the salespeople seem to know how much this item costs.
c. Neither of the salespeople seems to know how much this item cost.

18. Select the sentence that is written most correctly.
a. It's time to check the automobile to see whether its paint job has dried.
b. Its time to check the automobile to see whether it's paint job has dried.
c. It's time to check the automobile to see whether it's paint job has dried.

19. Select the sentence that is written most correctly.
a. Eaten as a delicacy in France for centuries, American diners are only now beginning to enjoy the culinary pleasures of escargot.
b. Eaten as a delicacy in France for centuries, escargot are only now beginning to bring culinary pleasure to American diners.
c. Escargot have been eaten as a delicacy in France for centuries, American diners are only now beginning to enjoy them.

20. Select the sentence that is written most correctly.
a. Some people say that jury duty is a nuisance that takes up their precious time and that we don't get paid enough.
b. Some people say that jury duty is a nuisance that takes up your precious time and that they don't get paid enough.
c. Some people say that jury duty is a nuisance that takes up one's precious time and that one doesn't get paid enough.

► Answers

1. c. The pretest is discussed in paragraph 2 of the passage. The passage states: "The first [stage] is the pretest, during which the subject engages in a casual interview with his or her interrogator." Thus, choice **c** is correct. Choice **a** describes the actual polygraph exam; choice **b** describes the design stage of the test; and choice **d** refers to information from a different part of the passage. Because the passage never states that the subject's heart rate and blood pressure fluctuate during the pretest, this cannot be the correct choice to an "According to the passage . . ." question.

2. a. *Skeptical* means *uncertain* or *doubtful*. *Irate* (choice **b**) means *angry*. *Intolerant* (choice **c**) means *unwilling to accept another's beliefs or customs*. *Enthusiastic* (choice **d**) means *excited*.

3. b. Use the process of elimination to answer this question. The tone of the passage is informative, not persuasive; furthermore, the author points out serious flaws in the polygraph test. Therefore, choice **a** cannot be correct. The author never discusses police forces, so choice **c** cannot be correct. Finally, the author reviews polygraph methods but does not suggest any new methods for improving the test; therefore, choice **d** cannot be correct.

4. c. In the final paragraph, the author reports: "Detractors argue that the test is stress-inducing, causing some people to register a 'false positive' (a test result indicating that they are lying even though they are telling the truth), *and that this is an uncorrectable flaw in the procedure*." The final part of the sentence supports the conclusion drawn in choice **c**. None of the other answer choices is mentioned or alluded to in the passage, so none of them can be correct.

5. d. The first paragraph states that polygraph tests measure respiratory rate. Choice **d**, *breathing rate*, is a good paraphrase of that information. Reread the first paragraph to see that the passage does not mention choices **a**, **b**, or **c**.

6. d. Of the answer choices, only choice **d** refers to the entire passage; the others refer to specific details from one portion of the passage. The answer to a main idea question must address the passage as a whole, not merely one section of the passage.

7. c. In the final paragraph, the passage states: "As for school revenues, reports are mixed." This, and the details that follow, support the conclusion that new school food policies have resulted in "a variety of positive and negative effects on school income from food sales." Choices **b** and **d** refer to data that is not provided in the passage and, therefore, cannot be correct; choice **a** is contradicted by the first sentence of the final paragraph.

8. a. Choice **a** is supported by paragraph 2, which explains how schools have become dependent on vending machine sales to pay for sports, arts programs, and other extracurricular activities. None of the other answers is mentioned in the passage and, therefore, cannot be correct.

9. b. The writer is indicating that he does not truly think that arts programs, sports, field trips, and extracurricular clubs are luxuries. He is being ironic. Irony is often indicated in writing by quotation marks.

10. **a.** Use context clues to answer this question. The sentence that follows the sentence in which *dubious* appears helps define the term. The schools "want to promote healthy eating," but "also relied on vending machines for cash." Their desires were at cross purposes and, therefore, the schools were *dubious*, or *uncertain*, about proposed changes.

11. **c.** The correct spelling is *appalling*.

12. **b.** The correct spelling is *memento*. Think of the words *memory* or *meme* to remember that *memento* starts with the letters *me*.

13. **a.** *Composure* means *a peaceful state of mind*. Of the three answer choices, *calm* (choice **a**) is closest in meaning.

14. **b.** *Potent* means *powerful*. *Ineffective* (choice **a**) is the opposite, or antonym, of *potent*.

15. **b.** *Jargon* means *technical language*. A *dialect* (choice **a**) is *a regional variation of a language*. *Jargon* is the better of the two choices because *jargon* is specifically associated with the technical specificity of engineers' conversation. *Vigilance* (choice **c**) means *watchfulness*.

16. **c.** Each incorrect answer contains capitalization errors. In choice **a**, the word *February* should be capitalized. In choice **b**, the word *family* should not be capitalized and the word *Canyon* should be capitalized (because it is part of a proper noun).

17. **a.** *Neither* takes a singular verb. Therefore, choice **b** is incorrect because it incorrectly states that *neither . . . seem* instead of *neither . . . seems*. Choice **c** is incorrect because *item* is singular and, therefore, must also take the singular verb *costs* instead of the plural verb *cost*.

18. **a.** The possessive form of *it* is *its*, not *it's*. The contraction *it's* means *it is*. Choice **b** uses the incorrect form of the word twice. Choice **c** incorrectly uses *it's paint job* when *its paint job* would be grammatically correct.

19. **b.** Choice **a** incorrectly states that *American diners* have been *eaten as a delicacy in France for centuries* when, in fact, it is *escargot*, not *American diners*, that have been eaten as delicacies there. Choice **c** contains two independent clauses but no conjunction or punctuation to connect them properly, making choice **c** a confusing run-on sentence.

20. **c.** Choices **a** and **b** contain ungrammatical pronoun shifts. Choice **a** uses *their* and *we* to describe the same group of people; choice **b** uses *your* and *they* similarly. Only choice **c** remains grammatically consistent, using *one* in both instances.

Civil Service
Skills

any civil service exams include skill tests specific to the job for which they are designed. Clerical exams, for example, may contain sections on alphabetizing and filing. Police exams often include sections on face recognition skills. The U.S. postal exam contains a section on address checking.

Three skill sets pop up most frequently on civil service exams: customer service, memory, and coding. These skills, and the questions used to test them, are the subject of this chapter.

▶ Customer Service

Customer service questions on civil service exams ask about a variety of situations and scenarios, but most can be answered by remembering a few basic principles.

- The top priority of customer service is a satisfied customer. Good customer service makes things as easy and comfortable for the customer as is reasonably possible.
- Always be polite to customers; any action that will upset the customer (e.g., telling the customer that he or she is being rude) is bad.
- Respect customers' right to privacy, especially when recording or handling personal information (e.g., Social Security numbers, addresses, birth dates, etc.).
- Try to resolve the customer's problem yourself, but if you can't, find someone who can. Whenever possible, resolve problems during a single visit or contact.
- Express regret when you cannot resolve the customer's problem.
- Handle complaints professionally.

Most customer service questions test these principles in one way or another.

Example: A customer asks you which form she must complete in order to apply for a certain government program. You are not sure of the answer. Which of the following should you do?

a. Give the customer the answer you think is most likely correct.
b. Direct the customer to another employee.
c. Inform the person that you are not sure but will find the answer for her.
d. Tell the customer that she must figure it out on her own.

Consider each answer choice. Choice **a** creates the real possibility that you will give the customer incorrect information. She may then fill out and submit the incorrect form, which will result in a delay in resolving

her matter and which may require her to make a return visit to your office. This is not a good answer choice; eliminate it.

Choice **b** suggests that you dump your problem onto another employee. This is not only poor customer service, but also the sort of workplace etiquette that will make you many enemies among your coworkers. Eliminate this answer choice.

Choice **c** looks good. You honestly inform the customer that you do not know the answer to her question, but you promise to find the answer for her. You are showing the customer the proper respect by telling her the truth, and you are attempting to resolve the problem in a single visit or contact. This is probably the correct answer, but we must look at choice **d** to be sure.

Choice **d** violates most of the basic principles tested by customer service questions. The response will certainly not result in a satisfied customer; it's not a polite response; it represents a failure on your part to try to resolve the customer's issue and it's unprofessional. This is definitely not the correct answer.

The correct answer to this question is choice **c**.

The Citizen Service Levels Interagency Committee (CSLIC) Report

In October 2005, the federal government released *The Citizen Service Levels Interagency Committee (CSLIC) Report*, a study commissioned by President Bush. The report contains "proposed performance measures, practices, and approaches for government-wide citizen contact activities" that focus on making government services "market-based, citizen-centric, and customer-focused." Simply put, the *CSLIC Report* is the federal government's official policy on what constitutes good customer service. Its recommendations have certainly had an impact on state and local governments as well. Because this report has become the government standard by which customer service is measured, you should be familiar with its contents. A summary of its most important points follows (those wishing to read the entire 36-page report will find it online by searching for *CSLIC Report*).

The report studies five areas: telephone service, e-mail service, traditional service such as walk-in and postal mail, cross-channel issues (e.g., customer complaints, multilingual service), and developing technologies (e.g., instant messaging, virtual meetings). Here's what it has to say about each.

In All Areas

Customer service must focus on ease of use for the customer, timely response, respect for privacy, quality service, consistency in service, and convenience for the customer. Applied to specific cross-function areas, this means that:

- **Customer complaints** should be counted and evaluated regularly in order to determine whether improvement in overall service is necessary. Customers should have a variety of options to choose from in registering complaints (in person, by telephone, via the Internet) and should be given a choice as to whether they would like a response. Complaints should be acknowledged promptly.

- **Queries should be resolved during first contact** whenever possible.

- **Plain language** (i.e., language that is easy for the general public to understand) should be used in all documents for the public and in all interactions with the public. Avoid using technical terms and acronyms. Prepared scripts for common queries should be prepared; they should utilize plain language.

- **Privacy policies** should be clearly posted and available in print, online, and e-mail form. Customers should be informed whenever their interactions are being recorded or otherwise

monitored, whether for training or quality assurance purposes. Customers should be informed that information they provide will be recorded for future reference in order to make future interactions with the customer easier, i.e., they will not have to repeat the process of providing name, birth date, Social Security number, etc.

- **Continuously available channels of contact** such as 24-hour help lines, web chat, and Internet sites should be made available and should be promoted in order to inform customers of their availability. Promotion should include placards and pamphlets displayed at customer service sites, recorded messages on government telephone lines, and reminders by agents at the conclusion of an interaction.

- **Language translation** services should be provided for customers with limited English skills. Quality of translation should be emphasized over quantity of available languages. In other words, it is better to have a great Spanish translator than a translator who translates Spanish, French, and Portuguese poorly. When used, auto translators should be checked regularly for accuracy and functionality.

- **Interagency contact information** (e.g., telephone extensions) should be updated regularly to ensure that agents always have the most current information.

- **Correspondences** should conform to an agency style guide that is regularly reviewed and updated. Styles should include a standard greeting and closing and sample instructions to customers.

- **Creative scheduling**, including flextime, should be used to meet customer needs by expanding hours of customer support. Hours of operation should be set to meet the needs and preferences of customers, and should be reevaluated regularly to ensure that customer needs continue to be met.

- **Supervisors** should be available to speak with customers in a timely manner when customers request such contact.
- **Overall customer satisfaction** should be regularly evaluated, with formal reviews at least once per year. Customers should be asked to assess their satisfaction with such services and to record their assessment on a uniform customer satisfaction survey, the results of which should be used to evaluate agency performance. Customer feedback should be incorporated into trainings and manuals.

Telephone Service

Even as options for contacting the government increase, the telephone remains the means of communication preferred by most of the government's customers. This is true across all age groups, not just for older citizens.

Contacting the government by telephone can be an unpleasant experience. Customers complain of prolonged hold times, repeated transfers among different agents within and between agencies, faulty automated answering and interactive voice response systems, unreturned voicemail and the delivery of inaccurate information by government agents. The *CSLIC Report* looks for ways to address these problems. Its recommendations:

- **Incoming calls during business hours** should be answered quickly. At least 80% of calls should be handled within 60 seconds. The abandonment rate—the rate at which customers hang up before they get to speak to a representative—should be kept below 4% annually.
- **Audio provided during hold time** should provide answers to frequently asked questions. If hold time is expected to be longer than 30 seconds, the customer should be periodically informed of the projected wait time.

- **Toll-free numbers** should be available to people calling from within the United States.
- **Interactive voice response (IVR) systems** should be used to free staff for other tasks and to allow customers to navigate their own way to the appropriate assistance. Speech recognition technology should be included in a government IVR system, allowing customers to navigate by voice as well as by keypad (e.g., "If you are calling to check on the status of your refund check, press or say 'one.'").
- **A common voice** should be used for all recorded messages. The voice should be calm; the speaker should speak slowly and clearly.
- **Recorded messages for those who call after business hours** should state the agency's hours of operation and should encourage callers to use online resources.
- **Return calls** for voicemail messages should be made no later than the next day. Agents should attempt to return the call three times at three different times of day before giving up.
- **Call transfers** should not be made until the customer is told to whom he or she is being transferred, the reason for the transfer, and the telephone number and extension of the person to whom he or she is being transferred.

E-mail and Internet

E-mail and Internet connection are preferred slightly over telephone contact by customers who have easy access to high-speed Internet connections (e.g., a cable modem). Customers who use these channels complain most often that e-mails are not always returned, requiring multiple submissions before a response arrives. Many agencies do not even generate an auto-reply confirming receipt, meaning that the customer cannot even be certain that his or her e-mail has reached its destination.

To address these issues, the CSLIC recommends:

- **Agency e-mail addresses** should be easy to find, both on the Internet and at the agency office. Accounts should be monitored throughout office hours.

- **Use of agents' individual e-mail accounts should be minimized** to reduce the likelihood that customer response will be delayed because of vacation or attrition.

- **An auto-reply** should be sent to a customer upon receipt of his or her query to confirm that the e-mail has been received. Auto-replies should suggest alternative means of resolution (telephone, walk-in visit, website) if such alternatives would yield a faster response.

- **Mandatory fields in customer e-mail submissions** should be kept to a minimum. In most instances, name, street address, e-mail address, and nature of query should provide enough information for the agent to identify and contact the customer.

- **Simple queries** should be answered within two business days. More complex queries should be answered within five business days; the customer should be informed of the approximate wait anticipated for response. Extremely complex queries may take longer; customers should be notified of the progress made toward resolution every five to ten business days.

- **E-mail responses should be concise** and should be written in plain language.

- **When an e-mail is not successfully delivered**, the agent should make at least two subsequent attempts to resend. This is not necessary when the e-mail is not delivered because the customer has incorrectly entered his or her e-mail address.

- **Misdirected e-mail**, which is e-mail sent to the wrong agency, should be sent to the U.S. General Services Administration's (GSA) USA Services center for redirection. Senders of misdirected e-mail should be notified and told that their inquiry is being forwarded to the appropriate office via USA Services. They should be advised to follow up on their inquiries if they do not receive a response within a reasonable amount of time.

- **Web response forms should be used whenever possible** to minimize spam. Such forms should include links to FAQs (frequently asked questions) and drop-down menus that allow the customer to categorize his or her query. Date and time of transmission should be automatically recorded.

Postal Mail, Fax, and Walk-In Service

Government employees must handle copious amounts of postal mail each day. Customers often prefer to use mail for urgent matters, complex inquiries, and issues that require them to disclose personal information. Civil servants must also interact with numerous walk-in customers and manage daily fax transmissions.

The CSLIC studied these matters and rendered the following recommendations:

- **Postal mail** should be acknowledged with an immediate response; the response should include an estimate of the time required to resolve the query if an answer cannot be delivered within 15 working days. Incoming mail should be logged, with topic, date of receipt, and date of response recorded. Agencies should have a clearly established policy for routing letters addressed to an agency's leadership.

- **Fax transmissions** should receive responses by postal mail for fax; rules for response are the same as those previously outlined for postal mail.

- **Walk-in customers** should be able to speak with a receptionist (or an employee serving the same function) immediately upon arrival at the office.

This greeter should inform the customer of the approximate wait time to see an agent and should inform the customer of the information required to address the query. Some sort of queuing system—take a number or electronic self-registration, for example—should be in operation in offices where more than a few customers are left waiting at any given time.

- **Appointments should be offered** by agencies whose walk-in customers typically wait more than 15 minutes to meet with an agent.
- **Extended hours of operation**, with possible extension into evening hours and Saturdays, should be considered by offices whose customers have difficulty visiting the office during regular business hours.

Web Chat, Etc.

Modern technology is rapidly changing the way citizens interact with the government. Websites allow citizens to retrieve information instantaneously, expediting transactions and freeing government employees to perform more important tasks. RSS (Really Simple Syndication) technology allows citizens to be notified immediately whenever a government webpage is updated. Other technologies—web chat, instant messaging, and videoconferencing to name a few—are being developed and adapted for use in government-citizen interactions.

The incorporation of new technology hasn't been a completely smooth ride for the government. Citizens have complained that some government websites are poorly organized, making it difficult to find important information. FAQs are not updated often enough to serve their purpose effectively.

To address these issues, the CSLIC recommends:

- **BOTs** (response software programmed to answer certain customer queries automatically) should

be reviewed at least once every three months to ensure that they work properly and provide accurate information.

- **Contact pages at websites** should include numerous options: telephone number(s), e-mail address(es), postal address(es), etc.
- **Links to other agencies' websites** should be provided, as appropriate.
- **FAQs** should be reviewed regularly for accuracy and relevance. Customers should have the option of having FAQs e-mailed to them.
- **RSS feeds** should be made available; feeds should include descriptions of updated material. Instructions should be provided to explain how to link to the agency's RSS feed. Agencies should inform USA.gov (a website that provides official information and services from the U.S. government; formerly FirstGov) when they establish a new RSS feed so the feed can be included in the government-wide RSS library.
- **Web chat** should be available for as many hours a day as possible. If 24-hour service is impossible, hours of operation should be clearly posted.
- **Websites should be designed** with low load times and minimal required scrolling; page layout should be kept clear and simple. Spelling should be carefully checked, as misspellings impede web searches; common misspellings of words appearing on a webpage should be included among the page's meta key words.

▶ Memory

Questions that test memory appear on a number of civil service exams. Practically all police exams include a memory section. Qualifying exams for most postal positions include them as well. Many other exams at the federal, state, and local level test memory.

The reason for this should be fairly obvious: Most jobs require you to remember procedures and protocols, and some jobs require you to remember a great deal more. Memory is certainly a more important skill in some jobs than in others—police officers, for example, rely on memory to solve crimes and, later, to testify accurately at criminal trials, making a good memory a crucial asset for their work—but nearly every job requires some ability to remember important facts and principles.

The most common format for memory questions asks you to study a picture for a fixed amount of time (typically five minutes). The image is then removed from view (on a computer test, the image simply disappears from the screen; on a paper-and-pencil test, you will be asked to close the "memory book" and turn to the test booklet), after which you must answer a number of questions about the image.

There are no shortcuts to finding the correct answers to memory questions; unfortunately, either you remember or you don't, and if you don't, you can only make your best guess and move on. Fortunately, there are several tricks for improving memory. We'll discuss two methods that are well suited to quick memorization:

- the **story** method
- the **peg** method

We will also discuss how to use each method to memorize details of an image or items on a list.

Story Method

To use the story method of memorization, take the items you are trying to memorize and weave a simple, memorable story out of them. The story method is well suited to memorizing images because an image helps suggest a narrative. Consider the image on page 130; it is the sort of image you might see on a memory test.

Before we can use the story method to remember this image, we have to decide what we are going to memorize from this picture. It's a busy picture with lots of detail; we must choose the details that we think the exam is most likely to test, and then memorize them. You should figure that the more prominent a detail, the more likely it is to be tested. Tiny details are least likely to be tested.

So what are the prominent features of this photograph?

People
    A bald man in sunglasses (or shades) and an
        Artie's Deli T-shirt
    A dark-haired man in a short-sleeve shirt with
        a bag across his shoulder
    A black woman carrying a purse

Stores
    Salon & Spa
    Newsstand (selling cigarettes, magazines, cold
        drinks, and phone cards)
    Photo shop
    Jeweler
    Japanese restaurant (Sushi-Time)

Other details
    Phone booth
    Billboard (automobile advertisement)
    Sign that reads "Podiatry"
    Jewelry sale, 20% to 60% off

That's about it. Yes, there are other details in the photograph, but they are pretty small and difficult to make out; they are unlikely to be the subject of a memory question. Now, let's write a story that incorporates the items we listed.

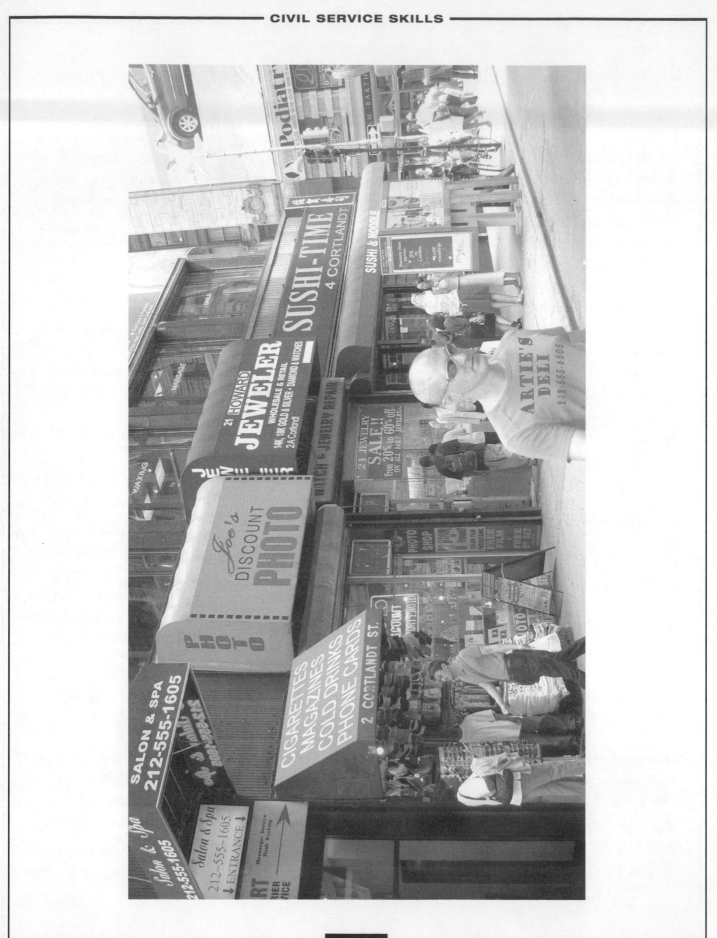

A <u>bald</u> man named <u>Artie Shades</u> took <u>photographs</u> of <u>jewelry</u> from <u>Japan</u> to sell to the <u>newspaper</u>. He went to the <u>salon and spa</u> to make a <u>phone</u> call to a <u>dark-haired man</u> who told him he would put the photos in his <u>shoulder bag</u> and deliver them by <u>automobile</u>. Artie would have rather walked, but his <u>podiatrist</u> told him he should reduce his walking by <u>20% to 60%</u>. His podiatrist was a <u>black woman</u> who <u>pursed</u> her lips while she talked.

Yes, the story is a little strange. It's certainly not the best story you ever heard. However, it is the sort of story you can write and memorize in five minutes. It contains memory cues (sometimes called *mnemonics*) for every item on the list we created. The fact that the story is ridiculous is good; the more ridiculous the story, the more likely you are to remember it. And although it doesn't repeat every item from the list word for word, it does contain key words that should trigger your memory (e.g., Artie Shades will trigger your memory that the bald man is wearing sunglasses and an "Artie's Deli" T-shirt).

Example: The dark-haired man walking past the newsstand is carrying a

a. briefcase.
b. shoulder bag.
c. suitcase.
d. basket.

If your mnemonic story works, you will remember that the man with the dark hair is carrying a shoulder bag (in the story, he puts the photos in it). If you can't remember the shoulder bag, you still might realize that your story does not mention a briefcase, a suitcase, or a

basket; therefore, they are probably not the correct answers. The correct answer to this question is choice **b**.

Peg Method

The peg method of memorization works by associating, or pegging, the items you wish to memorize with items on a list you have already memorized. The most commonly used peg list uses rhymes for the numbers 1 through 10:

1–gun
2–shoe
3–tree
4–door
5–hive
6–bricks
7–Kevin
8–gate
9–wine
10–hen

To use the peg method, you would first memorize this list. This would become, in effect, your permanent "peg board." Whenever you want to memorize a list of ten or fewer items, you would then be able to do so by pegging the item to your list. Say, for example, you wanted to memorize the following grocery list:

apples
lettuce
ground beef
cola
potato chips
napkins
paper plates

You would memorize this list by associating each item on the list with an item on the peg list. Imagine and form a solid mental image of:

a gun that shoots apples

a pair of shoes made of lettuce (or filled with lettuce)

a tree that grows ground beef

a door that is blocked by cases of cola piled on top of one another

bees returning to their hive carrying potato chips

bricks wrapped in napkins

Kevin having a picnic and eating off paper plates

Suppose you want to memorize more than ten items. You would have to memorize a longer peg list. The alphabet provides a good model for a 26-item peg list. Create a list that works best for you. For most people, a list of words beginning with the corresponding letter works best. Make up your own if you like or use this example:

A–ape
B–bee
C–car
D–dog
E–egg
F–frog
G–gold
H–hat
I–ice

J–jail
K–kangaroo
L–log
M–monkey
N–nose
O–owl
P–pig
Q–queen
R–rock
S–sun
T–truck
U–umbrella
V–vest
W–wig
X–X-ray
Y–yogurt
Z–zoo

The peg method is best suited to memorizing lists or charts, diagrams, tables, etc., that can be turned into lists. You might use it when a memory question asks you to study a table such as the one that follows. It lists the alternate side of the street parking regulations for streets surrounding a municipal office. If you work at this office and drive to work, you'll need to memorize this table if you don't want to get lots of parking tickets!

ALTERNATE SIDE OF THE STREET PARKING REGULATIONS	
STREET NAME	**ALTERNATE SIDE PARKING IN EFFECT**
Branson Street	Monday and Wednesday, 8 A.M. to noon
Franklin Avenue	Tuesday and Friday, 8 A.M. to noon
Park Row	Monday and Thursday, 8 A.M. to 11 A.M.
Water Street	Monday and Wednesday, noon to 4 P.M.
Independence Avenue	Tuesday and Friday, noon to 4 P.M.
Elm Street	Monday and Thursday, 11 A.M. to 2 P.M.

At first, this may seem like a lot of information to memorize. Before you start trying to commit it all to memory, however, study the table for a few moments. Note that two of the streets have alternate side parking on Monday and Wednesday, one in the morning and one in the afternoon. The same is true for Tuesday and Friday. Alternate side parking for the two Monday and Thursday streets is in effect for different hours (8 A.M. to 11 A.M. and 11 A.M. to 2 P.M.) rather than 8 A.M. to noon and noon to 4 P.M.).

Under the circumstances, it would be better for you to rearrange the information in the table this way:

Monday–Wednesday
Branson (early)
Water (late)

Tuesday–Friday
Franklin (early)
Independence (late)

Monday–Thursday
Park (early)
Elm (late)

The peg system requires you to memorize items in a list, so you'll really be memorizing:

Monday
Wednesday
Branson
Water
Tuesday
Friday
Franklin
Independence
Monday
Thursday
Park
Elm

The only information missing from this list is that the hours for alternate side of the street parking for Park and Elm are different from the hours for the other four streets. By listing them last, you should be able to remember that they are the two streets that are different from the other four.

To memorize the list, peg each item to one of your peg words. Because the list contains more than ten items, let's use the alphabet peg list. For each item, try to form a vivid mental picture. To peg "Monday," the first item on the list you want to memorize, to "ape," the first item on your peg list, picture an ape-faced monster in your mind. To peg "Wednesday" to "bees," imagine two bees having a wedding.

Here's how you might finish out your peg list. Remember to choose dramatic images; they will be easier to remember than mundane images.

An ape-faced monster
Two bees having a wedding
A car driving to Branson, Missouri, for vacation
A dog swimming through lots of water
An egg with lots of twos written on it (twos = Tuesday)
A fried frog
A statue of Benjamin Franklin made entirely of gold
A hat tossed in the deep end of a pool (in deep end = Independence; believe it or not, the wackier the mnemonics, the easier they will be to remember)
A monkey crawling on a tree made of ice
A thirsty man in jail (thirsty = Thursday)
A kangaroo parked at a parking meter
Michael Jordan sitting on a log

You can try other mnemonic techniques if the story method and the peg method don't seem right for you. Search for *mnemonics* online or look for books on memory at your local library.

▶ Coding

Government offices use a variety of coding systems to record information in shorthand. As a result, many government jobs require coding skills. Therefore, civil service exams include coding questions.

Also, coding questions test your ability to follow directions, an ability required in all government jobs. To answer a coding question correctly, you must read instructions carefully and follow them accurately.

Example: An office uses a code to record the e-mails it receives from citizens during the day. A code is assigned to each e-mail and logged on a spreadsheet; one spreadsheet is created for each day. The code is assigned according to the following rules:

Characters one through four
The time, in military-time format (e.g., 9:00 A.M. = 0900, 3:00 P.M. = 1500)

Characters five through eight
The first three letters of the sender's last name, and the sender's first initial (e.g., Bob Harris = HARB)

Example: An e-mail arrives at 4:25 P.M. from Catherine McDonald. Which of the following is the correct code for the e-mail?
  a. 1625MCDC
  b. 1625CATM
  c. 0425MCDC
  d. 0425CATM

There are two possible strategies for answering a coding question. The first is to create the correct code according to the information in the question, and then check your code against each of the answer choices until you find the one that matches. Try writing the proper code for the e-mail now.

This approach is certainly one alternative, but it is not without drawbacks. First, it requires you to create the code accurately. Then, it requires you to match your answer accurately with the corresponding answer choice. The problem with this strategy, then, is that it creates two opportunities for a careless mistake. Did you write the code 1625MCDC? Unless you did, there is no way you could answer this question correctly using this approach. And you would still have to match your code to the correct answer without making a careless mistake.

A better strategy is to check each rule, one at a time, against the answer choices, eliminating any answer that breaks the rule. Continue this process until you have eliminated three incorrect choices. The remaining choice must be the correct answer. You will have found the answer by process of elimination.

For example, you might first look at the rule stating that the final four characters should be the first three letters of the sender's first name, followed by the sender's first initial. The first three letters of this sender's last name are MCD; her first initial is C. Therefore, the correct answer must end MCDC. Check the answers and eliminate choices **b** and **d**, which end with CATM.

Now check the other rule, which states that the time should be recorded in military format. The time 4:25 P.M. is written "1625" in military format, meaning you can eliminate choice **c**. The correct answer, by process of elimination, is choice **a**.

Coding questions are typically more elaborate than the example we just studied. Usually they contain at least three rules and often several more than that. The more elaborate the rules for the code, the more effective the strategy of checking rules and eliminating incorrect answers, because you are more likely to make a careless mistake on a question with elaborate instructions.

Let's look at a more complicated example.

Example: All teachers in a state receive a license. The license is coded to reflect the duration of the license, the academic level for which the teacher is licensed, and the primary subject in which the teacher is licensed. The license code is generated according to the following rules.

First and second characters (type of license)
00—Teaching assistant
01—One-year license
02—Two-year license
03—Three-year license
04—Four-year license
05—Five-year license

Third and fourth characters (level)
10—Preschool
11—Elementary
12—Middle school
13—High school
14—All levels

Fifth, sixth, and seventh characters (primary subject)
200—Agriculture
201—Business
202—Computer science
203—Family education
204—Foreign language
205—Health science
206—Language arts
207—Mathematics
208—Natural science
209—Physical education
210—Social science
211—Special education
212—Technical education
213—Theater, music, and/or art

Eighth, ninth, and tenth characters (last name)
First three letters of license holder's last name (e.g., Fong = FON)

Example: A school principal receives notification that the school will soon have a new teacher and that the teacher's license number is 0212207JAC. Which of the following statements about the new teacher could be true?
  a. She is a middle school teacher whose name is Jacqueline Richardson.
  b. She holds a two-year license and teaches physical education.
  c. She is an elementary school teacher who teaches mathematics.
  d. She is a middle school teacher whose name is Mary Jackson.

This question asks you to look at a code and determine to whom it could belong. Once again, the best approach is to check the rules one by one, eliminating answer choices that break the rules.

Let's check the first two digits first. The digits 02 in the first two slots tell us that the teacher has a two-year license. This information tells us that choice **b** might be correct. Unfortunately, it does not allow us to eliminate any answer choices. Let's move on.

The second two digits are 12. These digits tell us that the teacher is a middle school teacher. This is enough information to eliminate choice **c**, which says the teacher is an elementary school teacher.

The fifth, sixth, and seventh digits are 207; they tell us that the teacher is a mathematics teacher. Therefore, she is not a physical education teacher; eliminate choice **b**. The answer must be choices **a** or **d**.

The final three letters of the code tell us that the teacher's last name begin with the letters JAC. This information allows us to eliminate choice **a**. The correct answer, by process of elimination, is choice **d**.

▶ Review Exercise

Customer Service—Questions 1 through 4

Select the best answer choice for each question.

1. A customer approaches you and immediately begins to list his many complaints with your agency's service. What should you do?

  a. Make a note of his complaints and check into their accuracy.

  b. Figure that the customer is having a bad day and listen patiently but ignore the complaints.

  c. Assume the complaints are accurate and take immediate action to remedy the indicated problems.

  d. Direct the customer to a complaint desk in another building.

2. Which of the following statements is most accurate?

  a. It is better to give a customer incorrect information than to admit that you do not know the answer to his question.

  b. When in doubt, you should instruct a customer that he or she should return to the line and wait for an employee who can answer his or her question.

  c. If you do not know the answer to a customer's question, write it down and tell him or her you will send your response within three weeks.

  d. When you cannot answer a question, find someone who can answer the question and make sure the answer is clearly conveyed to the customer.

3. A customer indicates her concerns about providing personal information. You should

  a. explain to the woman that the government handles thousands of people's personal information every day, so the odds of her privacy being compromised are low.

  b. assure her that the government respects and protects privacy, showing her the appropriate policy statements if she asks to see them.

  c. agree that her concerns are legitimate and advise her that she may want to reconsider seeking service from the government.

  d. advise her not to share any information she does not want to share and hope that her query is processed without the missing information.

4. When writing a letter to a customer, you should

  a. use an informal tone in order to make the customer comfortable.

  b. include as many technical terms and acronyms as you can.

  c. tell the customer to resolve future matters via the Internet.

  d. conform to the style mandated by agency policy.

Memory—Questions 5 through 12

Take five minutes to study the following picture. Then, answer questions 5 to 8 without looking back at the picture.

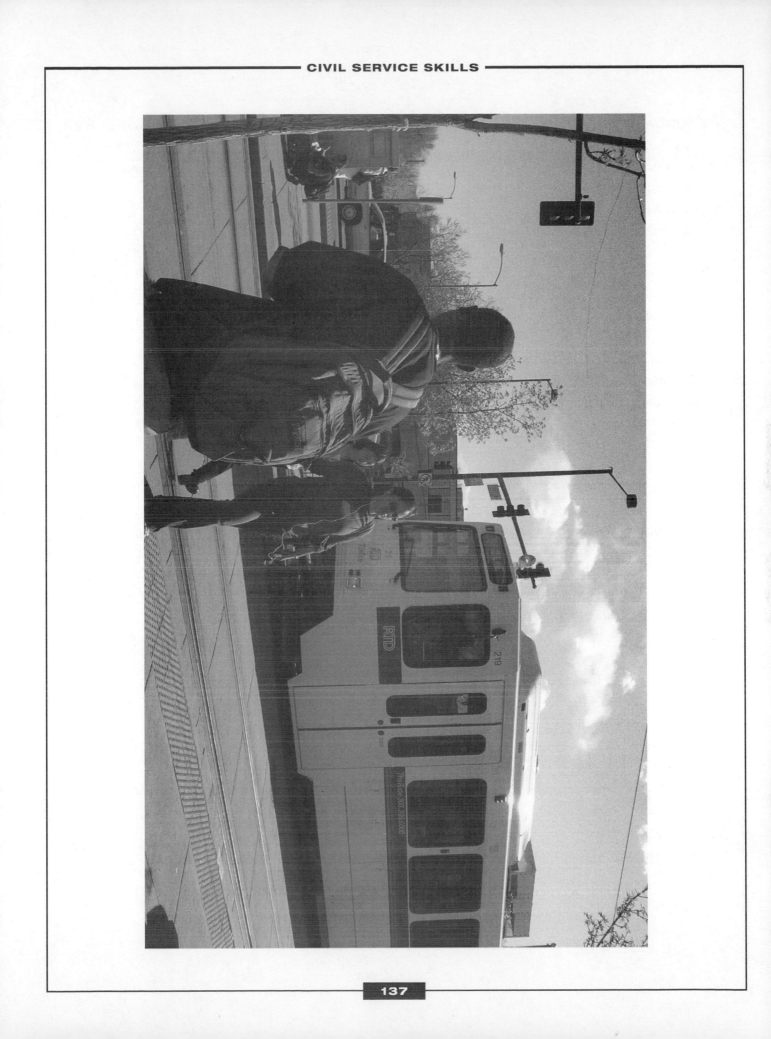

5. Based on the photo, the number of people crossing the street in front of the train is
   a. one.
   b. two.
   c. three.
   d. undeterminable from the photo.

6. Based on the photo, the number of people who are crossing the street while wearing a personal music device is
   a. one.
   b. two.
   c. three.
   d. undeterminable from the photo.

7. Other than those seen crossing the street in front of the train, how many other people or nontransit vehicles can be observed in the photo?
   a. one person and no vehicles
   b. one person and one vehicle
   c. two persons and no vehicle
   d. two persons and one vehicle

8. What is the total number of people seen in the photo?
   a. three
   b. four
   c. five
   d. six

Take five minutes to study the following flow chart. Then, answer questions 9 to 12 without looking back at the picture.

A government office used the flow chart below to determine which documents to save and where to save them.

9. Documents that pertain to an open investigation should be
 a. filed in the permanent file.
 b. filed in the short-term file.
 c. stored on computer.
 d. thrown away.

10. The permanent file includes
 a. only documents that the agency is required by law to save.
 b. documents that the agency is required by law to save and documents that pertain to an open investigation.
 c. documents that the agency is required by law to save and documents that relate to an agency ruling.
 d. all documents that the agency creates.

11. Documents stored in the short-term file should be reviewed once a
 a. day.
 b. week.
 c. month.
 d. year.

12. Andrew Distefano contacts the agency by e-mail. His correspondence is
 a. saved on a hard drive and CD-ROM.
 b. saved in the permanent file.
 c. saved in the short-term file.
 d. destroyed after it has been read.

Coding—Questions 13 to 20

To answer questions 13 through 20, refer to the following scenario.

A government office uses the following code to log every e-mail it receives:

First letter
A = received in the A.M.
P = received in the P.M.

Four digits
First two digits = month (e.g., February = 02)
Second two digits = date (e.g., February 4 = 0204)

Four letters
First three letters = first three letters of sender's last name
Fourth letter = first letter of sender's first name

Thus, an e-mail received at 10:45 A.M. on October 18 from Henry Watson would be coded:

A1018WATH

13. At 1:38 P.M. on March 16, the office received an e-mail from Janet Dubois. The e-mail should be coded
 a. 0138P0316JAND.
 b. P0316JAND.
 c. P316DUBJ.
 d. P0316DUBJ.

14. At 11:57 A.M. on December 14, the office received an e-mail from Martin Anderson. The e-mail should be coded
 a. A1214ANDM.
 b. A1157ANDM.
 c. A1214MARA.
 d. A1157MARA.

15. The office received an e-mail from David Levitsky at 9:38 A.M. on June 1. The e-mail should be coded
 a. DAVLA0601.
 b. LEVDA0601.
 c. A0601LEVD.
 d. A0938LEVD.

16. On August 30, the office received an e-mail from Sharon Douglas at 2:15 P.M. The e-mail should be coded
 a. 0830SHADP.
 b. P0830DOUS.
 c. P0215DOUS.
 d. P0830SHAD.

17. The code A1105FARB could represent an e-mail sent by
 a. Andrew Farber.
 b. Farley Benson.
 c. Frank Arbuckle.
 d. Betty Farmer.

18. The code P0311JANA represents an e-mail that arrived
 a. at 3:11 P.M.
 b. on the afternoon of November 3.
 c. on the afternoon of March 11.
 d. on the afternoon of January 11.

19. Which of the following people might have sent the e-mail coded P1010ANDR?
 a. Rachel Anderson
 b. Parker Andrews
 c. Andrea Rivera
 d. Annette Dreiser

20. An e-mail arrives at 2:48 P.M. on November 3 from Lorraine Drew. An employee codes the e-mail P113DREL. What error does the code contain?
 a. The date is incorrectly coded.
 b. The sender's last name is incorrectly coded.
 c. The time of day at which the e-mail arrived is incorrectly coded.
 d. The employee recorded the time of arrival where the date of arrival should be recorded.

► Answers

1. a. The customer's complaints may or may not be accurate; the only way to find out is to note and investigate them. You shouldn't figure that the customer is having a bad day, choice **b**, and you certainly shouldn't dismiss complaints without first determining whether they are accurate. You also shouldn't assume the complaints are accurate (choice **c**), because they may not be. Sending the complainant to another building (choice **d**), will probably make him angry, which is a big no-no.

2. d. Use process of elimination to get rid of incorrect answers. Giving a customer incorrect information (choice **a**) may get rid of him or her in the short term, but it almost guarantees that he or she will return, and when this person does, he or she will be angry because his or her time has been wasted. Instructing a customer to return to the line because you do not know the answer to his or her question (choice **b**) is unfair to the customer; this person is your responsibility, so you must find the answer for him or her. Three weeks is a long time to wait for resolution to a problem, choice **c**, and while such a wait may be appropriate in resolving complex problems, it is not universally appropriate. Choices **a**, **b**, and **c** are all poor answers; the correct answer must be choice **d**. Indeed, the proper course of action is to find the answer to the customer's question, even if that requires you to get assistance from a coworker.

3. b. The best course of action is to assure the customer that the government has strict policies in place to safeguard her privacy. Suggesting that it is unlikely that her personal information will be compromised (choice **a**) indicates that it *might* be compromised and so is unlikely to satisfy the customer; in addition, it presumably contradicts government policies that ensure privacy. Citizens should be able to seek government services with confidence and should not be discouraged from seeking those services; thus, choice **c** is incorrect. An incomplete submission to a government agency will not be processed; therefore, choice **d** is poor advice.

4. d. Letters should be written in accordance with agency policy. They should be written in plain language, but that is not the same as writing a letter in an informal tone (choice **a**); letters should still assume a tone appropriate for business. The plain language policy mandates that letters include as few technical terms and acronyms as possible; therefore, choice **b** is incorrect. A letter may suggest that the customer use other channels for future queries but should not tell him or her to do so (choice **c**); if this person wishes to continue to correspond via postal mail, he or she should not be discouraged from doing so.

5. c. Three people are seen crossing the street in the photo.

6. a. The woman in the center of the photo closest to the viewer is wearing headphones that appear to be connected to a personal music device.

7. d. On the left-hand side of the photo, two people are in the corner of the photo, one partially hidden by a wall and the other crouched in front of the wall. One vehicle can be seen in the background moving in the direction opposite the train.

8. c. Three people are seen crossing the tracks, and two people are visible in the left-hand portion of the photo.

9. b. According to the flow chart, if the answer to the question "Pertains to open investigation?" is "Yes," then the document is to be filed in the short-term file.

10. c. Arrows point to the permanent file for documents that the government is "required by law to save" and documents that "relate to agency rulings."

11. c. The flow chart states that the agency should "review contents [of the short-term file] every 30 days."

12. a. According to the flow chart, e-mails are stored on a computer hard drive and backed up on a CD-ROM.

13. d. The first letter of a correct code must be A or P; this information allows you to eliminate choice **a**. The code for the date must be four digits long; this information allows you to eliminate choice **c**. The code for the name of the sender must start with the first three letters of the sender's last name (in this case, DUB); this information allows you to eliminate choice **b**. The correct answer must be choice **d** by process of elimination.

14. a. The four digits following A or P in the code represent the date on which the e-mail was sent (in this case, 1214), not the time at which it was sent (1157). Use this information to eliminate choices **b** and **d**. The code for the name of the sender must start with the first three letters of the sender's last name (in this case, AND); this information allows you to eliminate choice **c**. The correct answer must be choice **a** by process of elimination.

15. c. The first letter of a correct code must be A or P; this information allows you to eliminate choices **a** and **b**. The four digits following A or P in the code represent the date on which the e-mail was sent (in this case, 0601), not the time

at which it was sent (0938). Use this information to eliminate choice **d**. The correct answer must be choice **c** by process of elimination.

16. b. The first letter of a correct code must be A or P; this information allows you to eliminate choice **a**. The four digits following A or P in the code represent the date on which the e-mail was sent (in this case, 0830), not the time at which it was sent (0215). Use this information to eliminate choice **c**. The code for the name of the sender must start with the first three letters of the sender's last name (in this case, DOU); this information allows you to eliminate choice **d**. The correct answer must be choice **b** by process of elimination.

17. d. Look at the final four letters of the code. The first three (FAR) represent the first three letters of the sender's last name. This information allows you to eliminate choices **b** and **c**. The fourth letter (B) is the sender's first initial; use this information to eliminate choice **a**. The correct answer must be choice **d** by process of elimination.

18. c. The four numbers following A or P represent the date on which the e-mail was received. Thus, this e-mail was received on March 11 (03 = March, so 0311 = March 11).

19. a. Look at the final four letters of the code. The first three (AND) represent the first three letters of the sender's last name. This information allows you to eliminate choices **c** and **d**. The fourth letter (R) is the sender's first initial; use this information to eliminate choice **b**. The correct answer must be choice **a** by process of elimination.

20. a. The date must be recorded with a four-digit code; thus, it should be recorded 1103, not 113.

Practice Exercises

Civil Service
Practice Exam 1

This is the first of three practice exams designed to prepare you for your civil service exam. As you read in Chapter 3, many state and local government jobs have a written exam as part of the selection process. The type of test varies greatly from job to job and from location to location, but most exams include at least some basic reading, writing, and sometimes math skills. The practice exams in this book also test spelling, vocabulary, grammar, civil service skills, memory, and coding.

The test that follows was created not to be identical to one particular civil service exam, but to allow you to practice the kinds of questions you may encounter on your exam. You can hone your skills in commonly tested areas by taking the practice exams and thoroughly reviewing the answers and explanations provided at the end of the chapter.

► Civil Service Practice Exam 1

1.	ⓐ	ⓑ	ⓒ	ⓓ	36.	ⓐ	ⓑ	ⓒ	ⓓ	71.	ⓐ	ⓑ	ⓒ	
2.	ⓐ	ⓑ	ⓒ	ⓓ	37.	ⓐ	ⓑ	ⓒ	ⓓ	72.	ⓐ	ⓑ	ⓒ	
3.	ⓐ	ⓑ	ⓒ	ⓓ	38.	ⓐ	ⓑ	ⓒ	ⓓ	73.	ⓐ	ⓑ	ⓒ	
4.	ⓐ	ⓑ	ⓒ	ⓓ	39.	ⓐ	ⓑ	ⓒ	ⓓ	74.	ⓐ	ⓑ	ⓒ	
5.	ⓐ	ⓑ	ⓒ	ⓓ	40.	ⓐ	ⓑ	ⓒ	ⓓ	75.	ⓐ	ⓑ	ⓒ	
6.	ⓐ	ⓑ	ⓒ	ⓓ	41.	ⓐ	ⓑ	ⓒ	ⓓ	76.	ⓐ	ⓑ	ⓒ	
7.	ⓐ	ⓑ	ⓒ	ⓓ	42.	ⓐ	ⓑ	ⓒ	ⓓ	77.	ⓐ	ⓑ	ⓒ	
8.	ⓐ	ⓑ	ⓒ	ⓓ	43.	ⓐ	ⓑ	ⓒ	ⓓ	78.	ⓐ	ⓑ	ⓒ	
9.	ⓐ	ⓑ	ⓒ	ⓓ	44.	ⓐ	ⓑ	ⓒ	ⓓ	79.	ⓐ	ⓑ	ⓒ	
10.	ⓐ	ⓑ	ⓞ	ⓓ	45.	ⓐ	ⓑ	ⓒ	ⓓ	80.	ⓐ	ⓑ	ⓒ	
11.	ⓐ	ⓑ	ⓒ	ⓓ	46.	ⓐ	ⓑ	ⓒ	ⓓ	81.	ⓐ	ⓑ	ⓒ	ⓓ
12.	ⓐ	ⓑ	ⓒ	ⓓ	47.	ⓐ	ⓑ	ⓒ	ⓓ	82.	ⓐ	ⓑ	ⓒ	ⓓ
13.	ⓐ	ⓑ	ⓒ	ⓓ	48.	ⓐ	ⓑ	ⓒ	ⓓ	83.	ⓐ	ⓑ	ⓒ	ⓓ
14.	ⓐ	ⓑ	ⓒ	ⓓ	49.	ⓐ	ⓑ	ⓒ	ⓓ	84.	ⓐ	ⓑ	ⓒ	ⓓ
15.	ⓐ	ⓑ	ⓒ	ⓓ	50.	ⓐ	ⓑ	ⓒ	ⓓ	85.	ⓐ	ⓑ	ⓒ	ⓓ
16.	ⓐ	ⓑ	ⓒ	ⓓ	51.	ⓐ	ⓑ	ⓒ	ⓓ	86.	ⓐ	ⓑ	ⓒ	ⓓ
17.	ⓐ	ⓑ	ⓒ	ⓓ	52.	ⓐ	ⓑ	ⓒ	ⓓ	87.	ⓐ	ⓑ	ⓒ	ⓓ
18.	ⓐ	ⓑ	ⓒ	ⓓ	53.	ⓐ	ⓑ	ⓒ	ⓓ	88.	ⓐ	ⓑ	ⓒ	ⓓ
19.	ⓐ	ⓑ	ⓒ	ⓓ	54.	ⓐ	ⓑ	ⓒ	ⓓ	89.	ⓐ	ⓑ	ⓒ	ⓓ
20.	ⓐ	ⓑ	ⓒ	ⓓ	55.	ⓐ	ⓑ	ⓒ	ⓓ	90.	ⓐ	ⓑ	ⓒ	ⓓ
21.	ⓐ	ⓑ	ⓒ	ⓓ	56.	ⓐ	ⓑ	ⓒ	ⓓ	91.	ⓐ	ⓑ	ⓒ	ⓓ
22.	ⓐ	ⓑ	ⓒ	ⓓ	57.	ⓐ	ⓑ	ⓒ	ⓓ	92.	ⓐ	ⓑ	ⓒ	ⓓ
23.	ⓐ	ⓑ	ⓒ	ⓓ	58.	ⓐ	ⓑ	ⓒ	ⓓ	93.	ⓐ	ⓑ	ⓒ	ⓓ
24.	ⓐ	ⓑ	ⓒ	ⓓ	59.	ⓐ	ⓑ	ⓒ	ⓓ	94.	ⓐ	ⓑ	ⓒ	ⓓ
25.	ⓐ	ⓑ	ⓒ	ⓓ	60.	ⓐ	ⓑ	ⓒ	ⓓ	95.	ⓐ	ⓑ	ⓒ	ⓓ
26.	ⓐ	ⓑ	ⓒ	ⓓ	61.	ⓐ	ⓑ	ⓒ		96.	ⓐ	ⓑ	ⓒ	ⓓ
27.	ⓐ	ⓑ	ⓒ	ⓓ	62.	ⓐ	ⓑ	ⓒ		97.	ⓐ	ⓑ	ⓒ	ⓓ
28.	ⓐ	ⓑ	ⓒ	ⓓ	63.	ⓐ	ⓑ	ⓒ		98.	ⓐ	ⓑ	ⓒ	ⓓ
29.	ⓐ	ⓑ	ⓒ	ⓓ	64.	ⓐ	ⓑ	ⓒ		99.	ⓐ	ⓑ	ⓒ	ⓓ
30.	ⓐ	ⓑ	ⓒ	ⓓ	65.	ⓐ	ⓑ	ⓒ		100.	ⓐ	ⓑ	ⓒ	ⓓ
31.	ⓐ	ⓑ	ⓒ	ⓓ	66.	ⓐ	ⓑ	ⓒ						
32.	ⓐ	ⓑ	ⓒ	ⓓ	67.	ⓐ	ⓑ	ⓒ						
33.	ⓐ	ⓑ	ⓒ	ⓓ	68.	ⓐ	ⓑ	ⓒ						
34.	ⓐ	ⓑ	ⓒ	ⓓ	69.	ⓐ	ⓑ	ⓒ						
35.	ⓐ	ⓑ	ⓒ	ⓓ	70.	ⓐ	ⓑ	ⓒ						

► Section 1: Mathematics

Select the best choice for each question.

1. Reduce $\frac{25}{35}$ to lowest terms.
- **a.** $\frac{3}{5}$
- **b.** $\frac{1}{10}$
- **c.** $\frac{5}{7}$
- **d.** $\frac{5}{9}$

2. A stock begins the day at the price $28\frac{3}{8}$ and ends the day at the price $26\frac{3}{4}$. Which choice best describes the change in the stock's price?
- **a.** The stock lost exactly $1 in value.
- **b.** The stock lost exactly $1\frac{1}{4}$ in value.
- **c.** The stock lost exactly $1\frac{5}{8}$ in value.
- **d.** The stock gained $1\frac{1}{2}$ in value.

3. Find the percent equivalent of $\frac{18}{25}$.
- **a.** 18%
- **b.** 43%
- **c.** 7%
- **d.** 72%

4. Jeanette went shopping with $100 and returned home with only $18.42. How much money did she spend?
- **a.** $81.58
- **b.** $72.68
- **c.** $72.58
- **d.** $71.68

5. $\frac{3}{5} - \frac{1}{3} =$
- **a.** $\frac{1}{2}$
- **b.** 1
- **c.** $\frac{4}{15}$
- **d.** $\frac{1}{4}$

6. $\frac{1}{2} + 4\frac{3}{4} + 2\frac{5}{6} =$
- **a.** $7\frac{3}{4}$
- **b.** $8\frac{1}{12}$
- **c.** $1\frac{1}{4}$
- **d.** $6\frac{3}{4}$

7. Harold wishes to leave a 15% tip for a restaurant meal. If the meal cost $16.80, how much money should Harold leave for the tip?
- **a.** $2.52
- **b.** $2.40
- **c.** $1.68
- **d.** $1.50

8. $8\frac{1}{5} =$
- **a.** $\frac{81}{5}$
- **b.** $\frac{5}{81}$
- **c.** $\frac{13}{5}$
- **d.** $\frac{41}{5}$

9. $7\frac{1}{10} - 5\frac{2}{3} =$
- **a.** $2\frac{1}{3}$
- **b.** $1\frac{13}{30}$
- **c.** $1\frac{2}{13}$
- **d.** $2\frac{2}{7}$

10. A farmer plants 75 rows of cabbage. Each row contains 40 cabbages. How many cabbages does the farmer plant?
- **a.** 115
- **b.** 1,150
- **c.** 1,500
- **d.** 3,000

Study the following graph, and then use it to answer questions 11 to 13.

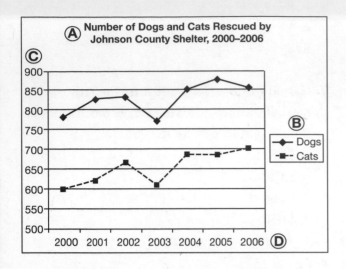

(A) Number of Dogs and Cats Rescued by Johnson County Shelter, 2000–2006

(C)

900
850
800
750
700 ◆ Dogs
650 ■ Cats
600
550
500

2000 2001 2002 2003 2004 2005 2006 (D)

(B)

11. Which letter corresponds to the legend of the graph?

a. A
b. B
c. C
d. D

12. Which letter corresponds to the *y*-axis of the graph?

a. A
b. B
c. C
d. D

13. Which letter corresponds to the title of the graph?

a. A
b. B
c. C
d. D

14. $\frac{4}{5} \times \frac{1}{8} =$

a. $\frac{1}{10}$
b. $\frac{1}{40}$
c. $\frac{4}{13}$
d. $\frac{5}{13}$

15. Mr. Stone commutes 15 miles from home to work. After driving $\frac{2}{5}$ of the way from home to work, Mr. Stone stops to buy some breakfast. How far is Mr. Stone from work when he stops for breakfast?

a. $14\frac{3}{5}$ miles
b. 6 miles
c. 4 miles
d. 9 miles

16. $14 \div \frac{3}{4} =$

a. $18\frac{2}{3}$
b. $10\frac{1}{2}$
c. $13\frac{1}{4}$
d. $20\frac{1}{4}$

17. Find the decimal equivalent of $\frac{5}{8}$.

a. 0.625
b. 0.58
c. 0.666
d. 0.13

18. Three teaspoons of water equal 1 tablespoon of water; 2 tablespoons of water equal 1 ounce of water. How many teaspoons of water are there in a pint of water (1 pint = 16 ounces)?

a. 23 teaspoons
b. 32 teaspoons
c. 96 teaspoons
d. 192 teaspoons

Study the following table, and then use it to answer questions 19 and 20.

AVERAGE LIFE SPAN AND WEIGHT OF DOGS, BY BREED		
BREED	AVERAGE LIFE SPAN IN YEARS	AVERAGE WEIGHT IN POUNDS
Jack Russell Terrier	13.6	15
Chihuahua	13	5
Corgi	11.2	25
Weimaraner	10	75
Rhodesian Ridgeback	9.1	80
Great Dane	8.4	160

19. The range of weights shown in the table is
   a. 160 pounds.
   b. 145 pounds.
   c. 80 pounds.
   d. 155 pounds.

20. Which of the following conclusions is best supported by the data in the table?
   a. Small dogs tend to live longer than large dogs.
   b. No dog has ever lived past the age of 15.
   c. A Chihuahua is an excellent house pet.
   d. A Great Dane weighs more than most humans.

21. During a sale, the price of a suit is reduced by 30%. If the suit sold for $350 before the sale, what is the sale price of the suit?
   a. $105
   b. $175
   c. $245
   d. $320

22. A train travels at an average rate of 90 miles per hour. How long does it take the train to travel 570 miles?
   a. 6 hours
   b. 6 hours 20 minutes
   c. 6 hours 30 minutes
   d. 7 hours

23. $\frac{12}{9} =$
   a. $1\frac{1}{3}$
   b. $\frac{3}{4}$
   c. $12\frac{1}{3}$
   d. $1\frac{1}{9}$

24. Reduce $\frac{12}{51}$ to lowest terms.
   a. $\frac{4}{5}$
   b. $\frac{14}{17}$
   c. $\frac{21}{25}$
   d. $\frac{1}{9}$

25. Jack ran for president of a community organization and received 30% of the votes cast. If Jack received 24 votes, what was the total number of votes cast for all candidates in the election?
   a. 54
   b. 70
   c. 74
   d. 80

Study the following graph, and then use it to answer questions 26 to 27.

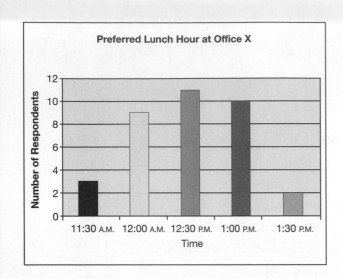

Preferred Lunch Hour at Office X

26. The workers at Office X were asked to choose their preferred time to start their lunch hour. The results of the survey are shown in the graph above. How many workers responded to the survey?

  a. 11

  b. 21

  c. 35

  d. 50

27. What is the range of the data shown?

  a. 9

  b. 10

  c. 11

  d. 35

28. $\frac{11}{15} \div \frac{3}{5} =$

  a. $\frac{4}{5}$

  b. $1\frac{2}{9}$

  c. $1\frac{1}{3}$

  d. $\frac{7}{10}$

29. Linda walks 15 miles in 4 hours. What is Linda's average speed during her walk?

  a. 3 miles per hour

  b. 3.5 miles per hour

  c. 3.75 miles per hour

  d. 4 miles per hour

30. Three of every 25 customers at a grocery store pays for his or her groceries with a check. What percentage of the customers pay for groceries with a check?

  a. 3%

  b. 12%

  c. 28%

  d. 75%

31. An automobile tank has a capacity of $14\frac{1}{2}$ gallons. Which of the following equals $14\frac{1}{2}$ gallons?

  a. $\frac{14}{3}$

  b. $\frac{1}{28}$

  c. $\frac{15}{2}$

  d. $\frac{29}{2}$

Study the following graph, and then use it to answer questions 32 to 33.

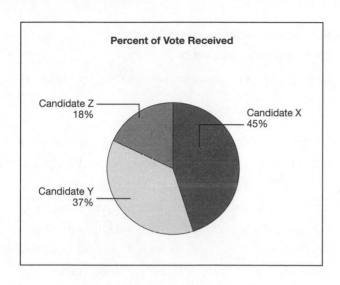

Percent of Vote Received

Candidate Z
18%

Candidate X
45%

Candidate Y
37%

32. The pie graph supports which of the following conclusions?

    a. More than 50% of eligible voters participated in the election.

    b. Two candidates each received more than 40% of the vote.

    c. Candidate X received the greatest number of votes.

    d. Voters would have preferred to vote for Candidate W, but she was not running.

33. If 600 voters voted in the election, how many votes did Candidate Z receive?

    a. 60

    b. 108

    c. 222

    d. 260

34. $5\frac{2}{5} + 7\frac{1}{3} =$

    a. $35\frac{2}{15}$

    b. $12\frac{3}{8}$

    c. $12\frac{11}{15}$

    d. $4\frac{1}{3}$

35. Of 300 consumers polled, 180 reported that they purchase household cleaning products at least once per week. Based on these results, approximately how many consumers out of 1,000 could be expected to buy household cleaning products at least once per week?

    a. 480

    b. 600

    c. 720

    d. 880

36. $\frac{7}{10} \times 2\frac{1}{5} =$

    a. $\frac{49}{50}$

    b. $1\frac{3}{5}$

    c. $\frac{7}{50}$

    d. $1\frac{11}{25}$

37. In 2005, a certain government agency employed 1,250 people. In 2006, the number of employees at the agency increased by 10%. How many people were employed by the agency in 2006?

    a. 1,250

    b. 1,320

    c. 1,350

    d. 1,375

38. An airplane flight takes exactly 4 hours to complete. If the airplane travels at an average speed of 480 miles per hour, how many miles long is the flight?
  a. 1,920 miles
  b. 2,000 miles
  c. 2,080 miles
  d. 2,400 miles

Study the following table, and then use it to answer questions 39 to 40.

PRICE OF LEADING DVD PLAYERS	
Ultrabox 4000	$89
Vizzione MR-1	$74.50
Clara 718	$95
Abomino 1	$61.50

39. What is the average (arithmetic mean) price of the leading DVD players?
  a. $61.50
  b. $76.00
  c. $80.00
  d. $95.00

40. What is the range of prices shown in the table?
  a. $28.50
  b. $27.50
  c. $32.50
  d. $33.50

▶ Section 2: Written Communication

Reading Comprehension— Questions 41–60

Read the following passage. Then, answer questions 41 to 44.

We generally think of libraries as publicly managed facilities offering books on a wide range of subjects, but, in fact, public libraries are only one highly visible facet of the library universe. Many offices—including many government offices—maintain large collections of reference materials, historical documents, and other relevant resources. In other words, such offices maintain libraries.

Any sizeable library collection must be organized in order to be useful. Librarians may organize a collection in any way they choose, but they generally choose between two options: the Dewey decimal classification system, which assigns a number between 000 and 999 to books based on their subject matter; and the Library of Congress classification system, which assigns an initial letter to books based on subject matter.

What are the differences between the two systems? The Dewey decimal system contains fewer subject classifications, with only ten general subject categories as opposed to the Library of Congress's 21. The latter system not only uses more general subject categories, but also subdivides each category into more, and more specific, subcategories. In the area of specificity, it is generally agreed that the Library of Congress system is more efficient.

When it comes to ease of use, however, the Dewey decimal system is typically the favorite. Users searching for books about dogs, for example, almost always find it easier to remember the Dewey code for such books (636) than the Library of Congress code (SF427). Furthermore, there is an internal logic to the entire Dewey system; the principles of code assignment are consistent throughout all ten subjects. Each Library of Congress subject category, on the other hand, was developed independently of the others, so each follows its own unique set of rules.

The differences between the two systems means that they are suited to <u>diverse</u> purposes. Ease of use makes the Dewey decimal system the system of choice for general public-use libraries. Research institutions, archives, and government agencies cataloging a great deal of highly specific or technical material, on the other hand, tend to prefer the Library of Congress system.

41. Which sentence best summarizes the main idea of the passage?
   a. The Library of Congress classification system is better than the Dewey decimal classification system.
   b. The differences between two cataloging systems makes each more appropriate for a particular purpose.
   c. More libraries should consider cataloging their collections alphabetically by the authors' last names, without regard to subject matter.
   d. There is an urgent need for librarians to develop a new classification system, because the two most common systems are deeply flawed.

42. In the passage, the word *diverse* is closest in meaning to
   a. unlike.
   b. unimportant.
   c. scientific.
   d. illogical.

43. The passage supports which of the following conclusions?
   a. Libraries that use the Dewey system typically contain more books about dogs than do libraries that use the Library of Congress system.
   b. Libraries must pay a licensing fee to use either the Dewey or the Library of Congress system, so they typically choose whichever system is cheaper.
   c. The Library of Congress system is more difficult to memorize than is the Dewey system.
   d. Books with certain subjects cannot be classified within the Dewey system because the system makes no place for them.

44. According to the passage, in comparison to the Dewey decimal system, the Library of Congress system is
   a. appropriate only to collections owned by the U.S. Congress.
   b. more likely to be used by public libraries.
   c. easier for casual library users to master.
   d. more specific in its categorization of books.

Read the following passage. Then, answer questions 45 to 48.

America's correctional facilities are in need of major reform, according to a June 2006 report by the Commission on Safety and Abuse in America's Prisons, a 20-member panel consisting of corrections professionals, government and private lawyers, judges, healthcare professionals, and community leaders. According to the group's report, titled "Confronting Confinement," the current penal system fails to provide adequately for the safety of inmates and corrections officers, provides only subpar healthcare and living conditions, and suffers from a lack of adequate oversight. The commission's report, a year in the making, was based on numerous visits to prisons, interviews with corrections officers, public hearings, and other research.

    Commissioners concluded that, among the penal system's many problems, medical care and prison violence are the most pressing. The report notes that prison medical facilities are dangerously understaffed; compounding the problem is the fact that penal systems have a difficult time attracting good healthcare professionals and are often forced to employ underqualified or subpar doctors. Making matters still worse is the common practice of requiring co-payments from prisoners, a practice that discourages prisoners from seeking medical help and thus further contributes to the spread of disease. Mental illness constitutes another major healthcare issue; the commission cited studies concluding that approximately 350,000 of the nation's inmates—nearly 20%—suffer from some serious mental illness, yet less than 2% receive 24-hour mental healthcare. Widespread mental illness among the general prison population no doubt contributes to the problems of prisoner-on-prisoner and prisoner-on-officer violence. A 2000 study recorded more than 50,000 such incidents.

The report offers a number of recommendations to improve federal, state, and local penal facilities, finding deficiencies in each system. Among its recommendations: eliminate co-payment policies and expand Medicare and Medicaid coverage to help more prisoners; screen incoming inmates more extensively for mental illness, and practice remediation and medication for those who need it; and, to combat violence, increase prisoner activity and productivity, address crowding issues, improve surveillance through new technology, and institute programs to encourage stronger connections between prisoners and their families. These programs will be difficult to implement, but they hold high promise of effectively addressing the penal system's most dramatic problems.

45. The word *constitutes* is closest in meaning to
    a. contradicts.
    b. reduces.
    c. implies.
    d. represents.

46. Which statement from the passage best summarizes the author's main idea?
    a. To combat violence, increase prisoner activity and productivity.
    b. Making matters still worse is the common practice of requiring co-payments from prisoners.
    c. America's correctional facilities are in need of major reform.
    d. Widespread mental illness among the general prison population no doubt contributes to the problems of prisoner-on-prisoner and prisoner-on-officer violence.

47. It can be inferred from the passage that the author
   a. is a professional working in the field of corrections.
   b. believes it is possible to reduce prison violence.
   c. does not agree with the conclusions of the Commission on Safety and Abuse in America's Prisons.
   d. believes the current penal system is basically sound.

48. According to the passage, the commission did all of the following while preparing its report EXCEPT
   a. test prisoners for mental health issues.
   b. visit prisons.
   c. interview relevant professionals.
   d. hold public hearings.

Read the following passage. Then, answer questions 49 to 52.

The state Department of Parks and Wildlife is seeking a recreational facility officer (Grade B) for permanent, full-time employment at its Williams Lake State Park location. A recreational facility officer (Grade B) enforces <u>pertinent</u> laws within the state park by ensuring that hunters and fishers have appropriate licenses and permits, by patrolling for violations, and when necessary, administering violations, making arrests, preparing cases, and testifying. In addition, the position requires public outreach work. A recreational facility officer (Grade B) gives educational speeches and presentations to the public, interacts with the media, and engages in fund-raising for the park. Management skills are also required, as the officer must coordinate staff projects including trail maintenance; prepare and submit budgets; and manage park safety, construction, and development.

Candidates must be certified as a B-level law enforcement officer by the state; this level of certification requires training in the use of firearms. Consequently, convicted felons are not eligible for this position, as under the laws of the state convicted felons are disallowed from using firearms. Candidates must also be U.S. citizens with a high school diploma. Employment to this position requires the applicant to submit to a drug screening test. If employed, the employee must consent to random drug screening tests throughout the term of employment. Applicant must also hold a valid state driver's license in good standing.

The recreational facility officer (Grade B) position offers an annual salary in the $38,000 to $44,000 range. Benefits include health insurance; life insurance; dental insurance; time-and-a-half pay on holidays; generous sick and vacation leave; and tuition reimbursement at any state college or university.

Applicants should complete a Department of Parks and Wildlife job application form, available at the state government website or from any Department of Parks and Wildlife office, including the ranger station at any state park. All applications must include a resume; three letters of recommendation from teachers, employers, or clergy; academic transcripts for all degree-bearing academic work completed; and a photocopy of the applicant's driver's license.

49. Convicted felons are not eligible for the position of recreational facility officer (Grade B) because
   a. the position requires someone who can legally use a firearm.
   b. convicted felons are disqualified from all government jobs.
   c. the job requires management skills that a convicted felon is unlikely to have.
   d. convicted felons are incapable of passing the mandatory drug screening test.

50. The main purpose of the passage is to
  a. interest students in a career in park management.
  b. advertise the availability of a civil service position.
  c. notify citizens that an important job has recently been filled.
  d. describe the procedure by which people can apply for civil service jobs.

51. It can be inferred from the passage that
  a. an applicant with a suspended driver's license would not be eligible for the position of recreational facility officer (Grade B).
  b. the state requires every recreational facility officer (Grade B) to continue his or her education while employed by the state.
  c. any citizen who is not a convicted felon is eligible for the position of recreational facility officer (Grade B).
  d. recreational facility officer (Grade B) is a good job for someone who does not like to interact with other people.

52. As used in the passage, the word *pertinent* is closest in meaning to
  a. potential.
  b. divisive.
  c. obscure.
  d. relevant.

Read the following passage. Then, answer questions 53 to 56.

The political activity of federal employees presents policy makers with a double-edged sword of a problem. On one hand, the integrity of the federal government requires that employees not pursue personal political goals through their offices; therefore, some restrictions on the political activities of federal employees seem <u>prudent</u> and even necessary. On the other hand, individual liberty and the right to participate in the political process are two bedrock principles of American government. Surely we cannot deny our government's employees rights so fundamental to the nation's identity.

Government leaders have been visiting and revisiting this question since the beginning of the republic. Thomas Jefferson issued an executive circular in 1801 advising federal employees to abstain from campaigning and electioneering. The Pendleton Act of 1883, which created a merit-based system for awarding civil service jobs, further codified proscribed political behavior.

These measures were deemed inadequate to check political coercion and patronage in the 1930s, when the massive expansion of the federal government created many new opportunities for the abuse of power. In response, Congress passed the Hatch Act of 1939, which prohibited a wide range of political activities by federal employees. The law made it illegal for federal civil servants to endorse candidates, seek political contributions, or run for office with the endorsement of a political party. Not all political activity was forbidden; Hatch allowed federal employees to vote, discuss politics privately, and contribute money to political parties.

The constitutionality of the Hatch Act has been challenged several times, with two such cases reaching the Supreme Court; in both instances, the court ruled that the Hatch Act was indeed constitutional. Nonetheless, discontent ultimately led to a 1993 amendment that allowed federal employees to participate in elections so long as their activity occurred outside their place of work. At the same time, the amendment increased penalties for those who abused the powers of their offices for political gain. At the signing ceremony, President Bill Clinton observed that "People who devote their lives to public service should not be denied the right to participate more fully in the democratic process. This law moves us in a more sensible direction."

53. As used in the passage, the word *prudent* is closest in meaning to
  a. optional.
  b. ill-advised.
  c. sensible.
  d. counterproductive.

54. The author's main purpose in writing this passage is to
  a. report the historical developments of a particular issue in American government.
  b. argue that the 1993 amendment to the Hatch Act had a destructive impact on good governance in the United States.
  c. describe the conditions under which the Hatch Act of 1939 was passed.
  d. propose the repeal of both the Pendleton Act of 1883 and the Hatch Act of 1939.

55. According to the passage, Thomas Jefferson did which of the following?
  a. oversaw the massive expansion of the federal government
  b. suggested to federal employees that they refrain from public politics
  c. signed an amendment to the Hatch Act
  d. endorsed the Pendleton Act

56. The passage supports which of the following conclusions?
  a. Under the Hatch Act, federal employees were prohibited from engaging in all political activity, including voting.
  b. Thomas Jefferson believed that there was no conflict in holding a federal office and engaging in such political activity as campaigning for candidates.
  c. The amendment to the Hatch Act aimed to preserve integrity in government while freeing federal employees to become more politically active as private citizens.
  d. Under the Hatch Act, federal employees could actively promote political parties but not individual candidates.

Read the following passage. Then, answer questions 57 to 60.

Community policing has frequently been touted as the best way to reform urban law enforcement. The idea of putting more officers on foot patrol in high crime areas, where relations with the police have frequently been strained, was most famously implemented in Houston in 1983 under then-Commissioner Lee Brown. Brown believed that officers should be accessible to the community at the street level. If officers were assigned to the same area over a period of time, those officers would eventually build a network of trust with neighborhood residents. As a result, merchants and residents in the community would be more likely to inform officers about criminal activities in the area and support police intervention.

Since Brown's <u>initiative</u>, many large cities have experimented with community-oriented policing services (COPS), with somewhat mixed results. Some have found that police and citizens are grateful for the opportunity to work together. Others have found that unrealistic expectations by citizens and resistance from officers have combined to hinder the effectiveness of COPS.

Overall, however, the verdict on community policing is positive, as the concept has evidently yielded notable successes. Since the federal government began funding COPS programs, national crime rates have declined measurably. Although this drop in crime rates has occurred nationwide (including areas that receive no federal assistance), the drops have been more pronounced in those locations that receive substantial COPS funding.

Unfortunately, stress on the federal budget in the post–9/11 era has resulted in a sharp decrease in federal assistance to local police. This decrease comes at a time when the federal government is expecting local law enforcement to contribute more to the national fight against terror, further increasing the strain on state and city government law enforcement budgets. As a result, many have had to reduce or even eliminate their COPS programs. The debate over the effectiveness of COPS programs might once and for all be settled as a result; if crime rates increase as COPS programs disappear, that would certainly provide a strong indicator that the programs are effective in reducing crime.

57. Which of the following best summarizes the main idea of the passage?
  a. Opponents of community policing correctly argue that such programs cause more problems than they solve.
  b. Community policing is a promising concept, but implementation of effective community policing programs faces several problems.
  c. Many local police forces lack the funding necessary to support community policing programs.
  d. Lee Brown is an innovative law enforcement leader whose talents should be utilized by the federal government.

58. As used in the passage, the word *initiative* most nearly means
  a. misfortune.
  b. blunder.
  c. victory.
  d. decision.

59. In paragraph 3, the author suggests that
  a. community policing programs have helped to reduce crime rates.
  b. community policing programs have had no effect on crime rates.
  c. community policing programs have resulted in an increase in crime rates.
  d. the government does not accurately track crime rates, making it impossible to determine the effectiveness of community policing programs.

60. According to Commissioner Brown, community policing is effective because
  a. criminals are less likely to commit crimes if they are familiar with their local police officers.
  b. community policing emphasizes the need for street patrols late at night, the time at which most crimes occur.
  c. community policing deputizes members of the community, allowing them to make arrests without an actual police officer present.
  d. citizens are more likely to cooperate with police if they have a closer relationship with local officers.

Spelling—Questions 61 to 65

Select the choice that is spelled correctly.

61. The _____ crew arrived with a wrecking ball and bulldozer.
   a. demolition
   b. demolishion
   c. demolishun

62. Rebecca _____ knocked over the coffee pot, spilling hot coffee all over the floor.
   a. accidently
   b. accidentaly
   c. accidentally

63. Jim's outburst was not planned; on the contrary, it was entirely _____.
   a. spontaneous
   b. spontainious
   c. spontaineus

64. Which of the following words is spelled incorrectly?
   a. frivolous
   b. embelish
   c. confound

65. Which of the following words is spelled incorrectly?
   a. lunar
   b. scapegoat
   c. retalliate

Vocabulary—Questions 66 to 70

Select the best answer for each question.

66. Find the word that is closest in meaning to the underlined word below.
   a valid hypothesis
   a. accusation
   b. theory
   c. mistake

67. Find the word that is closest in meaning to the underlined word below.
   a tentative effort
   a. uncertain
   b. misguided
   c. hasty

68. Find the word that is most nearly the opposite of the word below.
   the virtuoso musician
   a. amateur
   b. experimental
   c. unpopular

69. Find the word that best completes the sentence below.
   The _____ window shades kept the hotel room nice and dark well into the late morning.
   a. malfunctioning
   b. flimsy
   c. opaque

70. Find the word that best completes the sentence below.

Minimum wage is poor _____ for a fry cook's hard work.

a. reprisal

b. retribution

c. remuneration

Grammar—Questions 71 to 80

Select the best answer for each question.

71. Which of the following is a complete sentence?

a. The onset of the cold war, having been brought on by natural tensions between the communist and free worlds and the end of World War II.

b. Natural tensions between the communist and free worlds, the end of World War II, bringing on the onset of the cold war.

c. The onset of the cold war was brought on by natural tensions between the communist and free worlds and the end of World War II.

72. Select the sentence that is written most correctly.

a. Genetically modified to increase yield and reduce disease, many consumers do not trust crops developed recently by agricultural scientists.

b. Genetically modified to increase yield and reduce disease, crops developed recently by agricultural scientists are distrusted by many consumers.

c. Crops developed recently by agricultural scientists have been genetically modified to increase yield and reduce disease that consumers do not trust.

73. Select the sentence that is written most correctly.

a. The California quail can be found in grasslands, wooded areas, or canyons; its habitat is diverse because it can live anywhere that brush abounds.

b. The California quail can be found in grasslands, wooded areas, or canyons; their habitat is diverse because they can live anywhere that brush abounds.

c. The California quail can be found in grasslands, wooded areas, or canyons; its habitat is diverse because they can live anywhere that brush abounds.

74. Select the sentence that is written most correctly.

a. They say you can't judge a book by looking at its cover.

b. They say you cant judge a book by looking at it's cover.

c. They say you can't judge a book by looking at it's cover.

75. Select the sentence that is written most correctly.

a. The perpetrator was stopped by the police officer, and he struck him with a stick.

b. The perpetrator, striking him with a stick, was stopped by the police officer.

c. The police officer stopped the perpetrator, who then struck the officer with a stick.

76. Select the sentence that is written most correctly.

a. Augustana College is an evangelical lutheran school located in Rock Island, illinois, along the banks of the Mississippi River.

b. Augustana college is an Evangelical Lutheran school located in Rock island, Illinois, along the banks of the Mississippi river.

c. Augustana College is an Evangelical Lutheran school located in Rock Island, Illinois, along the banks of the Mississippi River.

77. Select the sentence that is written most correctly.

  a. Make sure that everyone in the office have turned off their desk lights before leaving for the day.

  b. Make sure that everyone in the office has turned off his or her desk light before leaving for the day.

  c. Make sure that everyone in the office has turned off their desk lights before leaving for the day.

78. Select the sentence that is written most correctly.

  a. The benefits of this therapy far outweigh its potential drawbacks.

  b. The positive benefits of this therapy far outweigh its potentially negative drawbacks.

  c. The benefits of this therapy far outweigh their potentially negative drawbacks.

79. Select the sentence that is written most correctly.

  a. After completing the obstacle course Renee proceeded to the shooting range.

  b. After completing the obstacle course, Renee proceeded to the shooting range.

  c. After completing the obstacle course, Renee proceeded, to the shooting range.

80. Select the sentence that is written most correctly.

  a. David asked me "whether I wanted to attend the baseball game with him tonight?"

  b. David asked me "whether I wanted to attend the baseball game with him tonight."

  c. David asked me whether I wanted to attend the baseball game with him tonight.

▶ Section 3: Civil Service Skills

Customer Service— Questions 81 to 85

Select the best answer for each question.

81. Records of an office's prior contacts with a customer should be maintained in order to

  a. document the amount of work done by the office so that staffing will not be reduced.

  b. make sure that no one customer overuses the office's facilities and services.

  c. minimize the need for the customer to provide the same basic information (e.g., address, Social Security number) repeatedly.

  d. prevent customers from asking for and receiving services that have already been provided.

82. When one is creating a recorded message to be heard by customers calling a government agency after hours of operation, which of the following pieces of information is least important?

  a. the agency's hours of operation

  b. the street address of the agency

  c. instructions on how to access the agency's website

  d. instructions on how to leave a message

83. An agency's phone system offers the capacity for audio during a customer's hold time. The agency would be best served to use this capacity to provide
   a. music to entertain customers while they are waiting.
   b. live programming from a local talk-radio station.
   c. live audio, transmitted via speaker phone, of the office with which they are waiting to speak.
   d. a recorded message providing choices to commonly asked questions.

84. The term *abandonment rate* refers to the
   a. frequency with which customers calling an office hang up before reaching a representative.
   b. number of times a customer must contact an office before receiving final resolution to an inquiry.
   c. average amount of time a customer visiting an office must wait on a service line before speaking with a representative.
   d. speed at which a government agent can redirect a telephone inquiry to the appropriate recipient.

85. An agency serving walk-in customers should consider offering appointments whenever
   a. customers cannot begin resolving their inquiry upon arrival.
   b. average wait times for customers exceed one hour.
   c. average wait times for customers exceed 15 minutes.
   d. such a policy would result in fewer visitors to the agency's office.

Memory—Questions 86 to 90

Take five minutes to study the following picture. Then, answer questions 86 to 87 without looking back at the picture.

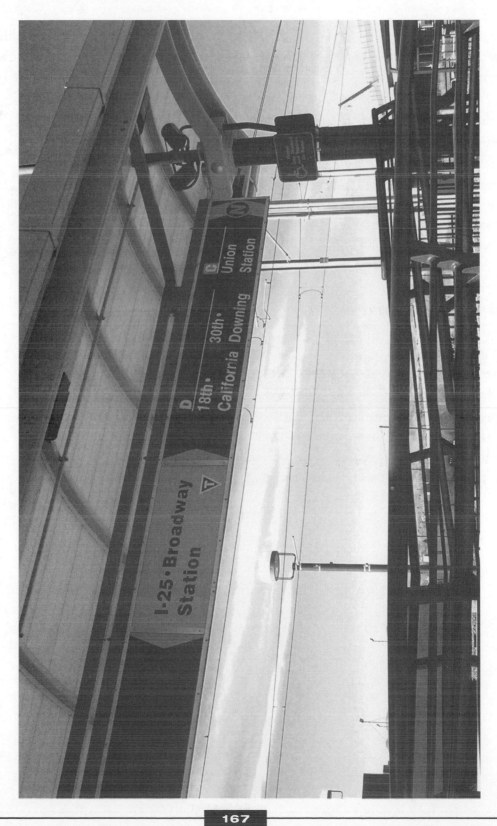

86. The number of destinations other than Broadway Station that are shown in the photo is
a. one.
b. two.
c. three.
d. zero; no other destinations are shown in the photo.

87. Based on the directional arrows on the signage at Broadway Station, a rail rider could correctly assume that the train will be heading _____ from Broadway Station to Union Station.
a. south
b. north
c. east
d. west

Take five minutes to study the following text. Then, answer questions 88 through 90 without looking back at the text.

A city is divided into five sectors. In each sector, garbage is collected twice a week and recycling is scheduled once a week, according to the schedule that follows.

SECTOR	GARBAGE	RECYCLING
1	Monday, Thursday	Friday
2	Tuesday, Saturday	Wednesday
3	Wednesday, Saturday	Thursday
4	Tuesday, Friday	Saturday
5	Monday, Friday	Tuesday

88. Recycling is collected in sector 2 on
   a. Monday.
   b. Tuesday.
   c. Wednesday.
   d. Saturday.

89. Garbage is collected Monday through Saturday. On which day is recycling NOT collected?
   a. Monday
   b. Wednesday
   c. Friday
   d. Saturday

90. In three of five sectors, the second garbage collection of the week occurs exactly three days after the first. In which two sectors is this NOT the case?
   a. 1 and 2
   b. 1 and 4
   c. 2 and 5
   d. 3 and 4

Coding—Questions 91 to 100

To answer questions 91 through 95, refer to the following scenario.

A municipal agency uses a code to log each visitor to its office. Each code is five characters long and is assigned according to the rules that follow. Each code is preceded by the time of the visit (format: 10:00 A.M.).

Gender
M = Male
F = Female

Citizenship
C = Citizen
N = Noncitizen

Age
1 – under age 18
2 – age 18 to 30
3 – age 31 to 65
4 – over age 65

Residence
V = northeast quadrant of city
W = southeast quadrant of city
X = northwest quadrant of city
Y = southwest quadrant of city
Z = outside the city

Purpose of Visit
5 = responding to summons
6 = filing complaint
7 = applying for employment
8 = other

91. A male citizen, age 38, who resides in the north-west quadrant of the city visits the office at 11:46 A.M. to file a complaint. How should this visit be coded?

a. MC3X6

b. MC38 11:46 A.M. X6

c. 11:46 A.M. MC3X6

d. MC 11:46 A.M. V6

92. A female citizen, age 67, who resides outside the city visits the office at 4:00 P.M. to solicit charitable contributions from employees. How should this visit be coded?

a. FC67Z 4:00 P.M.8

b. FC67X8 4:00 P.M.

c. 4:00 P.M. FC67Z8

d. 4:00 P.M. FC4Z8

93. A male noncitizen who resides in the southeast quadrant of the city visits the office at 10:45 A.M. to respond to a summons. He is 16 years old. How should the visit be coded?

a. 10:45 A.M. MN1W5

b. 10:45 A.M. MC1Z8

c. MNW 11:45 A.M. 168

d. MNW168 11:45 A.M.

94. Which of the following describes the visitor whose visit was coded 12:00 P.M. FC3Y6?

a. The visitor was a noncitizen residing in the southwest quadrant of the city.

b. The visitor was a female who filed a complaint.

c. The visitor was a male citizen over the age of 65.

d. The visitor was a female under the age of 18.

95. The visitor whose visit was coded 9:10 A.M. MC2Z7 visited the office in order to

a. respond to a summons.

b. file a complaint.

c. apply for employment.

d. none of the above

To answer questions 96 through 100, refer to the following scenario.

A state assigns numbers to the fishing licenses it issues using the following code:

2 letters = first two letters of county of residence

8 digits = license recipient's date of birth (e.g., September 30, 1957 = 09301957)

2 letters = license recipient's initials (e.g., Robert Sims = RS)

2 digits = license recipient's height in inches (rounded to nearest whole number)

3 letters = randomly assigned

96. Danielle Valenzuela receives a fishing license. She resides in Ardmore County and is 62 inches tall. Her date of birth is May 11, 1973. Which of the following could be her fishing license number?

a. AR05111973DV62

b. DV05111973AR62MPY

c. DV051173AR62

d. AR05111973DV62XLE

97. Milton Mazur, a resident of Hazelton County, receives a fishing license. His date of birth is December 7, 1948. He is 70.4 inches tall. Which of the following could be his fishing license number?

a. HA12071948MM70EEE

b. HA12071948MM70.4WQA

c. MM12071948HA70LBD

d. MMHC120714870.4

98. Jerome Fielding, a resident of Buncomb County, is 75 inches tall. His date of birth is August 26, 1980. The number assigned to his license, BU26081980JF75RBC, is incorrectly assigned. What error does his license number contain?

a. His height was incorrectly recorded.

b. His height and date of birth have been transposed.

c. The three randomly assigned letters have been omitted.

d. His date of birth is incorrectly recorded.

99. A fishing license with the number TR11151938WE72DVA could belong to an individual named

a. Toni Rouse.

b. Warren Evers.

c. David Van Allen.

d. Victoria Andrews.

100. A fishing license with the number LA08081967MU66ABO belongs to someone

a. born in 1967.

b. born in 1966.

c. who lives in Munroe County.

d. named Linda Almonte.

▶ Civil Service Practice Exam 1 Answers

Section 1: Mathematics

1. c. To reduce $\frac{25}{35}$ to lowest terms, divide both the numerator and denominator by 5. The resulting fraction, $\frac{5}{7}$, is the correct choice. If you chose choice **b**, you probably subtracted; this is incorrect, because you must divide, not subtract, to reduce a fraction.

2. c. To determine the change in the stock's price, first determine whether the price of the stock increased or decreased. Because the price decreased, you can immediately eliminate choice **d**. Next, subtract the smaller value from the larger value. You will have to rewrite the fractions $\frac{3}{8}$ and $\frac{3}{4}$ in common terms as $\frac{3}{8}$ and $\frac{6}{8}$. Because $\frac{6}{8}$ is larger than $\frac{3}{8}$, you will have to borrow to rewrite $28\frac{3}{8}$ as $27\frac{11}{8}$. Now you can subtract $\frac{6}{8}$ from $\frac{11}{8}$ and 26 from 27 to get the correct choice, $1\frac{5}{8}$.

3. d. To rewrite a fraction as a percent, create an equation that allows you to rewrite the fraction with a denominator of 100. Here's the equation you should write: $\frac{18}{25} = \frac{x}{100}$. Next, cross multiply to create the equation $1{,}800 = 25x$. Finally, divide both sides of the equation by 25 to produce the result $72 = x$. Because a percent is the numerator of a fraction when it is written with a denominator of 100, this is the correct choice.

4. a. To determine how much money Jeanette spent, subtract the amount of money she returned home with ($18.42) from the amount of money she left the house with ($100). The result, $81.58, is the correct choice. If you chose any of the incorrect choices, you probably miscalculated. You

should practice carrying and borrowing to avoid such careless errors in the future.

5. c. To answer this question, you must rewrite both fractions over a common denominator. You can easily find a common denominator by multiplying the denominators of the two fractions together; $5 \times 3 = 15$, so 15 is a good common denominator. Rewrite $\frac{3}{5} - \frac{1}{3}$ as $\frac{9}{15} - \frac{5}{15}$ and calculate to arrive at the answer $\frac{4}{15}$. If you chose choice **b**, you probably subtracted numerator from numerator and denominator from denominator; this is not the correct way to subtract fractions.

6. b. To answer this question, you must rewrite the fractions over a common denominator; 12 is a good common denominator because it is divisible by 2, 4, and 6, the denominators in the problem. Rewrite the problem as $\frac{6}{12} + 4\frac{9}{12} + 2\frac{10}{12}$. Next, add the fractions; $\frac{6}{12} + \frac{9}{12} + \frac{10}{12} = \frac{25}{12}$, which can be rewritten as the mixed number $2\frac{1}{12}$. Add $4 + 2 + 2$ to get 8. $8\frac{1}{12}$.

7. a. To calculate 15% of $16.80, multiply $16.80 by 0.15. The product, $2.52, is your correct answer. You might also try this shortcut: Find 10% of $16.80 by moving the decimal point one place to the left. Thus, 10% of $16.80 is $1.68. Immediately eliminate choices **c** and **d**, because 15% of $16.80 must be greater than 10% of $16.80. Next, find 5% of $16.80 by dividing $1.68 (10% of $16.80) in half. Half of $1.68 is $0.84. Therefore, 15% of $16.80 equals $1.68 + $0.84 = $2.52.

8. d. This question asks you to rewrite the mixed number $8\frac{1}{5}$ as an improper fraction. To do this, multiply the whole number 8 by the denominator 5 to get the product 40. Add 40 to the numerator 1 and rewrite the fraction $\frac{41}{5}$. Choices **a**, **b**, and **c** all represent results achieved by incorrect procedures; if you

chose one of these, review the correct procedure for rewriting mixed numbers as
improper fractions.

9. b. There are several ways to answer this question. One way is to rewrite each mixed number as an improper fraction, and then find a
common denominator for the two fractions
and subtract. By this method, you would
rewrite $7\frac{1}{10}$ as $\frac{71}{10}$ and $5\frac{2}{3}$ as $\frac{17}{3}$. You would
then rewrite the improper fractions over the
common denominator of 30 as $\frac{213}{30}$ and $\frac{170}{30}$.
Finally, you would subtract $\frac{213}{30} - \frac{170}{30}$ to get
$\frac{43}{30}$, which equals the mixed number $1\frac{13}{30}$.

10. d. The farmer plants 40 cabbages in each of 75
rows; therefore, he plants 40×75 cabbages,
which equals 3,000 cabbages.

11. b. The legend of a graph shows which line represents which set of data. In this graph, the
legend tells you which line represents the
number of dogs and which line represents the
number of cats.

12. c. The y-axis is the vertical axis of a graph.

13. a. The title tells you what information is contained in the graph. Choice **d** corresponds to
the x-axis of the graph.

14. a. To multiply fractions, multiply numerator by
numerator and denominator by denomina-
tor, and then reduce if necessary. $\frac{4}{5} \times \frac{1}{8} = \frac{4}{40}$,
which reduces to $\frac{1}{10}$. If you chose choice **c** or
d, you probably tried to add numerators and
denominators instead of multiplying them.
You should review the procedure for multiplying fractions to avoid this error in the
future.

15. d. To find the choice, first find $\frac{2}{5}$ of 15, the distance from Mr. Stone's home to his work, by
multiplying $\frac{2}{5}$ and 15. $\frac{2}{5}$ of 15 equals 6, meaning that Mr. Stone has driven 6 miles when he
stops for breakfast. The question asks how far

Mr. Stone is from work, however, so you must
subtract 6 (the distance traveled so far) from
15 (the entire distance of the trip) to determine how much distance remains in his trip.
Thus, the correct choice to the question is 9.

16. a. To divide fractions, multiply the dividend
(the first fraction in the equation) by the
reciprocal of the divisor (the second fraction
in the equation). Thus, $14 \div \frac{3}{4}$ should be
rewritten as $14 \times \frac{4}{3}$, which equals $\frac{56}{3}$. Rewrite
$\frac{56}{3}$ as $18\frac{2}{3}$ to identify the correct answer.

17. a. To find the decimal equivalent of a fraction,
divide the numerator by the denominator;
$5 \div 8 = 0.625$.

18. c. Because 3 teaspoons of water equal 1 tablespoon of water and 2 tablespoons of water
equal 1 ounce of water, 3×2 teaspoons of
water equal 1 ounce of water. Therefore, there
are 6 teaspoons of water in 1 ounce of water,
and there are 6×16 teaspoons of water in a
pint of water; $6 \times 16 = 96$, so 96 is the correct
answer to this question.

19. d. The range of a data set is the difference
between the greatest and least values in the
set. The greatest value in this set is 160 and
the least value is 5, so the range of the data is
$160 - 5$, which equals 155.

20. a. The data in the table show a correlation
between weight and expected life span. In
general, smaller dogs tend to live longer than
larger dogs. Choice **b** cannot be correct
because the table tells us about the average
age for an entire breed of dogs only, not the
lifespan of any individual member of that
breed. Choice **c** cannot be correct because the
table does not contain any information about
how good or bad a house pet each breed
makes. Choice **d** cannot be correct because

the table does not include any information about the weight of an average human.

21. c. You can solve this problem by finding 30% of $350 and subtracting the result from $350, the original price of the suit. Or, you can find 70% of the price of the suit, because a suit discounted by 30% will sell for 70% of its original price. Calculate 70% of $350 by finding 10% of $350 and multiplying the result by 7; 10% of $350 is $35, and $35 × 7 = $245.

22. b. To solve rate problems, apply the equation $rt = d$, where r equals rate, t equals time, and d equals distance. This problem provides the rate (90 miles per hour) and the distance (570 miles), so you can write the equation $90t = 570$. Divide both sides of the equation by 90 to get $t = 6\frac{1}{3}$. Remember that $\frac{1}{3}$ of an hour is 20 minutes; therefore, 6 hours 20 minutes is the correct answer.

23. a. The question asks you to rewrite the improper fraction $\frac{12}{9}$ as a mixed number. To do this, divide the numerator 12 by the denominator 9. The result is $1\frac{3}{9}$, which reduces to $1\frac{1}{3}$.

24. b. To reduce $\frac{42}{51}$, you must find a number that divides evenly into both 42 and 51. Both numbers are divisible by 3, so you can reduce $\frac{42}{51}$ to $\frac{14}{17}$.

25. d. The question tells you that Jack received 24 votes, which constituted 30% of all the votes cast. This is enough information to formulate the question "24 is 30% of what," which can be written as the equation $24 = \frac{30}{100}x$. Now solve the equation by multiplying both sides by 100 to get $2,400 = 30x$. Divide both sides by 30 to get $80 = x$, the solution to the problem.

26. c. To determine the number of workers who responded to the survey, add the number of workers who gave each response. Three work-

ers chose 11:30 A.M., nine workers chose 12 P.M., 11 chose 12:30 P.M., ten chose 1 P.M., and two chose 1:30 P.M.; $3 + 9 + 11 + 10 + 2 = 35$, the correct answer to this question.

27. a. The range of a data set is the difference between the greatest and least values in the set. The greatest value in this set is 11 and the least value is 2, so the range of the data is 11 − 2, which equals 9.

28. b. To divide fractions, multiply the dividend (the first fraction in the equation) by the reciprocal of the divisor (the second fraction in the equation). Thus, $\frac{11}{15} \div \frac{3}{5}$ should be rewritten as $\frac{11}{15} \times \frac{5}{3}$, which equals $\frac{55}{45}$. Rewrite $\frac{55}{45}$ as $1\frac{10}{45}$, then reduce $\frac{10}{45}$ by dividing both numerator and denominator by 5 to get $\frac{2}{9}$; $1\frac{2}{9}$.

29. c. To solve rate problems, apply the equation $rt = d$, where r equals rate, t equals time, and d equals distance. This problem provides the time (4 hours) and the distance (15 miles), allowing you to write the equation $4r = 15$. Now divide both sides of the equation by 4 to solve for r. The result is $r = 3.75$, the correct answer.

30. b. To rewrite a proportion as a percent, create an equation that allows you to rewrite the fraction with a denominator of 100. Here's the equation you should write: $\frac{3}{25} = \frac{x}{100}$. Next, cross multiply to create the equation $300 = 25x$. Finally, divide both sides of the equation by 25 to produce the result $12 = x$. Because a percent is the numerator of a fraction when it is written with a denominator of 100, this is the correct answer.

31. d. This question asks you to rewrite the mixed number $14\frac{1}{2}$ as an improper fraction. To do this, multiply the whole number 14 by the denominator 2 to get the product 28. Add 28 to the numerator 1; $\frac{29}{2}$.

32. c. The pie chart shows that Candidate X received 45% of the votes, more than any other single candidate received. Thus, the graph supports the conclusion that Candidate X received the greatest number of votes. The graph does not mention what percent of eligible voters participated in the election, so choice **a** cannot be correct. Only one candidate received more than 40% of the vote, so choice **b** is incorrect. The graph does not mention whether voters would have chosen Candidate W if she were running, so choice **d** cannot be correct.

33. b. A total of 600 votes were cast in the election. Candidate Z received 18% of the votes; therefore, Candidate Z received 18% of 600 votes; $\frac{18}{100} \times 600 = 108$, the correct answer.

34. c. There are several ways to answer this question. One way is to rewrite each mixed number as an improper fraction, and then find a common denominator for the two fractions and add. By this method, you would rewrite $5\frac{2}{5}$ as $\frac{27}{5}$ and $7\frac{1}{3}$ as $\frac{22}{3}$. Multiply the denominators to find a common denominator of 15, and then rewrite $\frac{27}{5}$ as $\frac{81}{15}$ and $\frac{22}{3}$ as $\frac{110}{15}$. Add $\frac{81}{15}$ and $\frac{110}{15}$ to get $\frac{191}{15}$, then divide 191 by 15 to get the mixed number $12\frac{11}{15}$.

35. b. 180 of 300 consumers polled purchases household cleaning products once per week. To find out how many of 1,000 consumers would be likely to purchase household cleaning products once per week, write the proportion $\frac{180}{300} = \frac{x}{1,000}$ and solve by cross multiplying to get $300x = 18,000$. Divide both sides by 300 to get $x = 600$, the solution to the problem.

36. d. To multiply fractions, multiply numerator by numerator and denominator by denominator, and then reduce if necessary. Because this problem includes a mixed number, you must

first rewrite the mixed number $2\frac{1}{5}$ as the improper fraction $\frac{11}{5}$. Next, multiply $\frac{7}{10}$ and $\frac{11}{5}$ to get $\frac{77}{50}$, which equals $1\frac{22}{50}$; $\frac{22}{50}$ reduces to $\frac{11}{25}$, so $1\frac{11}{25}$.

37. d. To answer this question, find 10% of 1,250, the number of employees in 2005. 10% of 1,250 is 125 (you can calculate 10% of a number quickly by moving its decimal point one place to the left). Now add 125 to 1,250 to get 1,375, the number of employees in 2006.

38. a. To solve rate problems, apply the equation $rt = d$, where r equals rate, t equals time, and d equals distance. This problem provides the time (4 hours) and the rate (480 miles per hour), allowing you to write the equation $4(480) = d$; 4×480 equals 1,920, the correct answer to the problem.

39. c. To find the mean price of the DVD players shown in the table, add all the prices together and divide by the number of DVD players shown. The sum of the four prices is $320. $320 divided by 4, the number of DVD players shown, is $80, so $80 is the average price.

40. d. The range of a data set is the difference between the greatest and least values in the set. The greatest value in this set is $95 and the least value is $61.50, so the range of the data is $95 − $61.50, which equals $33.50.

Section 2: Written Communication

41. b. The main idea of the passage is that there are significant differences between the Library of Congress classification system and the Dewey decimal classification system. The details of the passage enumerate those differences. An expression of the main idea of the passage should focus on the fact that there are important differences between the two systems; of the choices, choice **b** does that best. Choices

a, **c**, and **d** express opinions that the author never states, so neither can be the correct answer.

42. **a.** Reread the sentence, substituting each choice for the word *diverse*. Of the four choices, only choice **a** makes sense in context.

43. **c.** The passage points out that "Users searching for books about dogs, for example, almost always find it easier to remember the Dewey code for such books (636) than the Library of Congress code (SF427)" and also that "there is an internal logic to the entire Dewey system" while "[e]ach Library of Congress subject category . . . was developed independently of the others, so each follows its own unique set of rules." These statements all support the conclusion stated in choice **c**.

44. **d.** The passage states this clearly in paragraph 2. Of the incorrect choices, choice **a** covers information not mentioned in the passage, while choices **b** and **c** are directly contradicted by information in the passage.

45. **d.** Reread the sentence, substituting each choice for the word *constitutes*. Choices **a** and **b** make no sense in context; choice **c** arguably makes some sense, but the word *implies* means *suggests without stating directly*. The word *represents* is much closer in meaning to *constitutes*, so choice **d** is the best answer.

46. **c.** The purpose of the passage is to summarize a report that concludes that there is a strong need to reform America's penal system. Each of the incorrect choices summarizes one of the supporting details of the passage. The main idea must describe the entire passage, not just one detail or one section of the passage.

47. **b.** The passage suggests that the author believes it is possible to reduce prison violence in the final sentence, in which the author, after summarizing the commission's recommendations, states that "These programs will be difficult to implement, but they hold high promise of effectively addressing the penal system's most dramatic problems."

48. **a.** Choices **b**, **c**, and **d** are all mentioned at the end of the first paragraph. The commission suggests testing prisoners for mental health issues, but the passage never says that the commission actually conducted such testing on its own.

49. **a.** Paragraph 2 states that "Candidates must be certified as a B-level law enforcement officer by the state; this level of certification requires training in the use of firearms. Consequently, convicted felons are not eligible for this position, as under the laws of the state convicted felons are disallowed from using firearms."

50. **b.** The passage is a public announcement of a job opening with the state Department of Parks and Wildlife.

51. **a.** The passage states that the "Applicant must also hold a valid state driver's license in good standing," supporting the inference that someone with a suspended driver's license would not be considered for the advertised position.

52. **d.** Reread the sentence, substituting each choice for the word *pertinent*. Of the four choices, only choice **d** makes sense in context.

53. **c.** Use context clues here; the sentence tells us that the *prudent* restrictions are perhaps necessary. Could they be *optional*? No, they can't be optional and necessary, so choice **a** cannot be correct. Can they be *ill-advised* or *counterproductive* and also be necessary? No, so choices **b** and **d** must also be incorrect. The answer must be choice **c**, *sensible*.

54. a. The passage provides a summary of regulations on the political activity of federal employees. Both choices **b** and **d** suggest that the author has written a persuasive passage that argues a particular point of view; in fact, the author has written an informational passage that does not expound any opinion. Thus, choices **b** and **d** must both be incorrect. Choice **c** refers to a detail in the passage; the choice to a main idea question, however, must address the entire passage, not just one detail in it.

55. b. In paragraph 2, the passage states that "Thomas Jefferson issued an executive circular in 1801 advising federal employees to abstain from campaigning and electioneering." Choice **b** is a good paraphrase of this sentence.

56. c. This statement is supported in the final paragraph, which states that "discontent ultimately led to a 1993 amendment that allowed federal employees to participate in elections so long as their activity occurred outside their place of work. At the same time, the amendment increased penalties for those who abused the powers of their offices for political gain." Thus, the passage supports the conclusion drawn in choice **c**.

57. b. The passage discusses both the potential strengths and some of the possible problems with community policing programs; thus, choice **b** is a good summary of the entire passage. Choices **a** and **c** address specific details in the passage; the choice to a main idea question, however, must address the entire passage, not just one detail in it. Choice **d** offers an opinion that the author never states or implies.

58. d. Consider the context; *initiative* clearly connotes something positive, so choices **a** and **b** cannot be correct. Although Brown's *initiative* may have represented a victory, that is not the clear sense of the word here; therefore, choice **c** is not the best answer. Clearly Brown made a *decision* to implement the COPS program in Houston. Thus, the choice closest in meaning to *initiative* is **d**, *decision*.

59. a. Paragraph 3 states that "Although this drop in crime rates has occurred nationwide (including areas that receive no federal assistance), the drops have been more pronounced in those locations that receive substantial COPS funding." The fact that the drops have been greater in areas that receive COPS funding suggests that COPS programs have contributed to the drop in crime rates.

60. d. The passage points out that "Brown believed that officers should be accessible to the community at the street level. If officers were assigned to the same area over a period of time, those officers would eventually build a network of trust with neighborhood residents. As a result, merchants and residents in the community would be more likely to inform officers about criminal activities in the area and support police intervention." These sentences best support choice **d**. None of the other choices is supported by information in the passage.

61. a. The correct spelling is *demolition*.

62. c. The correct spelling is *accidentally*.

63. a. The correct spelling is *spontaneous*.

64. b. The correct spelling of choice **b** is *embellish*.

65. c. The correct spelling of choice **c** is *retaliate*.

66. b. A *hypothesis* is a theory.

67. a. Another word for *tentative* is *uncertain*.

68. a. A *virtuoso* musician is a musician with great expertise. An *amateur* musician is one who plays music for the love of playing, but who lacks the experience and/or skill to be considered a *virtuoso*.

69. c. The sentence provides necessary context clues. What sort of shade could keep a hotel room nice and dark? An *opaque* shade is one that does not let light through. Therefore, *opaque* is the best choice.

70. c. *Remuneration* means *payment*. *Reprisal* and *retribution* (choices **a** and **b**) both mean *revenge*.

71. c. Choice **a** has a subject (*the onset of the cold war*) but no predicate. Likewise, choice **b** has a compound subject that is never completed with a predicate.

72. b. Choice **a** begins with a misplaced modifier, thereby incorrectly indicating that *many consumers* have been genetically modified. Choice **c** also misplaces a modifying phrase (*that consumers do not trust*), thereby inaccurately indicating that the consumers do not trust *disease*.

73. a. Choice **b** incorrectly uses the plural pronouns *their* and *they* to refer to the singular antecedent *quail*. Choice **c** incorrectly uses the plural pronoun *they* to refer to the singular antecedent *quail*.

74. a. Choices **b** and **c** are incorrectly punctuated. The contraction *it's* means *it is*, not *belonging to it*. The possessive form of *it* is *its*.

75. c. In choices **a** and **b**, it is unclear whether the pronouns refer to the *perpetrator* or the *police officer*. Only choice **c** clearly identifies the antecedents to the pronouns.

76. c. Choices **a** and **b** contain capitalization errors. In choice **a**, the words *Evangelical* and *Lutheran* should be capitalized. In

choice **b**, the words *College* and *River* should be capitalized.

77. b. Choice **a** contains a subject-verb agreement error; *everyone* is a collective pronoun that should take the singular verb *has*, not the plural verb *have*. Also, *everyone* should take a singular pronoun such as *his* or *her*, not the plural pronoun *their*. The latter error appears in choice **c** as well.

78. a. Choice **b** contains a pronoun error; the singular pronoun *its* does not agree with its plural antecedent *benefits*. Choice **c** also contains a pronoun error; the pronoun *their* refers to *therapy*, not *benefits*, and, therefore, should be singular rather than plural.

79. b. Choices **a** and **c** both contain punctuation errors. In choice **a**, there should be a comma between *course* and *Renee*. In choice **c**, the comma after *proceeded* is confusing and ungrammatical.

80. c. Choices **a** and **b** are incorrectly punctuated; because the sentence includes no direct quotes, the quotation marks are incorrectly used. The question mark in choice **a** is also grammatically incorrect, because the sentence is a statement of fact, not a question.

Section 3: Civil Service Skills

81. c. The primary governing principle of customer service is to make things as easy and pleasant for the customer as possible. Thus, the primary reason for maintaining customer records is to minimize the need for the customer to provide redundant information. Choice **a** has nothing to do with customer service and, therefore, cannot be the correct answer to a question in this section of the test. Choice **b** falsely suggests that there is a limit to the amount of government service a citizen may receive. Choice **d** falsely suggests that citizens are not entitled to a government service if they have previously received it.

82. b. Callers should be able to find the street address of the agency via numerous accessible means (e.g., telephone book, Internet). The information mentioned in choices **a**, **c**, and **d** is not as easy to find. Furthermore, it is more immediately relevant to the needs of a person who calls an agency outside of business hours.

83. d. A recorded message providing choices to frequently asked questions should allow some callers to resolve their queries without speaking to a representative, a win for both the caller and the agency. Music, choice **a**, is a good second choice but is not as advantageous as the above-described recorded message. Choices **b** and **c** represent options likely to annoy callers.

84. a. Some customers left on hold for a long time will hang up before they get to speak with a representative. The number of total calls divided by the number of hang ups is used to calculate the *abandonment rate*. If 5 out of every 100 calls results in a hang-up, then the abandonment rate is 1 in $\frac{100}{5}$, or 1 in 20.

85. c. This is a common-sense question. It would not be economically feasible or practical to give appointments simply because customers cannot see a representative immediately (choice **a**); a short wait is reasonable. A one-hour wait (choice **b**), however, is far beyond reasonable. Fifteen minutes (choice **c**, the correct choice) is a reasonable amount of time to expect people to wait. Choice **d** falsely suggests that it is a good idea to implement policies that discourage citizens from using government services.

86. c. Three other station names are shown, 18th and California, 30th and Downing, and Union Station.

87. b. The arrow in the photograph indicates the train will be traveling north from the Broadway Station to Union Station.

88. c. Recycling is never collected on the same day as garbage, so if you remembered that Sector 2's garbage was collected on Tuesday and Saturday, you would have been able to eliminate choices **b** and **d**.

89. a. Recycling is collected Tuesday through Saturday; Monday is not a recycling-collection day.

90. c. In Sector 2, garbage is collected on Tuesday and on Saturday, creating a four-day break between the first and second collection. Garbage in Sector 5 is collected on Monday and Friday, which also leaves a four-day break between the first and second collection.

91. c. The instructions indicate that each code is preceded by the time of the visit it represents. Eliminate choices **a**, **b**, and **d**, none of which begins with the time. The correct answer, by process of elimination, must be choice **c**.

92. d. The instructions indicate that each code is preceded by the time of the visit it represents. Eliminate choices **a** and **b**, neither of which begins with the time. Choice **c** records the visitor's actual age of 67 rather than the code for her age (4 = over age 65). Therefore, choice **d** must be the correct answer.

93. a. Eliminate choices **c** and **d**, neither of which begins with the time. Choice **b** incorrectly includes the code Z, indicating that the visitor lives outside the city. In fact, the visitor lives in the southwest quadrant of the city, as choice **a** correctly indicates.

94. b. The F in the code indicates that the visitor was female. The Y in the code indicates that she filed a complaint. The code indicates that the visitor arrived at 12:00 P.M., was a female (F) citizen (C) between the ages of 31 and 65 (3) from the southwest quadrant of the city (W) who filed a complaint (6).

95. c. The question asks for the purpose of the visit, which is represented by the final digit of the code. That digit, 7, indicates "applying for employment," meaning that choice **c** is the correct answer.

96. d. The first two letters of the code correspond to the first two letters of the recipient's county of residence. The recipient lives in Ardmore County, so her license will begin with the letters AR. Eliminate choices **b** and **c**, which begin with the letters DV (the recipient's initials). The final three characters in the license must be randomly generated letters; choice **a** omits these characters and so cannot be correct.

97. a. The first two letters of the code correspond to the first two letters of the recipient's county of residence. The recipient lives in Hazelton County, so his license will begin with the letters HA. Eliminate choices **c** and **d**, which do not begin with these letters. Choice **b** does not round the recipient's height to the nearest whole inch as required by the rules; therefore, choice **a** must be the correct answer.

98. d. The rules state that the birth date should be recorded as month-date-year. Thus, the correct coding of the recipient's birth date would be 08261980, not 26081980 as it erroneously appears on the license.

99. b. The code indicates that the recipient's initials are WE. Therefore, the license could belong to someone named Warren Evers.

100. a. The recipient of this license lives in a county that begins with the letters LA; was born on August 8, 1967; has the initials MU; and is 66 inches tall.

Civil Service
Practice Exam 2

ike the first practice exam, this test was designed to prepare you for the kinds of questions you will encounter on your civil service exam. The 100 multiple-choice questions that follow will test your knowledge of math, reading, spelling, vocabulary, grammar, civil service skills, memory, and coding.

Make sure you take the time to score your test, and then read all the answer explanations, regardless of whether you answered the question correctly. Compare your score on this test with your score on the first test. Are there areas in which you need more improvement? If so, go back to the review chapters and keep studying before you take the third practice test.

► Civil Service Practice Exam 2

1.	ⓐ	ⓑ	ⓒ	ⓓ
2.	ⓐ	ⓑ	ⓒ	ⓓ
3.	ⓐ	ⓑ	ⓒ	ⓓ
4.	ⓐ	ⓑ	ⓒ	ⓓ
5.	ⓐ	ⓑ	ⓒ	ⓓ
6.	ⓐ	ⓑ	ⓒ	ⓓ
7.	ⓐ	ⓑ	ⓒ	ⓓ
8.	ⓐ	ⓑ	ⓒ	ⓓ
9.	ⓐ	ⓑ	ⓒ	ⓓ
10.	ⓐ	ⓑ	ⓒ	ⓓ
11.	ⓐ	ⓑ	ⓒ	ⓓ
12.	ⓐ	ⓑ	ⓒ	ⓓ
13.	ⓐ	ⓑ	ⓒ	ⓓ
14.	ⓐ	ⓑ	ⓒ	ⓓ
15.	ⓐ	ⓑ	ⓒ	ⓓ
16.	ⓐ	ⓑ	ⓒ	ⓓ
17.	ⓐ	ⓑ	ⓒ	ⓓ
18.	ⓐ	ⓑ	ⓒ	ⓓ
19.	ⓐ	ⓑ	ⓒ	ⓓ
20.	ⓐ	ⓑ	ⓒ	ⓓ
21.	ⓐ	ⓑ	ⓒ	ⓓ
22.	ⓐ	ⓑ	ⓒ	ⓓ
23.	ⓐ	ⓑ	ⓒ	ⓓ
24.	ⓐ	ⓑ	ⓒ	ⓓ
25.	ⓐ	ⓑ	ⓒ	ⓓ
26.	ⓐ	ⓑ	ⓒ	ⓓ
27.	ⓐ	ⓑ	ⓒ	ⓓ
28.	ⓐ	ⓑ	ⓒ	ⓓ
29.	ⓐ	ⓑ	ⓒ	ⓓ
30.	ⓐ	ⓑ	ⓒ	ⓓ
31.	ⓐ	ⓑ	ⓒ	ⓓ
32.	ⓐ	ⓑ	ⓒ	ⓓ
33.	ⓐ	ⓑ	ⓒ	ⓓ
34.	ⓐ	ⓑ	ⓒ	ⓓ
35.	ⓐ	ⓑ	ⓒ	ⓓ

36.	ⓐ	ⓑ	ⓒ	ⓓ
37.	ⓐ	ⓑ	ⓒ	ⓓ
38.	ⓐ	ⓑ	ⓒ	ⓓ
39.	ⓐ	ⓑ	ⓒ	ⓓ
40.	ⓐ	ⓑ	ⓒ	ⓓ
41.	ⓐ	ⓑ	ⓒ	ⓓ
42.	ⓐ	ⓑ	ⓒ	ⓓ
43.	ⓐ	ⓑ	ⓒ	ⓓ
44.	ⓐ	ⓑ	ⓒ	ⓓ
45.	ⓐ	ⓑ	ⓒ	ⓓ
46.	ⓐ	ⓑ	ⓒ	ⓓ
47.	ⓐ	ⓑ	ⓒ	ⓓ
48.	ⓐ	ⓑ	ⓒ	ⓓ
49.	ⓐ	ⓑ	ⓒ	ⓓ
50.	ⓐ	ⓑ	ⓒ	ⓓ
51.	ⓐ	ⓑ	ⓒ	ⓓ
52.	ⓐ	ⓑ	ⓒ	ⓓ
53.	ⓐ	ⓑ	ⓒ	ⓓ
54.	ⓐ	ⓑ	ⓒ	ⓓ
55.	ⓐ	ⓑ	ⓒ	ⓓ
56.	ⓐ	ⓑ	ⓒ	ⓓ
57.	ⓐ	ⓑ	ⓒ	ⓓ
58.	ⓐ	ⓑ	ⓒ	ⓓ
59.	ⓐ	ⓑ	ⓒ	ⓓ
60.	ⓐ	ⓑ	ⓒ	ⓓ
61.	ⓐ	ⓑ	ⓒ
62.	ⓐ	ⓑ	ⓒ
63.	ⓐ	ⓑ	ⓒ
64.	ⓐ	ⓑ	ⓒ
65.	ⓐ	ⓑ	ⓒ
66.	ⓐ	ⓑ	ⓒ
67.	ⓐ	ⓑ	ⓒ
68.	ⓐ	ⓑ	ⓒ
69.	ⓐ	ⓑ	ⓒ
70.	ⓐ	ⓑ	ⓒ

71.	ⓐ	ⓑ	ⓒ
72.	ⓐ	ⓑ	ⓒ
73.	ⓐ	ⓑ	ⓒ
74.	ⓐ	ⓑ	ⓒ
75.	ⓐ	ⓑ	ⓒ
76.	ⓐ	ⓑ	ⓒ
77.	ⓐ	ⓑ	ⓒ
78.	ⓐ	ⓑ	ⓒ
79.	ⓐ	ⓑ	ⓒ
80.	ⓐ	ⓑ	ⓒ
81.	ⓐ	ⓑ	ⓒ	ⓓ
82.	ⓐ	ⓑ	ⓒ	ⓓ
83.	ⓐ	ⓑ	ⓒ	ⓓ
84.	ⓐ	ⓑ	ⓒ	ⓓ
85.	ⓐ	ⓑ	ⓒ	ⓓ
86.	ⓐ	ⓑ	ⓒ	ⓓ
87.	ⓐ	ⓑ	ⓒ	ⓓ
88.	ⓐ	ⓑ	ⓒ	ⓓ
89.	ⓐ	ⓑ	ⓒ	ⓓ
90.	ⓐ	ⓑ	ⓒ	ⓓ
91.	ⓐ	ⓑ	ⓒ	ⓓ
92.	ⓐ	ⓑ	ⓒ	ⓓ
93.	ⓐ	ⓑ	ⓒ	ⓓ
94.	ⓐ	ⓑ	ⓒ	ⓓ
95.	ⓐ	ⓑ	ⓒ	ⓓ
96.	ⓐ	ⓑ	ⓒ	ⓓ
97.	ⓐ	ⓑ	ⓒ	ⓓ
98.	ⓐ	ⓑ	ⓒ	ⓓ
99.	ⓐ	ⓑ	ⓒ	ⓓ
100.	ⓐ	ⓑ	ⓒ	ⓓ

▶ Section 1: Mathematics

Select the best choice for each question.

1. Find the fraction equivalent of 45%.

  a. $\frac{4}{5}$

  b. $\frac{9}{20}$

  c. $\frac{1}{2}$

  d. $\frac{45}{10}$

2. $\frac{16}{5} =$

  a. $2\frac{1}{5}$

  b. $16\frac{1}{5}$

  c. $3\frac{1}{5}$

  d. $1\frac{5}{6}$

3. A tortoise crawls 3 feet per minute. How far does the tortoise crawl in 1 hour?

  a. 3 feet

  b. 30 feet

  c. 60 feet

  d. 180 feet

4. $6\frac{5}{7} =$

  a. $\frac{47}{7}$

  b. $\frac{65}{7}$

  c. $\frac{18}{7}$

  d. $\frac{6}{12}$

Study the following graph, and then use it to answer questions 5 to 7.

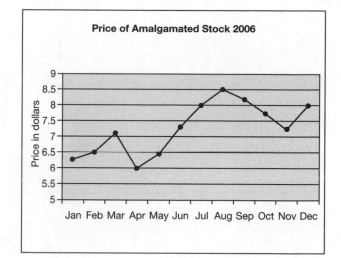

5. The graph shows the price of amalgamated stock throughout 2006. What is the range of the prices for which the stock sold in 2006?

  a. $1.25

  b. $1.75

  c. $2.25

  d. $2.50

6. A person who bought the stock in January and sold it in December would have realized a

  a. profit of $2.25.

  b. profit of $1.75.

  c. loss of $0.50.

  d. loss of $1.25.

7. What information is displayed on the *y*-axis of the graph?

  a. the months of the year

  b. the price of the stock in dollars

  c. the number of shares sold

  d. the title of the graph

8. $10\frac{2}{3} - 3\frac{1}{8} =$

   a. $7\frac{1}{5}$

   b. $7\frac{11}{24}$

   c. $7\frac{13}{24}$

   d. $7\frac{3}{11}$

9. Jamal invests $2,000 in a certificate of deposit that yields 6% simple interest compounded annually. How much is the certificate of deposit worth 2 years after Jamal's initial investment?

   a. $2,247.20

   b. $2,240

   c. $2,120

   d. $2,060

10. Reduce $\frac{28}{45}$ to lowest terms.

   a. $\frac{2}{3}$

   b. $\frac{4}{7}$

   c. $\frac{3}{5}$

   d. The fraction cannot be reduced.

11. Belinda walked a total of 18.6 miles in 4 days. On average, how many miles did Belinda walk each day?

   a. 14.6 miles

   b. 4.65 miles

   c. 4.6 miles

   d. 4.15 miles

12. A piece of ribbon 3 feet 4 inches long was divided into 5 equal parts. How long was each part?

   a. 1 foot 2 inches

   b. 8 inches

   c. 10 inches

   d. 6 inches

13. $2\frac{2}{5} + 3\frac{1}{3} + 1\frac{1}{2} =$

   a. $7\frac{7}{30}$

   b. $7\frac{4}{17}$

   c. $6\frac{2}{5}$

   d. $6\frac{1}{15}$

14. During a 20% off sale, the price of a widescreen television is reduced by $300. What was the price of the television before the sale?

   a. $1,500

   b. $2,400

   c. $3,000

   d. $6,000

15. $\frac{7}{8} \times 104 =$

   a. 78

   b. 91

   c. 96

   d. 97

16. A bread recipe calls for $3\frac{1}{2}$ cups of flour during the initial mixing process and an additional $\frac{1}{4}$ cup of flour during the kneading process. How much flour is used to produce the bread?

   a. $3\frac{1}{8}$ cups

   b. $3\frac{3}{4}$ cups

   c. $\frac{7}{8}$ cup

   d. $7\frac{1}{4}$ cups

Study the following graph, and then use it to answer questions 17 to 19.

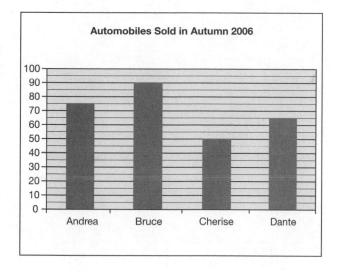

17. Andrea, Bruce, Cherise, and Dante sell automobiles for a living. The graph above shows the number of cars each sold during the autumn of 2006. What is the average number of automobiles sold by each salesperson?
   a. 280
   b. 240
   c. 80
   d. 70

18. What is the range of the data shown in the graph?
   a. 15
   b. 25
   c. 40
   d. 90

19. What information is displayed on the *x*-axis of the graph?
   a. the number of automobiles sold
   b. the names of the salespeople
   c. the title of the graph
   d. the months of autumn

20. $\frac{7}{8} - (\frac{1}{3} + \frac{1}{4}) =$
   a. $\frac{41}{56}$
   b. $\frac{19}{24}$
   c. $\frac{5}{24}$
   d. $\frac{7}{24}$

21. Find the decimal equivalent of 4%.
   a. 0.4
   b. 4.0
   c. 0.04
   d. 0.004

22. $\frac{5}{7} \div 10 =$
   a. $\frac{1}{70}$
   b. $\frac{7}{5}$
   c. $7\frac{1}{7}$
   d. $\frac{1}{14}$

23. The ratio of men to women attending a university is 5:4. If there are 7,650 students at the school, how many are men?
   a. 4,250
   b. 3,400
   c. 1,530
   d. 850

24. After receiving a 10% increase in salary, Marisol earns a salary of $55,000. What was Marisol's salary before she received the raise?
   a. $40,000
   b. $45,000
   c. $50,000
   d. $54,000

25. $\frac{1}{8} + \frac{5}{6} =$
   a. $\frac{3}{7}$
   b. $1\frac{1}{3}$
   c. $\frac{3}{4}$
   d. $\frac{23}{24}$

Study the following graph, and then use it to answer questions 26 to 28.

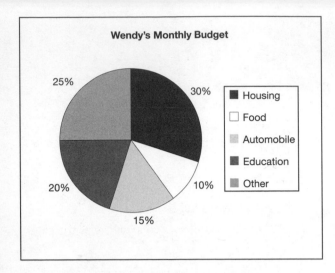

Wendy's Monthly Budget

30% Housing
25%
20%
15%
10%

- ■ Housing
- □ Food
- ▨ Automobile
- ■ Education
- ▨ Other

26. The legend of the graph tells you
   a. how much money Wendy has to spend each month.
   b. which categories correspond to which sections of the graph.
   c. what type of food Wendy buys each month.
   d. why type of expenses are classified under the category "other."

27. Which of the following conclusions is supported by the graph?
   a. Wendy spends half her monthly budget on housing and education.
   b. Automobile expenses are Wendy's single biggest monthly expense.
   c. Wendy does not spend any money on entertainment.
   d. If Wendy earned more money, she would spend more money on food.

28. Wendy budgets for $3,000 in expenditures each month. What is her monthly expenditure on education?
   a. $300
   b. $450
   c. $600
   d. $900

29. Over the course of a 63-mile-long bicycle ride, a cyclist averages a speed of 18 miles per hour. How long does it take the bicyclist to complete the ride?
   a. 3 hours
   b. 3 hours 9 minutes
   c. 3 hours 30 minutes
   d. 45 hours

30. A warbler that weighs 9 grams eats 80% of its body weight each day. How much food, in grams, does a warbler eat daily?
   a. 7.2 grams
   b. 8.0 grams
   c. 8.9 grams
   d. 9.8 grams

31. A television miniseries consists of three episodes. The first is $2\frac{1}{2}$ hours long, the second is $2\frac{3}{4}$ hours long, and the third is $2\frac{1}{3}$ hours long. What is the total length of the entire miniseries?
   a. 7 hours
   b. $7\frac{5}{9}$ hours
   c. $7\frac{1}{8}$ hours
   d. $7\frac{7}{12}$ hours

32. $8\frac{1}{2} \times 3\frac{1}{4} =$
   a. $27\frac{5}{8}$
   b. $24\frac{1}{8}$
   c. $24\frac{3}{4}$
   d. $11\frac{3}{4}$

33. $21 \div \frac{1}{2}$

a. $20\frac{1}{2}$

b. $10\frac{1}{2}$

c. 42

d. 43

34. Last Monday, 20% of the 140-member nursing staff was absent. How many nurses were absent on Monday?

a. 14

b. 20

c. 28

d. 112

35. Derek jogs for 2 hours 15 minutes at an average rate of 8 kilometers per hour. How far does Derek jog?

a. 19 kilometers

b. 18 kilometers

c. 17 kilometers

d. 16 kilometers

Study the following table, and then use it to answer questions 36 to 37.

DAVID'S TEST SCORES IN HIS HISTORY CLASS	
DATE	TEST SCORE
September 22, 2006	74
October 6, 2006	73
October 27, 2006	82
November 17, 2006	86
December 8, 2006	95

36. What was David's average (arithmetic mean) score for the five tests given in his history class?

a. 81

b. 82

c. 86

d. 88

37. The data in the table support which of the following conclusions?

a. David will earn a grade of an A in his history class.

b. The exam on December 5 will count most toward David's final grade.

c. David's grades tended to improve as the class progressed.

d. Test scores are not an accurate indicator of one's understanding of history.

38. Reduce $\frac{14}{35}$ to lowest terms.

a. $\frac{7}{17}$

b. $\frac{2}{5}$

c. $\frac{1}{21}$

d. $\frac{2}{3}$

39. Of the 840 crimes committed last month, 42 involved petty theft. What percent of crimes committed last month involved petty theft?

a. 5%

b. 0.5%

c. 0.05%

d. 2%

40. A recipe calls for $4\frac{1}{4}$ cups of flour. Which of the following equals $4\frac{1}{4}$ cups?

a. $\frac{5}{4}$ cup

b. $\frac{1}{16}$ cup

c. $\frac{9}{4}$ cup

d. $\frac{17}{4}$ cup

▶ Section 2: Written Communication

Reading Comprehension— Questions 41 to 60

Read the following passage. Then, answer questions 41 to 44.

What is the U.S. Constitution's position on the right to privacy? The answer is not a simple one. Many Americans are surprised to learn that the Constitution does not speak directly to the issue. They regard the Bill of Rights as a safeguard of fundamental individual rights against government power, and because they believe privacy is one of those fundamental rights, they assume that it is specifically protected.

One cannot assume that privacy rights are unprotected simply because they are not mentioned in the Constitution, however. After all, the Ninth Amendment of the Constitution states that "the enumeration in the Constitution, of certain rights, shall not be construed to deny or disparage others retained by the people." In other words, the Constitution acknowledges that the people may have other rights other than those it specifically protects.

Is privacy one of those rights? The Supreme Court addressed that question in 1965, in the case of *Griswold v. Connecticut*, in which Estelle Griswold challenged a state law prohibiting the use of contraceptives. The court ruled 7–2 in her favor, noting that the cumulative effect of the first nine amendments to the Constitution was an <u>implicit</u> right to privacy. The court reasoned that each of the first eight amendments relied upon the establishment of a zone of privacy, without which the amendments were meaningless. The Ninth Amendment, the court argued, bolstered that interpretation. Several of the justices added that the due process clause of the Fourteenth Amendment also required a right to privacy.

Griswold remains the law of the land, but that doesn't mean it is without its controversial aspects. The two dissenting justices argued that the majority had overreached in its decision, and opponents of privacy rights have continued pressing that argument into the present day. Because privacy rights play a critical role in such hot-button political topics as abortion rights and homosexual rights, the controversy remains a prominent one. With the Supreme Court shifting to a more conservative position in the early twenty-first century, it is possible that the court will revisit privacy rights someday soon. Its decision may mark the beginning of a new chapter in the story of privacy rights in the United States.

41. According to the passage, Americans' right to privacy was established by a
   a. law passed by the Congress.
   b. presidential ruling.
   c. public referendum.
   d. Supreme Court ruling.

42. As used in the passage, the word *implicit* most nearly means
   a. controversial.
   b. absent.
   c. understood.
   d. nominal.

43. The author suggests that the
  a. *Griswold* ruling would not be as controversial if it did not have implications in divisive social issues.
  b. court made an incorrect ruling when it decided the *Griswold* case.
  c. Bill of Rights should be amended to include a specific guarantee of privacy rights.
  d. current Supreme Court is likely to strengthen the privacy rights guaranteed in *Griswold* in the near future.

44. The main idea of the passage is that
  a. Estelle Griswold effectively used the Supreme Court to overturn an outdated Connecticut law.
  b. privacy rights in America were affirmed only relatively recently, and they remain a contentious subject.
  c. all the amendments to the Constitution are important, but the Fourteenth Amendment is the most important.
  d. Americans are likely to lose their privacy rights in coming years.

Read the following passage. Then, answer questions 45 to 48.

Each state and local government handles funding of public education somewhat differently, but as a general rule, public schools depend upon a combination of state education funds generated through sales and income tax, lotteries and other user fees, and local property taxes, which are contributed directly to the local school system. As a result of this system, every school receives a certain baseline amount of funding from the state. Schools in districts that generate high property taxes, however, tend to receive greater funding than those in districts that generate low property taxes. Thus, schools in wealthy areas are better funded than those in poorer areas.

This situation raises the issue of fairness. Should wealthy areas enjoy better funding for their public schools than do poor areas? The question is especially germane if one believes that America truly is a meritocracy, under which education should be the primary means by which citizens can elevate themselves from the lower to upper strata of society. Providing some students with better schools solely on the basis of their economic backgrounds runs counter to the notion that every child should be given an equal opportunity to achieve the American dream.

Those looking to reform the current system most often suggest a rebalancing in the mix of tax resources allocated to schools. They seek to increase the contributions made at the state level and decrease the contributions made at the local level, a policy that would result in more equitable funding for all public schools regardless of location. The question is, how to get more money from state governments, most of whose budgets are currently already overburdened?

One possible solution is to increase state income taxes while concurrently reducing local property taxes. Most citizens would feel little or no change in their current tax burden as a result, and those most likely to experience an increase would probably be those most capable of affording it; namely, the wealthy. The chief alternative—increasing state sales tax—is untenable because it has the opposite effect, most powerfully affecting the poor, who can least afford it.

Are such reforms possible? The sad truth is that advocates for low-income school districts have been proposing such changes for many years, with little effect. Many powerful forces are aligned against these proposals. That's not to say that change is impossible, however. Perhaps the best means of achieving these changes is through amendment of state constitutions. Well-funded campaigns that stressed fairness as the central issue may just be able to garner the support of the majority, particularly if the campaigns also made clear that the tax impact of the changes would be insignificant for most citizens.

45. The main idea of the passage is that
   a. state tax rates are already too high and should be decreased.
   b. states looking to increase funding for public schools should consider adding a lottery or adding to existing lottery programs.
   c. the way public schools are funded should be changed, but such change will probably be difficult.
   d. a campaign to rewrite state constitutions would probably succeed.

46. Which of the following represents a flaw in the author's reasoning?
   a. Local property taxes fund not only public schools but also garbage collection, sewer maintenance, and other important services.
   b. Most low-income taxpayers do not own property and thus would see an increase in their taxes if the author's plan were implemented.
   c. Some people argue that property taxes in most areas are already too low and, therefore, should not be reduced.
   d. The impact of an increase in sales tax on the poor could be offset by some form of income-tax tax credit at the end of the year.

47. As used in the passage, the word *germane* most nearly means
   a. relevant.
   b. frightening.
   c. tantalizing.
   d. inconsequential.

48. According to the passage, America's public schools face a problem caused by
   a. lack of motivation among students.
   b. a shortage of qualified teachers in technical fields.
   c. underfunding of science programs.
   d. disproportionate funding based on location.

Read the following passage. Then, answer questions 49 to 52.

This information sheet is provided courtesy of the Centers for Disease Control and Prevention (CDC). It is intended to help citizens make informed choices when deciding whether to consume raw oysters.

Nearly all oysters carry the *Vibrio vulnificus* bacteria, although in the vast majority of cases it is present in concentrations too low to affect humans adversely. The bacteria tends to be more active during the warmer months, making oysters harvested during this period substantially more dangerous. There is an old saying: "Never eat an oyster in a month that does not have an 'r' in it." The saying is grounded in fact, as there is a markedly increased danger of *Vibrio vulnificus* infection during these months.

In healthy adults, a *Vibrio vulnificus* infection usually manifests itself in symptoms commonly associated with food poisoning. These symptoms typically include stomach pain, diarrhea, and vomiting. The infection is much more dangerous to people with weakened immune systems, especially those who suffer from chronic liver disease. In such individuals, *Vibrio vulnificus* can infect the bloodstream, resulting in decreased blood pressure, fever, chills, and skin lesions. Such infections are fatal approximately half the time. Such individuals should avoid not only eating oysters, but also swimming in oyster-inhabited waters during the summer months, as infection can be transmitted in the water through open wounds.

People infected with *Vibrio vulnificus* should seek immediate help; antibiotics can be effective in reducing mortality. In the case of infection through an open wound on a limb, amputation may be necessary.

Fortunately, the incidence of *Vibrio vulnificus* is low, with only about 40 cases reported annually. Most cases occur in the Gulf Coast region. Researchers suspect that many low-grade cases of *Vibrio vulnificus*—those that result in food-poisoning-like symptoms—go unreported, making the actual incidence of infection difficult to calculate accurately. The CDC strongly urges patients and medical professionals to report such incidents, as it allows the agency to identify potentially risky oyster beds and thus to prevent <u>subsequent</u> infections. To reduce the risk of *Vibrio vulnificus* infection, eat only shellfish that has been fully cooked and wear gloves and other protective clothing when handling raw shellfish.

49. The author's main purpose is to
   a. convince readers to avoid all seafood.
   b. warn readers about a specific danger.
   c. refute an erroneous report.
   d. describe the life cycle of an oyster.

50. According to the passage, a *Vibrio vulnificus* infection is especially dangerous to
   a. children and the elderly.
   b. people who do not live on the Gulf Coast.
   c. those with compromised immune systems.
   d. amputees.

51. It can be inferred from the passage that
   a. one does not have to eat an oyster to contract a *Vibrio vulnificus* infection.
   b. it is safer to eat oysters in the summertime than in the wintertime.
   c. a *Vibrio vulnificus* infection is usually fatal to everyone who contracts it.
   d. there is currently no effective treatment for a *Vibrio vulnificus* infection.

52. As used in the passage, the word *subsequent* most nearly means
   a. vigilant.
   b. unnecessary.
   c. more dangerous.
   d. future.

Read the following passage. Then, answer questions 53 to 56.

The "broken window" theory was originally developed to explain how minor acts of vandalism or disrespect can quickly escalate to crimes and attitudes that break down the entire social fabric of an area. This theory can easily be applied to any situation in society. The theory contends that if a broken window in an abandoned building is not replaced quickly, soon all the windows will be broken. In other words, a small violation, if condoned, leads to other similar or greater violations. Thus, after all the windows have been broken, the building is more likely to be looted and perhaps even burned down.

According to the theory, violations increase exponentially. Thus, if disrespect to a superior is tolerated, others will be tempted to be disrespectful as well. A management crisis could erupt literally overnight. For example, if one firefighter begins to disregard proper housewatch procedure by neglecting to keep up the housewatch administrative journal, and if this firefighter is not <u>reproved</u>, others will follow suit by committing similar violations of procedure. The theory is that group members begin to reason, "If he can get away with it, why can't I?" Thus, what starts out as a minor problem, such as a violation that may not seem to warrant disciplinary action, may ultimately undermine efficiency throughout the entire firehouse, putting the people the firehouse serves at risk.

There are, of course, dangers inherent to implementing the broken window theory. Many conclude that the theory mandates a zero tolerance policy toward malfeasance and even toward legal but disrespectful behavior. In practice, such a policy can quickly result in the abuse of power by authority figures, whether they be police officers patrolling a community, firefighters maintaining a firehouse, or managers supervising a team of employees. Excessive exertion of authority typically gives rise to its own set of problems, such as resentment of authority and disobedience as an act of defiance.

53. Which of the following best expresses the main idea of the passage?
   a. A theory explains how disorder can escalate under certain conditions.
   b. If order is not maintained in a firehouse, public safety can be compromised.
   c. Some bosses are too demanding, which results in employee insubordination.
   d. The housewatch administrative journal is the most important document in a firehouse.

54. As used in the passage, the word *reproved* most nearly means
   a. condoned.
   b. ostracized.
   c. fired.
   d. scolded.

55. With which of the following statements would the author most likely agree?
   a. The broken window theory is a fatally flawed concept.
   b. The broken window theory may help explain certain behavior.
   c. The broken window theory should be applied to all situations.
   d. The broken window theory really pertains to firehouses only.

56. According to the passage, the broken window theory helps explain
   a. how disciplinary problems can arise quickly seemingly from nowhere.
   b. why cities today are more successful in combating vandalism than they have been in the past.
   c. which organizations the broken window phenomenon is mostly likely to affect adversely.
   d. what personality traits drive a citizen to disrespect authority.

Read the following passage. Then, answer questions 57 to 60.

If you are looking for a new pet in your life, please consider adopting one from the county animal shelter. Every year the county takes custody of thousands of stray cats and dogs. Those pets that the county cannot find homes for, sadly, must be euthanized. By adopting a pet from the county, you'll be saving the life of an innocent animal and adding a new and wonderful member to your family.

As an <u>inducement</u> to adopt, the county provides a number of valuable services for your pet. Your dog will receive his or her first round of bordatella, parvo, parainfluenza, distemper, and hepatitis vaccinations; if your pet is old enough, he or she will also receive the first rabies shot and implantation of an identifying microchip. Your dog will also be wormed and given a full physical examination by our in-house veterinarian. Cats receive their first round of vaccinations for calici virus, chlamydia, panleukopenia, and rhinotracheitis. If he or she is old enough, your cat will also receive the first rabies shot and implantation of an identifying microchip.

The county charges a uniform adoption fee of $60 for all pets. Please note that you are required to have your pet spayed or neutered. The county does not perform these operations; however, it will provide you with a certificate that pays for the entire cost of the operation, redeemable at a number of local veterinarian hospitals. Failure to have your pet spayed or neutered will result in a $100-per-month fine, so please fulfill your obligation.

Keep in mind that owning a pet is a big responsibility. We hope that you will decide to adopt one of our animals, but only if you make the commitment to care for your pet correctly. The shelter offers regular evening seminars in pet care. You may wish to enroll in one before you adopt an animal to learn more about a pet owner's responsibilities so you can decide whether a pet is right for you.

57. The author's main purpose in this passage is to
 a. persuade all citizens to adopt at least one pet.
 b. warn citizens of fines they may face.
 c. inform citizens of the details regarding pet adoption.
 d. explain why the county shelter must put down so many animals each year.

58. It can be inferred from the passage that
 a. most people are not responsible enough to take care of a pet.
 b. the author believes the adoption fee charged by the county is too high.
 c. cats and dogs must reach a certain age before they can be implanted with a microchip.
 d. it is less expensive to care for a cat than to care for a dog.

59. According to the passage, dogs adopted from the county shelter receive vaccinations for all of the following EXCEPT
 a. parvo.
 b. distemper.
 c. bordatella.
 d. panleukopenia.

60. As used in the passage, the word *inducement* most nearly means
 a. imperative.
 b. encouragement.
 c. evasion.
 d. ultimatum.

Spelling—Questions 61 to 65
Select the choice that is spelled correctly.

61. We will be able to move forward after the planning office _____ a policy.
 a. formalates
 b. formulates
 c. formulaits

62. The _____ inspected the corpse and found no evidence of foul play.
 a. coroner
 b. corroner
 c. coronor

63. Which of the following words is spelled incorrectly?
  a. congeal
  b. sirmount
  c. personnel

64. Which of the following words is spelled incorrectly?
  a. bilingual
  b. monatary
  c. vehement

65. Which of the following words is spelled incorrectly?
  a. grotesque
  b. instigate
  c. contemptabul

Vocabulary—Questions 66 to 70
Select the best choice for each question.

66. Find the word that is closest in meaning to the underlined word below.
an <u>excruciating</u> experience
  a. enlightening
  b. boring
  c. painful

67. Find the word that is closest in meaning to the underlined word below.
a <u>trite</u> saying
  a. biblical
  b. nonsensical
  c. overused

68. Find the word that is most nearly the opposite of the underlined word below.
a <u>monotonous</u> speech
  a. annoying
  b. interesting
  c. short

69. Find the word that best completes the sentence below.
The employer offered a large signing bonus as an _____ to persuade the applicant to accept the job offer.
  a. inducement
  b. affront
  c. impediment

70. Find the word that best completes the sentence below.
The spies arranged a secret _____ to exchange secrets.
  a. liaison
  b. confection
  c. premonition

Grammar—Questions 71 to 80
Select the best choice for each question.

71. Which of the following is a complete sentence?
  a. Because of spending increases in both discretionary programs and entitlements, the federal budget deficit has increased greatly in recent years.
  b. Because of spending increases in both discretionary programs and entitlements, causing the federal budget deficit to increase greatly in recent years.
  c. Spending increases in both discretionary programs and entitlements causing the federal budget deficit to increase greatly in recent years.

72. Select the sentence that is written most correctly.
  a. An effort to remedy the problem will be made as soon as possible by the school principal.
  b. The school principal will make an effort to remedy the problem as soon as possible.
  c. As soon as possible, the school principle will make an effort to remedy the problem soon.

73. Select the sentence that is written most correctly.

    a. The reason we are switching to an automated phone system is because it is more efficient.

    b. We are switching to an automated phone system because it is more efficient.

    c. There is a reason that we are switching to an automated phone system, and that reason is because it is more efficient.

74. Select the sentence that is written most correctly.

    a. The bill reached the desk of governor Williams on Friday, but she did not sign it until monday.

    b. The bill reached the desk of Governor Williams on Friday, but she did not sign it until Monday.

    c. The Bill reached the Desk of Governor Williams on Friday, but she did not sign it until Monday.

75. Select the sentence that is written most correctly.

    a. Please make sure that Mr and Mrs Anderson receive an invitation to the meeting.

    b. Please make sure that Mr. and Mrs. Anderson receive an invitation to the meeting.

    c. Please make sure that Mr. and Mrs Anderson receive an invitation to The Meeting.

76. Select the sentence that is written most correctly.

    a. Unlike other pianists, Thelonious Monk played in a style that is difficult to trace to that of an earlier musician.

    b. Unlike other pianists, the style of Thelonious Monk is difficult to trace to an earlier musician.

    c. Unlike other pianists, whose styles can be traced to an earlier musician, Thelonious Monk's cannot.

77. Select the sentence that is written most correctly.

    a. William Morrison the president of the local Chamber of Commerce will address the class next Thursday.

    b. William Morrison, the president of the local Chamber of Commerce will address the class next Thursday.

    c. William Morrison, the president of the local Chamber of Commerce, will address the class next Thursday.

78. Select the sentence that is written most correctly.

    a. The use of electronic devices, including cellular phones, are prohibited on airplanes when the aircraft is in flight.

    b. The use of electronic devices, including a cellular phone, are prohibited on airplanes when the aircraft are in flight.

    c. The use of electronic devices, including cellular phones, is prohibited on airplanes when the aircraft are in flight.

79. Select the sentence that is written most correctly.

    a. Miguel has been assigned to work on the project with Leticia and I.

    b. Miguel has been assigned to work on the project with Leticia and me.

    c. Miguel, he has been assigned to work on the project with Leticia and I.

80. Select the sentence that is written most correctly.

    a. Roberta went to the store to pick up some butter, sugar, milk, and flour.

    b. Roberta went to the store to pick up some butter sugar milk and flour.

    c. Roberta went to the store to pick up some butter, sugar, milk and, flour.

▶ Section 3: Civil Service Skills

Customer Service— Questions 81 to 85

Select the best choice for each question.

81. Customers who complain about government service should
- **a.** receive a response even if they request that no response be provided.
- **b.** be offered a variety of outlets through which to complain (e.g., complaint desk, e-mail, website).
- **c.** register their complaints in person so they can receive an immediate response.
- **d.** be allowed to complain only if they can register the complaint in English.

82. Quality-assurance agents focus primarily on
- **a.** citizens' level of satisfaction in their government interactions.
- **b.** government employees' level of satisfaction with their pay and benefits.
- **c.** the speed and frequency at which agencies update their websites.
- **d.** the punctuality of government employees.

83. An office that offers language translation services should have as its highest priority
- **a.** offering the greatest number of languages possible.
- **b.** providing accurate translation of those languages it offers.
- **c.** requiring non-English-speaking users to enroll in English courses.
- **d.** making sure that all forms are available in multiple languages.

84. When transferring a call, which of the following pieces of information is least important to provide the customer?
- **a.** the number of the extension to which they are being transferred
- **b.** the reason they are being transferred
- **c.** the number to call in case they are disconnected
- **d.** the name of your supervisor

85. The term *web chat* refers to
- **a.** a list of frequently asked questions and choices posted on a website.
- **b.** a telephone line dedicated to customer queries about how to navigate a website.
- **c.** a training program designed to teach government employees how to use the Internet.
- **d.** live interactive online help from an agency representative.

Memory—Questions 86 to 90

Take five minutes to study the following picture. Then, answer questions 86 to 87 without looking back at the picture.

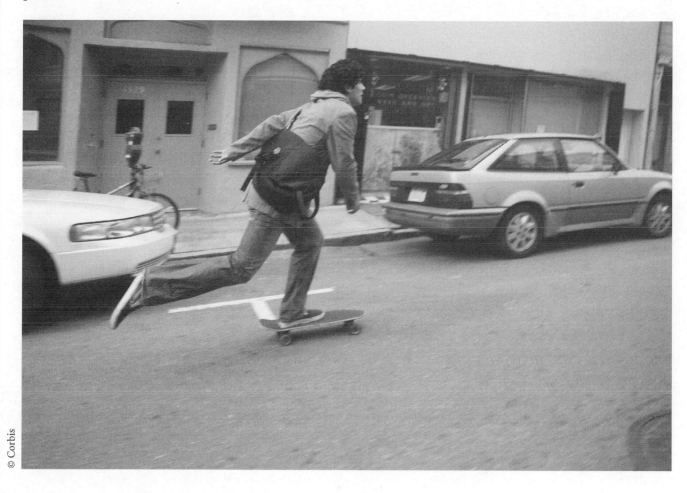

© Corbis

86. The automobile on the right-hand side of the photograph is a
a. two-door sedan.
b. station wagon.
c. sport-utility vehicle.
d. motorcycle.

87. The skateboarder is wearing
a. a large hat.
b. a jacket.
c. Bermuda shorts.
d. a cape.

Take five minutes to study the following text. Then, answer questions 88 through 90 without looking back at the text.

You are about to begin a meeting with six professional peers you have never met before. Their images and names follow.

Sylvia Martinez

Victor Dinapoli

Janet Barnes

Arthur Jones

Maureen Cho

Carlos Domingo

88. Sylvia Martinez's hair
   a. is worn in an afro style.
   b. is blonde.
   c. is shoulder-length.
   d. covers her ears.

89. Arthur Jones is distinguished from all the other people by all of the following details EXCEPT for which?
   a. He is the only one with dark hair.
   b. He is the only one wearing a hat.
   c. He is the only one with a beard and moustache.
   d. He is the only one wearing sunglasses.

90. Which is a complete list of all the people who are wearing glasses?
   a. Sylvia Martinez, Victor Dinapoli
   b. Victor Dinapoli, Arthur Jones, Maureen Cho
   c. Victor Dinapoli, Janet Barnes, Carlos Domingo
   d. Arthur Jones, Carlos Domingo

Coding—Questions 91 to 100

To answer questions 91 through 95, refer to the following scenario.

A record of all correspondences sent from a particular government office must be entered into a log. The following code is used to record the information.

5 letters = first four letters of the recipient's last name and the first letter of the recipient's first name

2 digits = first two digits of the recipient's street address; if the address is one digit long, precede that digit with a zero (0)

1 letter = I if the correspondence represents an inquiry originating in the government office;

R if the correspondence represents a response to an inquiry from the recipient

1 digit = 0 if the letter is high priority; 1 if the letter is medium priority; 2 if the letter is low priority

3 letters and 2 digits = First three letters of the month and date correspondence was sent (e.g., July 6 = JUL06)

91. In response to an inquiry from Denise Fong of 3724 Haywood Boulevard, the office sends a letter graded medium priority on November 15. How should this correspondence be entered into the log?
   a. RFONGD37241NOV15
   b. FONGD37R1NOV15
   c. FONG3724RNOV15
   d. 37R1NOV15FONG

92. The office originated an inquiry to Martin Ramirez of 8 Elm Court on June 2. The office graded the letter high priority. How should this correspondence be entered into the log?
   a. MARTR8I0JUN2
   b. MARTR08I0JUN02
   c. RAMIM8I0JUN2
   d. RAMIM08I0JUN02

93. In response to a letter from John Davis of 1277 Highland Road on October 15, the office sent a low priority letter on October 23. How should the office's response be entered into the log?
   a. JOHND12R2OCT15
   b. DAVIJ12R2OCT15
   c. JOHND12R2OCT23
   d. DAVIJ12R2OCT23

94. A log entry reading BERNM35I0FEB05 could represent

    a. a reply sent to Martin Bernstein of 3 Fifth Avenue on February 5.

    b. an inquiry sent to Bernard Moskowitz of 3 Fifth Avenue on February 5.

    c. an inquiry sent to Martin Bernstein of 35 Michigan Drive on February 5.

    d. a reply sent to Bernard Moskowitz of 35 Michigan Drive on February 5.

95. The following log entry for a response to Harold McCarthy of 5 Stevenson Road, sent high priority on March 6, was coded MCCAH5R0MAR06. It contains which of the following errors?

    a. It omits a zero (0) that should appear between H and 5.

    b. It incorrectly codes the recipient's name.

    c. The date on which the letter was sent is recorded incorrectly.

    d. The priority level of the letter is miscoded.

To answer questions 96 through 100, refer to the following scenario.

A city health department inspects salad bars in grocery stores as well as the areas in which foods for the salad bars are prepared. It logs violations of the health code according to the following rules:

Major Infraction (subtract 5 points for each incident; infraction must be remedied immediately)

A—Cooked foods not cooked through
B—Cooked foods stored under 140° F
C—Cold food stored above 41° F
D—Raw and cooked foods stored together, allowing for cross-contamination
E—Improper cleaning of knives and other utensils

F—Employee with contagious condition (e.g., flu) preparing food
G—Employee fails to wash hands thoroughly
H—Presence of animal droppings detected

Minor infraction (subtract 3 points for each incident; infraction must be remedied within two business days)

j—Hand-washing facilities not immediately accessible to food preparers
k—Lack of soap or towels at hand-washing facility
m—Improper temperature or water pressure in automatic dishwasher or washing machine
n—Inaccurate labeling of food items
p—Inaccurate labeling or improper storage of toxic cleaning materials
r—Consumer advisories (e.g., notices about safety of shellfish) improperly displayed
s—Smoking in the food preparation area

Multiple infractions are logged multiple times (e.g., an inspector who observes three incidents of undercooked food would log the code AAA). A health code score is tabulated by adding the value of all infractions and subtracting the sum from 100.

96. An inspector visits Wilson's Supermarket to observe its salad bar and preparation areas. During her visit, she notes one incident of cold food stored at too high a temperature. She also finds animal droppings in two separate areas of the store. Finally, she notes that one food item is improperly labeled. What code does the inspector record for this visit?

    a. CCHp

    b. CHp

    c. CHHp

    d. CHHppp

97. An inspector visits Hungry Bob's Mini-Mart to inspect its salad bar and preparation areas. The inspector observes three incidents of improper storage of toxic cleaning materials. He also notes that a consumer advisory that should be posted clearly is not posted. What code should he assign for his visit?

a. pppr

b. EEEn

c. En

d. pr

98. An inspector visits Hungry Bob's Mini-Mart to inspect its salad bar and preparation areas. The inspector observes three incidents of improper storage of toxic cleaning materials. He also notes that a consumer advisory that should be posted clearly is not posted. What score should the inspector assign for this visit?

a. 88

b. 80

c. 90

d. 94

99. An inspector visits Mega-Mart and logs the following code:

EGkss

The inspector observed more than one incident of

a. poor cleaning of utensils.

b. poor hand-washing technique.

c. insufficient amount of soap or towels.

d. smoking where food is prepared.

100. An inspector visits Mega-Mart and logs the following code:

EGkss

What score should the inspector assign for the report?

a. 75

b. 81

c. 79

d. 85

► Civil Service Practice Exam 2 Answers

Section 1: Mathematics

1. b. To find the fraction equivalent of a percent, rewrite the percent as a fraction with 100 in the denominator and reduce. $45\% = \frac{45}{100}$. Divide numerator and denominator by 5 to produce the result $\frac{9}{20}$, the correct answer.

2. c. The question asks you to rewrite the improper fraction $\frac{16}{5}$ as a mixed number. To do this, divide the numerator 16 by the denominator 5. The result is $3\frac{1}{5}$.

3. d. It is easiest to solve this as a proportion problem. Write a proportion with *feet* in the numerator and *minutes* in the denominator. Don't get fooled by the fact that the question asks you about both minutes AND hours; just convert 1 hour to 60 minutes so that your time units remain constant throughout your calculations. Write the following proportion: $\frac{3}{1} = \frac{x}{60}$. Now cross multiply to solve; $x = 180$, so 180 is the answer to the question.

4. a. This question asks you to rewrite the mixed number $6\frac{5}{7}$ as an improper fraction. To do this, multiply the whole number 6 by the denominator 7 to get the product 42. Add 42 to the numerator 5 to get 47; $\frac{47}{7}$.

5. d. The range of a data set is the difference between the greatest and least values in the set. The greatest value in this set is $8.50 and the least value is $6, so the range is $8.50 − $6.00, which equals $2.50.

6. b. To answer this question, first determine whether the stock price in December was higher or lower than it was in January. Because it was higher, you know that the stock showed a profit for 2006. Eliminate choices **c** and **d**, because they say the stock took a loss. Next, subtract the December

price from the January price. $8.00 − $6.25 equals $1.75, so the stock showed a $1.75 per share profit between January and December.

7. b. The *y*-axis is the vertical axis of a graph.

8. c. To solve this problem, rewrite each mixed number as a fraction. Rewrite $10\frac{2}{3}$ as $\frac{32}{3}$ and $3\frac{1}{8}$ as $\frac{25}{8}$. Next, find a common denominator by multiplying the two denominators. 3×8 equals 24, so rewrite each fraction with 24 in its denominator. $\frac{32}{3} \times \frac{8}{8}$ equals $\frac{256}{24}$; $\frac{25}{8} \times \frac{3}{3} = \frac{75}{24}$. Now you can subtract. $\frac{256}{24} − \frac{75}{24} = \frac{181}{24}$. Divide 181 by 24 to get the result $7\frac{13}{24}$.

9. a. To solve this problem, first determine the value of Jamal's certificate of deposit after one year. The certificate of deposit is worth $2,000 and it earns 6% interest, so it increases in value by 6% of $2,000, which is $120. After one year, then, the certificate of deposit is worth $2,120. In the second year, the certificate of deposit earns 6% interest on its entire value of $2,120. Therefore, it earns another $127.20, meaning that after two years, its value is $2,247.20.

10. d. In order to reduce a fraction, the numerator and the denominator must be divisible by a common factor. 28 and 45 have no common factors; therefore, $\frac{28}{45}$ cannot be reduced.

11. d. To solve rate problems, apply the equation $rt = d$, where r equals rate, t equals time, and d equals distance. This question provides the time (4 days) and the distance (18.6) miles, so you can write the equation $4r = 18.6$. Next, divide both sides by 4 to get $r = 4.15$. Therefore, Belinda walks 4.15 miles per day.

12. b. When solving problems that include two different units, convert to one of the units. In this problem, both feet and inches are included. Convert 3 feet 4 inches to 40 inches by converting 3 feet to 36 inches. Next, divide 40 inches by 5 to determine that each of the five pieces of ribbon is 8 inches long.

13. a. To add mixed numbers with uncommon denominators, first convert all mixed numbers to improper fractions. Convert $2\frac{2}{5}$ to $\frac{12}{5}$, $3\frac{1}{3}$ to $\frac{10}{3}$, and $1\frac{1}{2}$ to $\frac{3}{2}$. Next, multiply the denominators 2, 3, and 5 to find a common denominator of 30. Now, rewrite all three fractions so that 30 is in the denominator of each; $\frac{12}{5} \times \frac{6}{6} = \frac{72}{30}$; $\frac{10}{3} \times \frac{10}{10} = \frac{100}{30}$; $\frac{3}{2} \times \frac{15}{15} = \frac{45}{30}$. Now you can add the fractions: $\frac{72}{30} + \frac{100}{30} + \frac{45}{30} = \frac{217}{30}$. Finally, divide 217 by 30 to produce the result $7\frac{7}{30}$.

14. a. Use the equation translation technique to write an equation for this problem. 20% of the price of the television equals $300; translate that sentence into the equation $\frac{20}{100}x = 300$. Now solve by multiplying both sides by 100 to get $20x = 30,000$, and then divide both sides by 20 to get $x = \$1,500$.

15. b. To multiply a whole number by a fraction, first multiply the whole number by the numerator of the fraction; then, divide the product by the denominator of the fraction: $7 \times 104 = 728$; $728 \div 8 = 91$.

16. b. This question asks you to add $3\frac{1}{2}$ and $\frac{1}{4}$. Fractions can be added together only if they have a common denominator, so rewrite $\frac{1}{2}$ as $\frac{2}{4}$. Now you can add $3\frac{2}{4}$ and $\frac{1}{4}$ to get $3\frac{3}{4}$, the correct answer. If you chose choice **a**, you probably tried to add the fractions without first finding a common denominator. If you chose choice **c**, you probably multiplied the two numbers.

17. d. To find the average number of cars sold by each salesperson, add up all the cars sold by all the salespeople, and then divide by the number of salespeople. The total number of cars sold was $75 + 90 + 50 + 65$, which equals 280. (If you chose choice **a**, you added correctly but forgot to divide the sum by 4, the number of salespeople.) Now divide 280 by 4 to get 70, the correct answer.

18. c. The range of a data set is the difference between the greatest and least values in the set. The greatest value in this set is 90 and the least value is 50, so the range of the data is $90 - 50$, which equals 40.

19. b. The x-axis is the horizontal axis of a graph.

20. d. To add and subtract fractions, first rewrite the fractions over a common denominator. The parentheses in the problem tell you that you must first add $\frac{1}{3}$ and $\frac{1}{4}$, so rewrite them over the common denominator 12 to get $\frac{4}{12} + \frac{3}{12}$, which equals $\frac{7}{12}$. Next, rewrite $\frac{7}{8}$ and $\frac{7}{12}$ over the common denominator 24 to get $\frac{21}{24} - \frac{14}{24} = \frac{7}{24}$.

21. c. One way to find the decimal equivalent of a percent is to rewrite the percent as a fraction: 4% equals $\frac{4}{100}$. Now, write $\frac{4}{100}$ as a decimal. If seeing the fraction "four hundredths" isn't enough to help you write the correct decimal, simply divide the numerator by the denominator to get the correct answer, 0.04.

22. d. To divide fractions, multiply the dividend (the first fraction in the equation) by the reciprocal of the divisor (the second fraction in the equation). Thus, $\frac{5}{7} \div 10$ should be rewritten as $\frac{5}{7} \times \frac{1}{10}$, which equals $\frac{5}{70}$. Divide both numerator and denominator by 5 to reduce $\frac{5}{70}$ to $\frac{1}{14}$.

23. a. To solve this problem, deduce a fraction from the ratio provided. The ratio of men to women at the school is 5:4, which means that 5 out of every 9, or $\frac{5}{9}$, of all students are men.

Next, calculate $\frac{5}{9}$ of 7,650 by multiplying to get 4,250.

24. c. You can solve this problem algebraically by setting Marisol's original salary equal to x. After receiving a 10% raise, Marisol's salary will be $1.1x$. Set $1.1x$ equal to $55,000 and divide both sides by 1.1 to determine that x equals $50,000. Another way to solve this problem is to look at the choices and work backward. Which choice, when increased by 10%, would result in a salary of $55,000? 10% of $50,000 is $5,000, so someone with a $50,000 salary who receives a 10% raise would earn a new salary of $55,000.

25. d. Fractions can only be added together if they have a common denominator, so rewrite $\frac{1}{8}$ and $\frac{5}{6}$ over the common denominator 24; $\frac{1}{8} \times \frac{3}{3} = \frac{3}{24}$ and $\frac{5}{6} \times \frac{4}{4} = \frac{20}{24}$, so $\frac{1}{8} + \frac{5}{6}$ equals $\frac{3}{24} + \frac{20}{24}$; $20 + \frac{3}{24} = \frac{23}{24}$, the correct answer to this problem.

26. b. The legend of a circle graph shows which sections represents which set of data.

27. a. Add the sections of the pie that represent housing and education. Wendy spends 30% of her budget on housing and 20% on education; therefore, she spends 50%, or half, her monthly budget on housing and education. Because housing is Wendy's biggest single expense, choice **b** is incorrect. Because entertainment spending could be included in the "other" category, choice **c** is not necessarily true. The graph includes no information about what Wendy would do if she had more money, so choice **d** cannot be correct.

28. c. Wendy spends 20% of her budget on education, so if her total monthly budget is $3,000, then her education spending is 20% of $3,000. Calculate 20% of $3,000 by translat-

ing the question into the equation $\frac{20}{100} \times 3{,}000$ and solving to get $600.

29. c. To solve rate problems, apply the equation $rt = d$, where r equals rate, t equals time, and d equals distance. This question provides the rate (18 miles per hour) and the distance (63 miles), so you can write the equation $18t = 63$. To solve, divide both sides of the equation by 18 to get $t = 3\frac{1}{2}$. Remember that there are 60 minutes in an hour; therefore, $\frac{1}{2}$ an hour equals 30 minutes; 3 hours 30 minutes is the correct answer.

30. a. Use the percent equation translation technique to write an equation for this question. The problem states that a warbler weighs 9 grams and eats an amount equal to 80% of its body weight. This means that the warbler eats $\frac{80}{100} \times 9$, which equals $\frac{720}{100}$. In decimal form, $\frac{720}{100}$ equals 7.2.

31. d. To add mixed numbers with uncommon denominators, first convert all mixed numbers to improper fractions. Convert $2\frac{1}{2}$ to $\frac{5}{2}$, $2\frac{3}{4}$ to $\frac{11}{4}$, and $2\frac{1}{3}$ to $\frac{7}{3}$. Next, find a common denominator. 12 is a good common denominator, because it is divisible by 2, 3, and 4, the three denominators in this question; $\frac{5}{2} \times \frac{6}{6} = \frac{30}{12}$, $\frac{11}{4} \times \frac{3}{3} = \frac{33}{12}$, and $\frac{7}{3} \times \frac{4}{4} = \frac{28}{12}$. Now, add $\frac{30}{12}$, $\frac{33}{12}$, and $\frac{28}{12}$ to get $\frac{91}{12}$. Convert to a mixed fraction by dividing 91 by 12 to get 7 with a remainder of 7; $7\frac{7}{12}$ hours is the correct answer.

32. a. To multiply mixed numbers, first rewrite them as improper fractions; $8\frac{1}{2}$ should be rewritten as $\frac{17}{2}$, and $3\frac{1}{4}$ should be rewritten as $\frac{13}{4}$. Next, multiply numerator by numerator and denominator by denominator; $\frac{17 \times 13}{2 \times 4} = \frac{221}{8}$. Next, rewrite the product as a mixed number by dividing the numerator by the denominator. The result is 27 with a remainder of 5, so $27\frac{5}{8}$.

33. c. To divide fractions, multiply the dividend (the first fraction in the equation) by the reciprocal of the divisor (the second fraction in the equation). Thus, $21 \div \frac{1}{2}$ should be rewritten $21 \times \frac{2}{1}$, or 21×2, which equals 42. If you chose choice **a**, you subtracted instead of dividing. If you chose choice **b**, you divided 21 by 2 rather than by $\frac{1}{2}$.

34. c. 20% of 140 equals 28.

35. b. To solve rate problems, apply the equation $rt = d$, where r equals rate, t equals time, and d equals distance. This question provides the time (2 hours 15 minutes) and the rate (8 kilometers per hour). Before plugging these numbers into the equation, rewrite the time as a mixed number. 2 hours 15 minutes equals $2\frac{1}{4}$ hours, so use the mixed number $2\frac{1}{4}$; $8 \times 2\frac{1}{4} = d$; $8 \times 2\frac{1}{4}$ equals $8 \times \frac{9}{4}$, which equals $\frac{72}{4}$, which reduces to 18.

36. b. To find David's average score for all tests, add the scores and divide by 5, the number of tests David has taken. The sum of David's scores is 410; $410 \div 5$ equals 82.

37. c. David's grades, in chronological order, were 74, 73, 82, 86, and 95. His first two grades were nearly identical, and each subsequent grade was better than the one before. Thus, the data supports the conclusion that David's grades tended to improve over time.

38. b. Reduce fractions by dividing numerator and denominator by a common factor. 14 and 35 are both divisible by 7, so $\frac{14}{35}$ can be reduced to $\frac{2}{5}$.

39. a. According to the problem, last month 42 out of 840 crimes involved petty theft. You can convert this proportion to a percent using the equation $\frac{42}{840} = \frac{x}{100}$. Cross multiply to get

$4{,}200 = 840x$, and then divide both sides of the equation by 840 to get $x = 5$. The correct answer is 5%.

40. d. This question asks you to rewrite the mixed number $4\frac{1}{4}$ as an improper fraction. To do this, multiply the whole number 4 by the denominator 4 to get the product 16. Add 16 to the numerator 1 to get 17. The result is $\frac{17}{4}$.

Section 2: Written Communication

41. d. Paragraph 3 of the passage explains how the Supreme Court ruling in *Griswold v. Connecticut* established a Constitutional basis for the right to privacy.

42. c. Reread the sentence, substituting each choice for the word *implicit*. In context, *understood* makes the most sense. Yes, the Supreme Court ruling was *controversial* (choice **a**), but the passage discusses the controversy in paragraph 4, not in paragraph 3 where the word *implicit* appears. The word *nominal* (choice **d**) means "in name only." Because Americans' right to privacy is real, it is not *nominal*.

43. a. In paragraph 4, the author states that "Because privacy rights play a critical role in such hot-button political topics as abortion rights and homosexual rights, the controversy remains a prominent one." This statement supports the inference drawn in choice **a**. The author points out that some justices disagreed with the ruling but never states or suggests his own opinion; therefore, choice **b** is incorrect. Similarly, the author is silent on the issues central to choice **c**. He suggests that the current Supreme Court might weaken privacy rights, so choice **d** cannot be correct.

44. b. This passage discusses the basis for privacy rights in the Constitution; choice **b** best summarizes all the information in the passage.

Choice **a** refers to one detail in the passage; the answer to a main idea question, however, must address the entire passage, not just one detail in it. Choice **c** is never discussed or implied by the passage, so it cannot be correct. Choice **d** overstates the author's suggestion in paragraph 4 and, furthermore, refers only to a detail of the passage, not the main idea of the entire passage.

45. c. The passage discusses problems with the current system for funding public schools, offers a possible solution to the problems, and then explains why implementing the solution may be difficult. Choice **c** comes closest to summarizing the passage. Choices **a** and **d** attribute opinions to the author that are contradicted in the passage. Choice **b** refers to one detail in the passage; the choice to a main idea question, however, must address the entire passage, not just one detail in it.

46. b. The author argues that "One possible solution is to increase state income taxes while concurrently reducing local property taxes. Most citizens would feel little or no change in their current tax burden as a result." However, people who do not own property would not receive any benefit from the reduction in property taxes. Choice **a** is off topic, because the passage is concerned only with school funding, not funding for garbage collection, etc. Choice **c** offers an opinion that may or may not be valid; therefore, it does not substantially weaken the author's argument. Choice **d**, like choice **a**, is off topic, because the author's discussion of sales tax is tangential to her central argument.

47. a. Reread the sentence, substituting each choice for the word *germane*. Is the question *frightening*? Not really, so choice **b** cannot be cor-

rect. *Tantalizing* means *attractive*, which makes no sense in context; therefore, choice **c** is incorrect. *Inconsequential* means *unimportant*; the question is important, however, so choice **d** cannot be the correct answer.

48. d. The author suggests this throughout the passage, stating it clearly at the end of paragraph 1 and the beginning of paragraph 2: ". . . schools in wealthy areas are better funded than those in poorer areas. This situation raises the issue of fairness."

49. b. The passage is an information sheet about a particular food-borne illness. The main purpose of the passage is to warn readers about the dangers of contracting *Vibrio vulnificus* bacteria from oysters. Of the incorrect choices, choice **a** is too strongly worded; the passage suggests cooking all seafood but does not advise readers to avoid all seafood. No erroneous report is referenced in the passage, so choice **c** cannot be correct. Similarly, the life cycle of oysters is not discussed, so choice **d** cannot be correct.

50. c. In paragraph 2, the passage states: "The infection is much more dangerous to people with weakened immune systems, especially those who suffer from chronic liver disease."

51. a. Choice **a** is supported by the following statement from the passage: "Such individuals should avoid not only eating oysters, but also swimming in oyster-inhabited waters during the summer months, as infection can be transmitted in the water through open wounds." Choices **b**, **c**, and **d** are all contradicted by information in the passage.

52. d. Reread the sentence, substituting each choice for the word *subsequent*. In the context, only choice **d** makes sense.

53. a. The main purpose of the passage is to describe the "broken window" theory, which explains how disorder escalates if it is not checked early. Choices **b** and **d** refer to conditions in a firehouse; the example of the firehouse, however, is offered as a detail in support of the main idea. The answer to a main idea question must summarize the entire passage, not just one part of the passage. Choice **c** summarizes an idea presented in the final paragraph; however, this idea is not the main idea of the entire passage, so this cannot be the correct answer.

54. d. This is a tricky question because several of the choices are potentially challenging vocabulary words. *Condoned* (choice **a**) means *approved*, making it the opposite of *reproved*. *Ostracized* (choice **b**) means *to be outcast*, which like *reproved* has a negative connotation but is not the right word for the context; the passage suggests that the firefighter should be disciplined, not that he or she should be kicked off the fire department. For this reason, choice **c** is also incorrect.

55. b. Use process of elimination to get rid of answers that cannot be correct. The author discusses the merits of the broken window theory throughout the first two paragraphs of the passage; therefore, it is inaccurate to say that the author finds the theory "fatally flawed," so choice **a** cannot be correct. The author devotes paragraph 3 to situations in which the broken window theory causes as many problems as it addresses; therefore, choice **c** cannot be correct. Because the author describes the broken window theory as one "that can easily be applied to any situation in society," choice **d** cannot be correct.

56. a. The author makes this point most clearly at the beginning of paragraph 2: ". . . if disrespect to a superior is tolerated, others will be tempted to be disrespectful as well. A management crisis could erupt literally overnight."

57. c. The main purpose of the passage is to outline the procedure for adopting a pet. Because the passage warns that not all citizens make good pet owners, choice **a** cannot be correct. Choices **b** and **d** refer to details in the passage; neither of these details, though important, can be described as the main idea of the passage.

58. c. The passage states that adopted dogs and cats receive implantation of an identifying microchip if they are old enough. Therefore, it can be assumed that some animals are too young to be implanted with a microchip; thus, the passage supports the statement in choice **c**.

59. d. According to the passage, cats receive vaccination for panleukopenia. Dogs do not receive that vaccination.

60. b. This is a tricky question because several of the choices are potentially challenging vocabulary words. The word *imperative* (choice **a**) means *order* or *command*. Neither makes sense in the context of the sentence, so choice **a** cannot be correct. *Evasion* (choice **c**) means *the act of trying to avoid*. This also makes no sense in the context of the sentence. The word *ultimatum* (choice **d**) means *challenge*, which again does not fit the context of the sentence. An *inducement* is a type of *encouragement* (choice **b**).

61. b. The correct spelling is *formulates*.

62. a. The correct spelling is *coroner*.

63. b. The correct spelling is *surmount*.

64. b. The correct spelling is *monetary*.

65. c. The correct spelling is *contemptible*.

66. c. *Painful* is the word that is closest in meaning to *excruciating*.

67. c. *Overused* is the word that is closest in meaning to *trite*.

68. b. The word *monotonous* means *boring*, so the word most nearly its opposite is *interesting*.

69. a. A signing bonus would certainly provide strong motivation to accept a job offer. The word *inducement* means *motivation* or *encouragement*. Choice **b**, *affront*, means *insult*. Choice **c**, *impediment*, means *obstacle*. Neither fits the context of this sentence, and so neither can be the correct answer.

70. a. The word *liaison* means *meeting*; a *liaison* is usually held in secret. Choice **b**, *confection*, means *candy*. Choice **c**, *premonition*, means *hunch* or *suspicion*.

71. a. Choices **b** and **c** are not complete sentences because each is made up entirely of dependent clauses.

72. b. Choice **a** uses the passive voice when a better alternative written in the active voice—choice **b**—is available. Choice **c** uses the incorrect spelling of the word *principal* and also is redundant (because it uses the word *soon* twice when one use is all that the sentence requires).

73. b. Sentences **a** and **c** contain forms of the redundant construction *the reason . . . is because*.

74. b. Sentences **a** and **c** contain capitalization errors. In choice **a**, the words *Governor* and *Monday* should be capitalized. In choice **c**, the word *bill* should not be capitalized.

75. b. Choice **a** is incorrectly punctuated; there should be periods after *Mr.* and *Mrs.* Choice **c** incorrectly capitalizes the words *the meeting*.

76. a. Choice **b** contains an apples and oranges error, comparing *other pianists* to *the style of Thelonious Monk*. A properly formulated sentence must either compare one pianist to another or one pianist's style to another's style. Choice **c** is awkwardly and confusingly worded; choice **a** is a much better formulation of the same idea, so it is the better answer.

77. c. In choice **a**, the phrase *the president of the local Chamber of Commerce* is an appositive that should be set apart with commas. Choice **b** makes a similar error, failing to conclude the appositive phrase *the president of the local Chamber of Commerce* with a comma.

78. c. Choices **a** and **b** contain a subject-verb agreement error; the subject *use* requires a singular verb, not the plural verb *are*.

79. b. Choices **a** and **c** incorrectly use *I* where they should use *me*. Omit *Leticia* from the sentence to see why; would you say *Miguel has been assigned to work on the project with me* or *Miguel has been assigned to work on the project with I*? Because the sentence calls for an indirect object, the word *me* should be used, not *I*.

80. a. When you write a list of items, separate each item on the list with a comma, including the item preceding the word *and*. There should be no comma after the word *and*, as there is in the incorrect choice **c**.

Section 3: Civil Service Skills

81. b. The primary governing principle of customer service is to make things as easy and pleasant for the customer as possible. Choice **b** makes things easier for customers by offering them a variety of means by which to register their complaints. Choice **a** incorrectly suggests that it is good to offer services customers do not want. Choices **c** and **d** make it more difficult and inconvenient for customers to register complaints.

82. a. Once again, the focus of this exam is customer service, so choose the answer that indicates that customer service is the primary priority. Of the choices, only choice **a** focuses on customer satisfaction, so it is the best answer.

83. b. Inaccurate translation creates unnecessary problems and can, in certain circumstances, be even less desirable than no translation service at all (because inaccurate translation typically results in the transmission of incorrect information). Offering the greatest number of languages possible (choice **a**) would be extremely desirable in large diverse communities like New York City, but in most areas the availability of many languages is not that important; translating the most common foreign languages accurately would certainly be more important. Choice **c** would discourage non-English speakers from using government services. Choice **d** represents an important priority but not as important as the one presented in choice **b** because many forms have extremely limited applicability and because all forms, regardless of the language in which they are written, can be filled out with the assistance of an able and accurate translator.

84. d. Choices **a**, **b**, and **c** all provide information that will help the customer resume his or her query should he or she be disconnected during the transfer. Knowing the name of your supervisor will not help the customer continue his or her query, so it is the least important of the four.

85. d. The term *web chat* is used to describe live help provided via the Internet. Web chat is delivered via text in a chat window.

86. a. The only automobile visible in its entirety is a two-door sedan.

87. b. The skateboarder is wearing a jacket. He is hatless and is wearing long trousers. He is not wearing a cape.

88. c. Sylvia Martinez has dark shoulder-length hair. Janet Barnes is the only person whose hair is in an afro style (choice **a**).

89. a. Arthur Jones is the only person wearing a hat, the only one with a beard and moustache, and the only one wearing sunglasses. Sylvia Martinez and Janet Barnes also have dark hair.

90. b. Victor Dinapoli, Arthur Jones, and Maureen Cho all wear glasses. Carlos Domingo wears an eye patch but does not wear glasses.

91. b. The first four letters of the code must be the first four letters of the recipient's last name; therefore, the code for this entry should begin with the letters FONG. Choices **a** and **d** do not start with the letters FONG and, therefore, can be eliminated. The fifth letter in the code must be the recipient's first initial; therefore, the fifth letter of the code should be D. Only choice **b** has D as its fifth letter, so it must be the correct answer.

92. d. The first four letters of the code must be the first four letters of the recipient's last name; therefore, the code for this entry should begin with the letters RAMI. This information allows you to eliminate choices **a** and **b**. Study choices **c** and **d** to detect differences. You should see that choice **c** records the date of the correspondence JUN2, while choice **d** records the date JUN02. Check the rules to see that JUN02 is the proper format; the correct answer is choice **d**.

93. d. The code for this response should be: the first four letters of the recipient's last name (DAVI); the recipient's first initial (J); the first two digits of the recipient's street address (12); response (R); low priority (2); on October 23 (OCT23). The correct code is DAVIJ12R2OCT23.

94. c. This letter was sent to a recipient whose last name begins with the letters BERN; therefore, only choices **a** and **c** can be correct. Eliminate choices **b** and **d**. The first two digits of the recipient's address are 35; therefore, choice **a** cannot be correct. By process of elimination, the answer must be choice **c**.

95. a. The code states that two digits are to be used to indicate the recipient's street address; if the address is only one digit long, that digit should be preceded by a zero (0).

96. c. One incident of cold food stored at too high a temperature should be coded C. Two inci-dents of animal droppings should be coded HH. One incident of improperly labeled food should be coded p. The correct code for this set of violations is CHHp.

97. a. Three incidents of improper storage of toxic cleaning materials should be coded ppp. One incident of a misplaced consumer advisory should be coded r. The correct code for this set of violations is pppr.

98. a. All four of the incidents described earn a three-point deduction from 100, a perfect score: 4×3 equals 12; $100 - 12$ equals 88.

99. d. The inspector observed multiple incidents of the violation coded *s*. The letter *s* is the code for smoking in the food preparation area.

100. b. Each of the violations coded with a capital letter results in a five-point deduction; each of the violations coded with a lower-case letter results in a three-point deduction: 2×5 equals 10 and 3×3 equals 9; $10 + 9$ equals 19, and $100 - 19$ equals 81.

Civil Service Practice Exam 3

This is the last practice exam in this book, but it is not designed to be any harder than the other two. It is simply another representation of the kinds of questions you might expect to see on your civil service exam.

For this exam, pull together all the tips you've been practicing since the first practice exam. Give yourself the time and space to work. Because you won't be taking the real test in your living room, you might want to take this one in an unfamiliar location, such as a library. Make sure you have plenty of time to complete the exam in one sitting. In addition, use what you have learned from reading the answer explanations on the previous practice exams. Remember the types of questions that have caused problems for you in the past, and when you are unsure, try to consider how those answers were explained.

Once again, use the answer explanations at the end of the exam to understand questions you may have missed.

A version of this practice test is available through the LearningExpress online link if you prefer to take it on a computer. See the back of this book for complete details.

▶ Civil Service Practice Exam 3

1.	ⓐ	ⓑ	ⓒ	ⓓ	36.	ⓐ	ⓑ	ⓒ	ⓓ	71.	ⓐ	ⓑ	ⓒ	
2.	ⓐ	ⓑ	ⓒ	ⓓ	37.	ⓐ	ⓑ	ⓒ	ⓓ	72.	ⓐ	ⓑ	ⓒ	
3.	ⓐ	ⓑ	ⓒ	ⓓ	38.	ⓐ	ⓑ	ⓒ	ⓓ	73.	ⓐ	ⓑ	ⓒ	
4.	ⓐ	ⓑ	ⓒ	ⓓ	39.	ⓐ	ⓑ	ⓒ	ⓓ	74.	ⓐ	ⓑ	ⓒ	
5.	ⓐ	ⓑ	ⓒ	ⓓ	40.	ⓐ	ⓑ	ⓒ	ⓓ	75.	ⓐ	ⓑ	ⓒ	
6.	ⓐ	ⓑ	ⓒ	ⓓ	41.	ⓐ	ⓑ	ⓒ	ⓓ	76.	ⓐ	ⓑ	ⓒ	
7.	ⓐ	ⓑ	ⓒ	ⓓ	42.	ⓐ	ⓑ	ⓒ	ⓓ	77.	ⓐ	ⓑ	ⓒ	
8.	ⓐ	ⓑ	ⓒ	ⓓ	43.	ⓐ	ⓑ	ⓒ	ⓓ	78.	ⓐ	ⓑ	ⓒ	
9.	ⓐ	ⓑ	ⓒ	ⓓ	44.	ⓐ	ⓑ	ⓒ	ⓓ	79.	ⓐ	ⓑ	ⓒ	
10.	ⓐ	ⓑ	ⓒ	ⓓ	45.	ⓐ	ⓑ	ⓒ	ⓓ	80.	ⓐ	ⓑ	ⓒ	
11.	ⓐ	ⓑ	ⓒ	ⓓ	46.	ⓐ	ⓑ	ⓒ	ⓓ	81.	ⓐ	ⓑ	ⓒ	ⓓ
12.	ⓐ	ⓑ	ⓒ	ⓓ	47.	ⓐ	ⓑ	ⓒ	ⓓ	82.	ⓐ	ⓑ	ⓒ	ⓓ
13.	ⓐ	ⓑ	ⓒ	ⓓ	48.	ⓐ	ⓑ	ⓒ	ⓓ	83.	ⓐ	ⓑ	ⓒ	ⓓ
14.	ⓐ	ⓑ	ⓒ	ⓓ	49.	ⓐ	ⓑ	ⓒ	ⓓ	84.	ⓐ	ⓑ	ⓒ	ⓓ
15.	ⓐ	ⓑ	ⓒ	ⓓ	50.	ⓐ	ⓑ	ⓒ	ⓓ	85.	ⓐ	ⓑ	ⓒ	ⓓ
16.	ⓐ	ⓑ	ⓒ	ⓓ	51.	ⓐ	ⓑ	ⓒ	ⓓ	86.	ⓐ	ⓑ	ⓒ	ⓓ
17.	ⓐ	ⓑ	ⓒ	ⓓ	52.	ⓐ	ⓑ	ⓒ	ⓓ	87.	ⓐ	ⓑ	ⓒ	ⓓ
18.	ⓐ	ⓑ	ⓒ	ⓓ	53.	ⓐ	ⓑ	ⓒ	ⓓ	88.	ⓐ	ⓑ	ⓒ	ⓓ
19.	ⓐ	ⓑ	ⓒ	ⓓ	54.	ⓐ	ⓑ	ⓒ	ⓓ	89.	ⓐ	ⓑ	ⓒ	ⓓ
20.	ⓐ	ⓑ	ⓒ	ⓓ	55.	ⓐ	ⓑ	ⓒ	ⓓ	90.	ⓐ	ⓑ	ⓒ	ⓓ
21.	ⓐ	ⓑ	ⓒ	ⓓ	56.	ⓐ	ⓑ	ⓒ	ⓓ	91.	ⓐ	ⓑ	ⓒ	ⓓ
22.	ⓐ	ⓑ	ⓒ	ⓓ	57.	ⓐ	ⓑ	ⓒ	ⓓ	92.	ⓐ	ⓑ	ⓒ	ⓓ
23.	ⓐ	ⓑ	ⓒ	ⓓ	58.	ⓐ	ⓑ	ⓒ	ⓓ	93.	ⓐ	ⓑ	ⓒ	ⓓ
24.	ⓐ	ⓑ	ⓒ	ⓓ	59.	ⓐ	ⓑ	ⓒ	ⓓ	94.	ⓐ	ⓑ	ⓒ	ⓓ
25.	ⓐ	ⓑ	ⓒ	ⓓ	60.	ⓐ	ⓑ	ⓒ	ⓓ	95.	ⓐ	ⓑ	ⓒ	ⓓ
26.	ⓐ	ⓑ	ⓒ	ⓓ	61.	ⓐ	ⓑ	ⓒ		96.	ⓐ	ⓑ	ⓒ	ⓓ
27.	ⓐ	ⓑ	ⓒ	ⓓ	62.	ⓐ	ⓑ	ⓒ		97.	ⓐ	ⓑ	ⓒ	ⓓ
28.	ⓐ	ⓑ	ⓒ	ⓓ	63.	ⓐ	ⓑ	ⓒ		98.	ⓐ	ⓑ	ⓒ	ⓓ
29.	ⓐ	ⓑ	ⓒ	ⓓ	64.	ⓐ	ⓑ	ⓒ		99.	ⓐ	ⓑ	ⓒ	ⓓ
30.	ⓐ	ⓑ	ⓒ	ⓓ	65.	ⓐ	ⓑ	ⓒ		100.	ⓐ	ⓑ	ⓒ	ⓓ
31.	ⓐ	ⓑ	ⓒ	ⓓ	66.	ⓐ	ⓑ	ⓒ						
32.	ⓐ	ⓑ	ⓒ	ⓓ	67.	ⓐ	ⓑ	ⓒ						
33.	ⓐ	ⓑ	ⓒ	ⓓ	68.	ⓐ	ⓑ	ⓒ						
34.	ⓐ	ⓑ	ⓒ	ⓓ	69.	ⓐ	ⓑ	ⓒ						
35.	ⓐ	ⓑ	ⓒ	ⓓ	70.	ⓐ	ⓑ	ⓒ						

▶ Section 1: Mathematics

Select the best answer for each question.

1. Patrolman Peterson drove $3\frac{1}{2}$ miles to the police station. Then he drove $4\frac{3}{4}$ miles to his first assignment. Next, he drove $3\frac{2}{3}$ miles back to the police station for a meeting. Finally, he drove $3\frac{1}{2}$ miles home. How many miles did Patrolman Peterson drive?

  a. $15\frac{5}{12}$

  b. $14\frac{5}{12}$

  c. $14\frac{1}{4}$

  d. $13\frac{11}{12}$

2. $\frac{28}{15} =$

  a. $1\frac{2}{3}$

  b. $1\frac{13}{15}$

  c. $2\frac{8}{15}$

  d. $28\frac{1}{15}$

3. $\frac{9}{10} - \frac{2}{5} =$

  a. $\frac{1}{2}$

  b. $\frac{7}{5}$

  c. $\frac{5}{7}$

  d. $1\frac{3}{10}$

4. A bus travels along a highway at a constant rate of 55 miles per hour. How far does the bus travel in 3 hours 24 minutes?

  a. 165 miles

  b. 178.2 miles

  c. 187 miles

  d. 192.5 miles

5. Reduce $\frac{18}{24}$ to lowest terms.

  a. $\frac{1}{24}$

  b. $\frac{2}{3}$

  c. $\frac{9}{12}$

  d. $\frac{3}{4}$

Study the following graph, and then use it to answer questions 6 to 8.

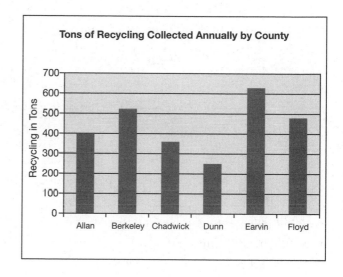

6. The data on the *x*-axis represents the

  a. amount of recycling collected, in tons.

  b. names of the counties.

  c. time period during which the data was collected.

  d. names of the companies hired to collect recycling.

7. The data on the *y*-axis represents the

  a. amount of recycling collected in tons.

  b. names of the counties.

  c. time period during which the data was collected.

  d. names of the companies hired to collect recycling.

8. The graph best supports which of the following conclusions?

    a. The population of Berkeley County is greater than the population of Floyd County.

    b. Of all the state's residents, the people of Berkeley County are most enthusiastic about recycling.

    c. Dunn County does not need to collect its recycling as frequently as does Earvin County.

    d. The people of Floyd County are more avid newspaper readers than are the people of Chadwick County.

9. Joanne must complete three tasks at work. She estimates that the first two tasks will each take her 45 minutes to complete and that the third task will take her 2 hours 10 minutes to complete. If Joanne's estimate is correct, how long will it take her to complete all three tasks?

    a. 2 hours 40 minutes

    b. 3 hours

    c. 3 hours 20 minutes

    d. 3 hours 40 minutes

10. $\frac{4}{5} \times 60 =$

    a. 8

    b. 45

    c. 48

    d. 85

11. $\frac{4}{5} + \frac{1}{6} =$

    a. $\frac{29}{30}$

    b. $\frac{5}{11}$

    c. $\frac{2}{15}$

    d. $\frac{5}{6}$

12. Reduce $\frac{33}{121}$ to lowest terms.

    a. $\frac{1}{4}$

    b. $\frac{3}{11}$

    c. $\frac{1}{3}$

    d. The fraction cannot be reduced.

13. Mary earns $1\frac{1}{2}$ times her standard hourly pay when she works overtime. If her hourly pay is $8.50, how much overtime pay does Mary earn when she works 6 hours of overtime?

    a. $12.75

    b. $51

    c. $72

    d. $76.50

14. $\frac{72}{10} =$

    a. $7\frac{1}{10}$

    b. $\frac{10}{72}$

    c. $\frac{5}{36}$

    d. $7\frac{1}{5}$

Study the following graph, and then use it to answer questions 15 to 17.

PRICE AND MILES PER GALLON BY MAKE OF AUTOMOBILE		
MAKE	RETAIL PRICE (STICKER)	MILES PER GALLON (CITY/HIGHWAY)
Voltero	$16,600	31/38
Accellator	$22,100	22/28
Montannic	$27,800	16/20
GXC 501	$31,500	27/32

15. Which conclusion is best supported by the data in the table?

    a. There is no correlation between the price of a car and its gas mileage.

    b. The more an automobile costs, the poorer its gas mileage.

    c. The chief factors in determining the price of an automobile are its size and weight.

    d. Most people pay considerably less than retail price for a new car.

16. What is the range of highway mileage shown in the table?

    a. 38

    b. 15

    c. 10

    d. 18

17. The average (arithmetic mean) retail price of the automobiles is

    a. $24,500

    b. $22,100

    c. $27,800

    d. $24,950

18. The star of a baseball team earns a salary of $8.5 million per year. A second-string player on the team earns a salary equal to 5% of the star's salary. What is the second-string player's salary?

    a. $50,000

    b. $425,000

    c. $850,000

    d. $8 million

19. $7\frac{1}{5} - 4\frac{4}{5} =$

    a. $2\frac{2}{5}$

    b. $3\frac{2}{5}$

    c. $1\frac{3}{5}$

    d. 0

20. Find the percent equivalent of 0.7.

    a. 7%

    b. 70%

    c. 0.7%

    d. 700%

21. Mr. Wallace is writing a budget request to upgrade his personal computer system. He wants to purchase 256 mb of SDRAM, which costs $80; two new software programs that cost $350 each; a 2 GB flash memory card for $65; and a new scanner for $165. What is the total amount Mr. Wallace should write on his budget request?

    a. $660

    b. $1,010

    c. $1,356

    d. $1,366

22. A migrating bird flies 12 hours per day. If the bird flies at an average speed of 20 miles per hour, how far does the bird fly in one day?

    a. 400 miles

    b. 240 miles

    c. 200 miles

    d. 32 miles

23. $\frac{2}{5} \div \frac{4}{7} =$

    a. $\frac{8}{35}$

    b. 1

    c. $\frac{1}{2}$

    d. $\frac{7}{10}$

24. A serving of potato chips contains 140 calories, 60% of which come from fat. How many calories of fat are in one serving of potato chips?

    a. 60

    b. 25

    c. 84

    d. 80

25. $2\frac{3}{8} =$
  a. $\frac{19}{3}$
  b. $\frac{19}{8}$
  c. $\frac{13}{8}$
  d. $\frac{5}{8}$

26. Find the fraction equivalent of 0.0034.
  a. $\frac{34}{100}$
  b. $\frac{34}{1,000}$
  c. $\frac{34}{10,000}$
  d. $\frac{34}{100,000}$

Study the following graph, and then use it to answer questions 27 to 28.

Causes of Household Fires in Percentages

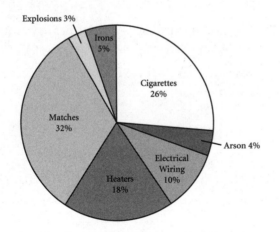

27. According to the circle graph, the most common cause of household fires is
  a. matches.
  b. cigarettes.
  c. heaters.
  d. arson.

28. The city of Grandee had 500 household fires last year. Based on the information in the graph, how many of those fires were most likely caused by explosions?
  a. 3
  b. 5
  c. 15
  d. 30

29. A community service organization has a staff of 40 people. At any given time, six members of the staff are on duty. What percent of the staff is on duty at the organization?
  a. 6%
  b. 8%
  c. 12%
  d. 15%

30. Mr. Anderson plans to divide his estate among his three children as follows: his eldest daughter, Melissa, will receive 40% of the estate, and his two younger children, Richard and Arlene, will divide the remainder of the estate evenly. If Mr. Anderson's estate is worth $180,000, how much will Arlene receive when the estate is divided?
  a. $54,000
  b. $60,000
  c. $72,000
  d. $108,000

31. Bill leaves his house and walks directly toward Melissa's house at a rate of 110 yards per minute. Melissa leaves her house at the same time and walks directly toward Bill's house at a rate of 95 yards per minute. Bill and Melissa's houses are exactly 2,870 yards apart. In how many minutes will Bill and Melissa meet?

   a. 11 minutes

   b. 14 minutes

   c. 26 minutes

   d. 30 minutes

32. Forty percent of Raleigh's postal service employees are women. If 160 women work for the Raleigh postal service, how many men work for the Raleigh postal service?

   a. 120

   b. 180

   c. 200

   d. 240

33. $\frac{7}{9} + \left(\frac{2}{3} - \frac{1}{6}\right) =$

   a. $1\frac{1}{9}$

   b. $1\frac{5}{18}$

   c. $\frac{5}{18}$

   d. $2\frac{13}{54}$

34. $5\frac{1}{3} \div 1\frac{5}{9} =$

   a. $3\frac{3}{7}$

   b. $3\frac{7}{9}$

   c. $6\frac{8}{9}$

   d. $4\frac{289}{42}$

35. An empty swimming pool is filled by two inlet pipes. One pipe can fill $\frac{1}{10}$ of the swimming pool in one hour. The other can fill $\frac{1}{8}$ of the swimming pool in one hour. If both inlet pipes are used to fill the pool, how many hours will it take to fill the empty pool?

   a. 8 hours

   b. 6 hours

   c. 4 hours 6 minutes

   d. 2 hours 45 minutes

36. By weight, a granola bar is 5% dietary fiber. If the weight of the dietary fiber in the granola bar is 1.5 grams, what is the weight of the granola bar?

   a. 7.5 grams

   b. 150 grams

   c. 6.5 grams

   d. 30 grams

37. $6\frac{1}{3} \times 75 =$

   a. 450

   b. $71\frac{1}{5}$

   c. 465

   d. $522\frac{3}{5}$

Study the following graph, and then use it to answer questions 38 to 40.

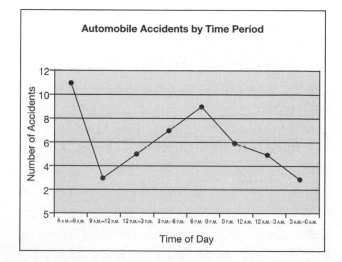

Automobile Accidents by Time Period

38. What is the range of the data shown in the graph?

a. 3

b. 8

c. 11

d. 14

39. The average (arithmetic mean) number of accidents per three-hour time period is

a. between 3 and 4.

b. between 4 and 5.

c. between 5 and 6.

d. between 6 and 7.

40. The number of accidents per time period is represented by the

a. scale.

b. x-axis.

c. y-axis.

d. legend.

▶ Section 2: Written Communication

Reading Comprehensions— Questions 41 to 60

Read the following passage. Then, answer questions 41 to 44.

Federal, state, and local courts produce a mountain of documents every day. Those documents need to be recorded and stored accurately in order for the various legal systems to function. The person who maintains these records is called the clerk of the court.

The parameters of the clerk of the court's job is defined by statute and so varies somewhat from <u>jurisdiction</u> to jurisdiction, but most clerks share a number of responsibilities in common. First and foremost, the clerk maintains the court's clerical records. Everything from the court's seal to the contracts and the orders it approves, to the judgments it issues to the verdicts it hands down must be accurately recorded and filed. The clerk also maintains official records of all marriages, leases, mortgages, deeds, and other property transfers.

Most localities assign additional responsibilities to the clerk of the court. In many jurisdictions, the clerk is empowered to perform marriages; the clerk of the court in St. Mary's County, Maryland, for example, conducts more than 3,000 marriages per year. Many clerks are responsible for issuing passports and jury summons, distributing jurors' pay, and overseeing the collection and distribution of court fines and court-ordered child support and alimony. As if those jobs weren't enough to keep a clerk busy, in some jurisdictions the clerk is also the chief financial officer of the court, responsible for making sure that budgets are met, that paychecks are issued, and that court expenditures all conform with the law.

With such a formidable list of tasks, it's no wonder that most clerks' offices are busy places. The operation of the clerk's duties requires a well-trained, dedicated, and efficient staff. Organizational skill is obviously required of anyone working for the clerk, but people skills are also important; the clerk's office deals with the public on a regular basis, often under stressful circumstances. Although demanding, work in a clerk's office brings with it the satisfaction of knowing that one has performed an essential role in allowing our court system to function properly.

41. The author's primary purpose in writing this passage is to

a. argue that most clerks of the court deserve salary increases.

b. inform people of the number of marriages performed annually in the United States.

c. describe the many functions of the clerk of the court.

d. define the term *clerical records*.

42. The final paragraph of the passage suggests that
   a. very few people are qualified to work in the clerk of the court's office.
   b. the clerk of the court's office is a satisfying place to work.
   c. all one needs to succeed in the clerk of the court's office is good people skills.
   d. the court's seal is an extremely important document.

43. As used in the passage, the word *jurisdiction* most nearly means
   a. domain.
   b. nation.
   c. individual.
   d. political party.

44. According to the passage, the clerk of courts
   a. decides verdicts in criminal cases.
   b. determines alimony levels in divorce cases.
   c. exists only in the state of Maryland.
   d. maintains the court's records.

Read the following passage. Then, answer questions 45 to 48.

State and local governments are almost always under-funded, a situation that compels them to constantly seek new ways to cut costs. Of course, the same governments are run by elected officials who, as a consequence of the conditions of their employment, must concern themselves with their constituents' satisfaction with government services. Thus, government leaders face a near-impossible challenge: reduce costs while improving—or at least, not diminishing—the quality of service.

In recent years, governments have increasingly turned to outsourcing as a solution to their problems. Working on the belief that the private sector operates more efficiently than does the government, state and local governments have started contracting private companies to perform jobs previously managed publicly. The results have been mixed.

One of the great success stories of government outsourcing is found in New York City. The city owns 13 public golf courses, which, under city management, fell into disrepair. The courses were not only poorly kept, they were dangerous; one course in the Bronx became a notorious dumping ground for garbage and the occasional corpse. Making matters worse, the city lost an average of $2 million per year on the golf courses. Since contracting out operations, the city has reversed that $2 million loss, instead realizing an annual profit of $2 million; best of all, they've done it without significantly increasing course income. Furthermore, conditions on the courses have greatly improved, as the private operators have invested substantially in material upgrades.

Texas has not been quite as fortunate, however, in its effort to privatize management of welfare benefits. With its caseload increasing and federal funding shrinking, the state naturally looked for a way to reduce costs. Privatization seemed the best choice: Contract bids suggested that the states could save hundreds of millions of dollars by shifting benefits administration services to a private company. The relationship started promisingly: The company replaced the state's <u>antiquated</u> computer program with a modern database, and then opened four new call centers to handle client queries. Unfortunately, the quality of service was initially poor, with many clients complaining that the call centers were difficult to reach and that the information they provided was often inaccurate. As a result, clients quickly grew to distrust the new system. The state and its contractor are now attempting to address the problems; it is too early to know whether they will succeed.

Outsourcing offers some benefits to governments eying the bottom line. It is by no means a guaranteed panacea, however, and public officials must consider each situation closely before deciding whether outsourcing is an appropriate solution.

45. The author's main idea is best summarized by which of the following?
  a. The municipal golf courses of New York have both grown more profitable and improved in quality since their management was outsourced.
  b. The state of Texas may never be able to undo the damage caused by its experiment in outsourcing social services.
  c. State and local governments always save money and improve services when they outsource.
  d. Outsourcing of government services can be successful, but by no means is it guaranteed to solve more problems than it causes.

46. As used in the passage, the word *antiquated* most nearly means
  a. outdated.
  b. broken.
  c. slow.
  d. uncertain.

47. According to the passage, clients of Texas's outsourced social service programs complained that
  a. call center operators did not speak Spanish.
  b. benefits checks were slow in arriving.
  c. clients were often given incorrect information.
  d. user fees discouraged them from taking advantage of the programs.

48. The passage suggests that the contractors who took control of New York City's golf courses
  a. had little previous experience in golf course management.
  b. used course income more efficiently than did the city.
  c. charged golfers much higher user fees than did the city.
  d. were difficult to reach by telephone.

Read the following passage. Then, answer questions 49 to 52.

The state Department of Transportation, Division of Highways seeks an experienced archaeologist for full-time employment. The chief responsibility of the archaeologist is to assess the impact that proposed highway projects will have on existing and potential archaeological sites. The archaeologist must be familiar with state and federal historic preservation laws and have the ability to assist the department in complying with those laws.

This position requires substantial knowledge of the prehistory, history, and archaeology of the state, including a familiarity with the various Native American tribes that have inhabited the region in the past. A working knowledge of the state's extensive research facilities in these areas is also <u>mandatory</u>. The candidate is expected to be well versed in modern archaeological techniques and practices. An artifact-recognition test will be administered to all candidates. This test requires not only recognition of various local artifacts, but also a description of each artifact's regional and cultural context.

Applicants must have at least a four-year undergraduate degree with a major in archaeology, anthropology, or a related field. Preference will be given to candidates with a master's degree. Extensive related field experience will also enhance the application of any candidate regardless of his or her highest academic degree.

This is a full-time position offering a salary range between $33,000 and $48,000 per year. Candidates should be aware that this job requires much work in the field and may be considered physically demanding by some. This job also requires someone comfortable working around heavy equipment; the archaeologist will be required to supervise crews that include heavy-machine operators and other laborers.

All applicants must apply via the state employment website. Only unopened official academic transcripts sent by the issuing institution will be considered. Applicant must be available for an in-person interview in the state capital during the final week of August.

49. As used in the passage, the word *mandatory* most nearly means
   a. preferred.
   b. admired.
   c. essential.
   d. tolerable.

50. Which of the following best summarizes the main idea of the passage?
   a. Some of the state's proposed highway routes pass through Native American burial grounds.
   b. The artifact recognition test required of all applicants is too difficult.
   c. Interviews for the archaeologist position must be conducted in person.
   d. There is a position available with the state Department of Transportation.

51. It can be inferred from the passage that which of the following applicants would have the best chance of being hired by the state Department of Transportation?
   a. an individual with a master's degree in anthropology and eight years of experience in the field
   b. a high school archaeology teacher with a bachelor's degree in English
   c. a Native American highway worker with a high-school diploma
   d. a person who recently graduated from college with a degree in archaeology

52. Applicants for the job described in the passage should be physically fit because
   a. the state requires all its employees to be physically fit.
   b. the job requires the holder to teach physical education classes.
   c. the state will not insure employees whose health is poor.
   d. the job requires physically challenging work on outdoor sites.

Read the following passage. Then, answer questions 53 to 56.

Did you ever wonder how the U.S. Postal Service chooses the images that appear on postage stamps? Nearly all the subjects of stamps originate with a suggestion from the public. The Citizens' Stamp Advisory Committee (CSAC), a 15-member board appointed by the Postmaster General, is charged with reviewing suggestions and selecting approximately 25 commemorative stamps each year.

Upon receiving a suggestion, the CSAC first determines whether the stamp meets the 12 major criteria for selection. Among the qualifying characteristics: The subject must be American or related to America; the subject must be of national, rather than regional or local, interest; if human, the subject must been deceased for at least ten years (except for former presidents, who can be honored immediately after their deaths); and, if commemorating an historic event, the stamp must be released on an anniversary that is a multiple of 50. Prohibited subjects include individual towns, cities, elementary and secondary schools, hospitals, and libraries; fraternal, political, sectarian, and service organizations; and religious groups.

If a nominee meets all the qualifications, it is added to the roster for consideration at the upcoming meeting of the CSAC, which meets four times each year. The committee may decide to reject the nominee, or it may set it aside for consideration of future issuance. All stamps in the latter category must undergo a second round of review before they can be scheduled for design and their subsequent release.

If you've submitted a suggestion to the CSAC, don't expect to be notified of the committee's decision; the committee has no staff, and announcements of upcoming stamp subjects are made by press release only. In other words, if you want to see whether your stamp has been chosen, you'll have to read the newspaper or check the U.S. Postal Service website. You should also be aware that the entire selection process typically takes three years. If you're the impatient type, suggesting subjects for stamps is probably not the right hobby for you!

53. As used in the passage, the word *commemorative* most nearly means
   a. funereal.
   b. mnemonic.
   c. celebratory.
   d. exclusive.

54. The author's purpose in writing this passage is to
   a. explain a process.
   b. define terms.
   c. persuade an audience.
   d. propose a new idea.

55. According to the passage, the Citizens' Stamp Advisory Committee
   a. determines the rules for selecting stamps.
   b. meets four times each year.
   c. is made up of former Postmaster Generals of the United States.
   d. contacts everyone who suggests a subject for a stamp.

56. Based on information in the passage, which of the following is the subject most likely to be honored with a U.S. postage stamp?
   a. the city of Chicago
   b. the current president of the United States
   c. the Republican Party
   d. Yellowstone National Park

Read the following passage. Then, answer questions 57 to 60.

Hazelwood County is home to more than 1,000 food service establishments operating under county permits. Each of these establishments offers the opportunity to enjoy a delicious meal away from home. Each, however, is also the source of a potential public-health outbreak. That is why the Hazelwood County government maintains a <u>rigorous</u> inspection regimen, visiting the majority of these establishments twice annually to conduct surprise examinations of their facilities.

Hazelwood County inspectors make a thorough investigation of kitchen and food storage areas, monitoring food handling procedures to ensure that raw food is kept at the proper temperature and that employees follow hygienic standards. Inspectors also examine all equipment to ascertain that it is operating in a safe and sanitary manner. Tap water temperatures are measured to determine whether they are hot enough to sterilize dining ware and cookware adequately during washing.

When a problem is detected, the inspector immediately issues a violation ticket and instructs establishment staff in the proper procedure or method for avoiding future violations. At the end of the inspection, the inspector assigns the establishment a sanitation grade between 60 and 100 and a letter grade between A and F. Any restaurant receiving a grade below B must close immediately and may not reopen until a subsequent inspection certifies it at least the B-grade level. All food service establishments must at all times display their current sanitation grade in a place clearly visible to patrons.

Violations of the health code are divided into two categories. *Minor infractions* are those that reflect substandard maintenance and sanitation but are unlikely to make diners ill. Minor infractions include poor labeling of food, poor storage of cooking and dining utensils, and poor kitchen ventilation. *Major infractions* are those that are more likely to result in food-borne illness. These include foods cooked to insufficiently high internal temperatures, raw foods stored at too high a temperature, and poor hygiene among kitchen and service staff.

In addition to conducting inspections, the health department conducts regular on-site educational sessions for the benefit of food-service employees. Hazelwood County works hard to enforce its food-service sanitation laws to protect the safety of their citizens and guests.

57. According to the passage, Hazelwood County inspectors check a restaurant's tap water to make sure that
   a. it is hot enough to sterilize eating utensils.
   b. it is not so hot that it will burn patrons' hands during washing.
   c. it is suitable for drinking.
   d. water pressure is sufficient to provide continuous running water.

58. Which of the following best summarizes the main idea of the passage?
   a. Hazelwood County is home to more than 1,000 food service establishments.
   b. The Hazelwood County government maintains a rigorous inspection regimen.
   c. Minor infractions are those that reflect substandard maintenance and sanitation but are unlikely to make diners ill.
   d. Any restaurant receiving a grade below B must close immediately.

59. As used in the passage, the word *rigorous* most nearly means
   a. unpredictable.
   b. haphazard.
   c. militaristic.
   d. thorough.

60. According to the passage, which of the following would most likely NOT be an acceptable location for displaying the restaurant's current sanitation grade?
   a. by the front door of the restaurant
   b. in the main dining room of the restaurant
   c. in the kitchen of the restaurant
   d. outside the restrooms of the restaurant

Spelling—Questions 61 to 65

Select the choice that is spelled correctly.

61. Would you prefer artificial sweetener or _____ sugar with your coffee?
  a. granalated
  b. granilated
  c. granulated

62. Davis could not hide his _____ at being caught shopping online when he was supposed to be working.
  a. embarrassment
  b. embarassment
  c. embarrissment

63. Which of the following words is spelled incorrectly?
  a. subside
  b. feesable
  c. impersonal

64. Which of the following words is spelled incorrectly?
  a. recktify
  b. narrate
  c. transcribe

65. Which of the following words is spelled incorrectly?
  a. atrocious
  b. infernal
  c. detearierating

Vocabulary—Questions 66 to 70

Select the best choice for each question.

66. Find the word that is closest in meaning to the underlined word below.
a <u>susceptible</u> asset
  a. vulnerable
  b. valuable
  c. insignificant

67. Find the word that is most nearly the opposite of the underlined word below.
an <u>inevitable</u> conclusion
  a. unexpected
  b. satisfying
  c. avoidable

68. Find the word that is most nearly the opposite of the underlined word below.
the <u>pompous</u> professor
  a. uneducated
  b. humble
  c. strict

69. Find the word that best completes the sentence below.
If you collect my mail while I am on vacation, I will _____ by mowing your lawn when I return.
  a. renege
  b. reciprocate
  c. rejuvenate

70. Find the word that best completes the sentence below.
The defendant's fingerprints on the murder weapon provided the most _____ evidence against her.
  a. incriminating
  b. exonerating
  c. dubious

Grammar—Questions 71 to 80

Select the best choice for each question.

71. Which of the following is a complete sentence?
   a. Because of the worsening weather conditions, the cancellation of tonight's event.
   b. The worsening of weather conditions has caused the cancellation of tonight's event.
   c. The cancellation of tonight's event on account of there being worsening weather conditions.

72. Select the sentence that is written most correctly.
   a. "Would you prefer sugar or artificial sweetener with your coffee?" Humphrey inquired.
   b. Would you prefer sugar or artificial sweetener with your coffee, Humphrey inquired?
   c. "Would you prefer sugar or artificial sweetener with your coffee?" Humphrey inquired?

73. Select the sentence that is written most correctly.
   a. Located along the railroad tracks, the noise of passing trains disrupted performances at the community theater.
   b. Located along the railroad tracks, the community theater had, by the noise of passing trains, its performances disrupted.
   c. Because it was located along the railroad tracks, the community theater had its performances disrupted by the noise of passing trains.

74. Select the sentence that is written most correctly.
   a. Mr. and Mrs. Harrison decided to have a picnic to celebrate Labor Day.
   b. Mr. and mrs. Harrison decided to have a picnic to celebrate Labor day.
   c. Mr. and Mrs. Harrison decided to have a Picnic to celebrate Labor day.

75. Select the sentence that is written most correctly.
   a. Each member of the Jameson family holds an advanced degree in either science or mathematics.
   b. Each member of the Jameson family hold an advanced degree in either science or mathematics.
   c. Each and every member of the Jameson family hold an advanced degree in either science or mathematics.

76. Select the sentence that is written most correctly.
   a. Call the boys' and girls' in from the playground, because its time for lunch.
   b. Call the boys and girls in from the playground, because it's time for lunch.
   c. Call the boys and girls in from the playground, because its time for lunch.

77. Select the sentence that is written most correctly.
   a. A decision was made by the manager and will be followed by her subordinates.
   b. A decision was made by the manager her subordinates will follow it.
   c. The manager made a decision and her subordinates will follow it.

78. Select the sentence that is written most correctly.
   a. The committee did their work very effectively.
   b. The committee did their work very effective.
   c. The committee did its work very effectively.

79. Select the sentence that is written most correctly.

   a. The athletes' integrity was called into question by the high incidence of positive drug tests among their top performers.

   b. The athlete's integrity was called into question by the high incidence of positive drug tests among their top performers.

   c. The athletes' integrity was called into question by the high incidence of positive drug test's among their top performer's.

80. Select the sentence that is written most correctly.

   a. The consensus of opinion among the advertisers was that customers would be enticed by a free gift.

   b. The consensus of opinion among the advertisers was that customers would be enticed by a gift.

   c. The consensus among the advertisers was that customers would be enticed by a gift.

▶ Section 3: Civil Service Skills

Customer Service— Questions 81 to 85

Select the best choice for each question.

81. Government offices strive to address customers' queries during a single visit or exchange whenever possible, a principle known as

   a. self-service communication.

   b. first contact resolution.

   c. interactive voice response.

   d. the abandonment rate.

82. Responses to citizen complaints should be

   a. processed twice annually to ensure uniformity of response.

   b. approved by a supervisor before they are delivered.

   c. delivered as quickly and accurately as possible.

   d. withheld until the citizen completes a customer satisfaction evaluation.

83. When scheduling an agency's office hours, a supervisor's primary consideration should be

   a. employees' personal commitments outside work.

   b. the schedules of other agencies with which the agency sometimes interacts.

   c. the time of year and its effect on electricity usage.

   d. the schedules of citizens who most often contact the agency.

84. Customers who request to speak to a supervisor should be

   a. allowed to do so in a timely manner whenever possible.

   b. informed that the help of a supervisor is not necessary to resolve their situation.

   c. prevented from distracting the supervisor from his or her duties.

   d. given an appointment at a later date to meet the supervisor.

85. Customers who contact an office by telephone and are put on hold more than one minute should

   a. not be informed of the projected wait time because inaccurate estimates anger customers.

   b. be informed of the projected wait time so they can make an informed decision about whether to wait.

   c. hear a recorded message encouraging them to resolve their matter via mail or in person.

   d. be offered a face-to-face appointment on the following day if their call is not handled within five minutes.

Memory—Questions 86 to 90

Take five minutes to study the following picture. Then, answer question 86 without looking back at the picture.

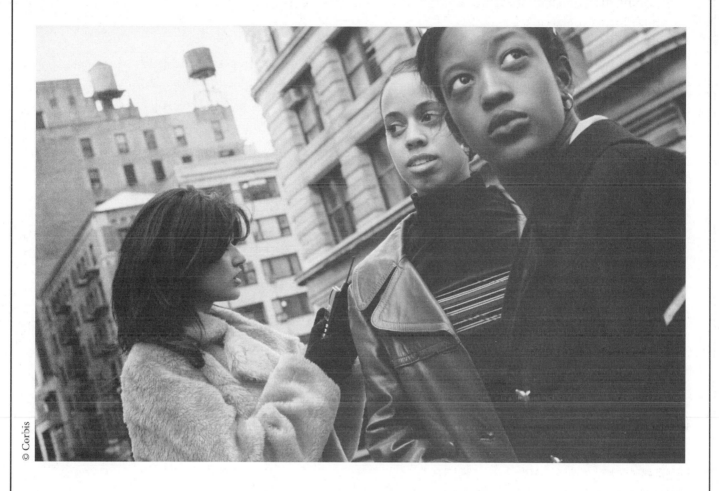

© Corbis

86. Who is holding a cellular telephone in the photograph?

   a. only the woman on the left

   b. only the woman in the middle

   c. only the woman on the right

   d. all three women

Take five minutes to study the following picture. Then answer questions 87 to 88 without looking back at the picture.

© Corbis

87. There are two women in the photograph. Which woman has hair long enough to cover her shoulder?
   a. only the woman on the left
   b. only the woman on the right
   c. both women
   d. neither woman

88. Which type of vehicle is visible in the photograph?
   a. a city bus
   b. a cable car
   c. a locomotive
   d. an airplane

Take five minutes to study the text that follows. Then, answer questions 89 through 90 without looking back at the text.

The following is the text of a notice posted in a government office. It instructs employees on the proper procedure for evacuating the office during a fire.

- Know the location of all stairwells, emergency exits, and fire extinguishers. Learn how to operate a fire extinguisher.
- If you see a fire, activate the nearest fire alarm. If you have a cell phone or are near a public telephone, call 911 to alert the fire department.
- If you do not have access to an alarm or a phone, inform other building occupants that they should vacate the building.
- If possible, assist others in evacuating the building.
- If the fire is small, use a fire extinguisher to extinguish the fire. Remember that you should never attempt to extinguish a fire when:

—you do not know what is fueling the fire (e.g., chemicals)
—you cannot keep a clear path between yourself and a fire exit
—the fire might block your path of escape
—the fire has spread to many locations
—the fire is spreading rapidly
—the fire is producing copious amounts of smoke

- Evacuate the building. If possible, close windows and doors if you are the last one to leave.
- Exit the building by stairwells. Do not use elevators.
- If you have not yet done so, notify the fire department. Report the location and nature of the fire.
- Do not reenter the building without the permission of the fire department.

89. According to the notice, people should not try to extinguish a fire on their own if they
   a. can detect the color blue in the burning flames.
   b. do not have the assistance of at least one other person.
   c. cannot maintain ready access to a fire exit.
   d. can contain the fire to a contained location.

90. According to the notice, why should people not use elevators during a fire?
   a. The fire might interrupt electrical service, rendering elevators inoperative.
   b. It is impossible to determine the fire conditions in an elevator shaft.
   c. An elevator is not always the quickest way to leave a building.
   d. The notice does not provide a reason people should not use elevators.

Coding—Questions 91 to 100

To answer questions 91 through 95, refer to the following scenario.

Each employee at a government office is assigned a unique identification code. The code is created according to the following rules:

4 digits = the first two digits represent an employee's last name; the second two digits represent the employee's first name. Digits are assigned accordingly:

0 = ABC
1 = DEF
2 = GHI
3 = JKL
4 = MNO
5 = PQR
6 = STU
7 = VWX
8 = YZ

1 letter = job grade. Jobs are graded 1 through 19; letters are assigned based on the numerical equivalent of the letter (i.e., A = 1, B = 2, C = 3, D = 4, etc.)

4 digits = month and date of birth (e.g., April 7 = 0407)

91. Marlene Romanoff is a grade 12 employee. Her birthday is December 24. What is her identification code?
 a. 4053AB2412
 b. 4053M2412
 c. 5440M1224
 d. 5440AB1224

92. Abdul Qoph is a grade 5 employee. His birthday is July 8. What is his identification code?
 a. 5400E0708
 b. 5400E78
 c. 0054E0708
 d. 0054E78

93. To whom might the identification code 6521R1115 belong?
 a. Barry Felton
 b. Spencer Henderson
 c. William Trieste
 d. Gerald Springer

94. Which of the following statements about the employee with identification code 0524D1102 must be true?
 a. The employee's birthday is May 24.
 b. The employee's birthday is November 2.
 c. The employee's last name begins with the letter D.
 d. The employee is a grade 8 employee.

95. Create an identification code for the following employee:
 Name: Rodriguez, Alexis
 Date of Birth: September 22
 Job Grade: 8
 a. 03540922H
 b. 03542209H
 c. 5403H0922
 d. 54032209H

To answer questions 96 through 100, refer to the following scenario.

A county animal control uses a code to log all complaints it receives. Each call receives a single code even if it includes multiple complaints. The code follows the rules below:

Subject of complaint

    C = cat
    D = dog
    H = horse
    R = reptile
    Z = none of the above

Nature of complaint (record all that apply)

    0 = noise
    1 = animal not properly restrained (e.g., no leash, not contained in enclosed area)
    2 = animal improperly fed, watered, or sheltered
    3 = animal not properly licensed
    4 = animal behaves menacingly toward human or other animal
    5 = abandoned animal
    6 = illegal animal breeding

The nature of complaint or complaints directly follows the code for the animal that is the subject of the complaint.

96. A citizen called animal control to complain that a neighbor's dog was barking and that the same neighbor owns a horse that is not properly fenced in. How should this complaint be coded?
   a. D0H1
   b. DH01
   c. 0DH1
   d. H10D

97. An animal control officer is flagged down by a citizen who directs the officer to a neighbor's house. There, the citizen points out that the neighbor owns a dog and a cat; he further notes that the dog is not receiving food or water and that neither the dog nor cat is properly licensed. How should this complaint be coded?
   a. DC23
   b. D3C23
   c. D23C3
   d. D2C3

98. Animal control receives a complaint of an abandoned horse that is not properly fed or watered. How should this complaint be coded?
   a. 25
   b. H5
   c. H2
   d. H25

99. The code Z5 could refer to
   a. a barking dog.
   b. an underfed horse.
   c. an abandoned pig.
   d. a menacing reptile.

100. An inspector discovers an illegal breeding facility at which the owner is breeding dogs, cats, horses, and ferrets. How should the inspector code this discovery?
   a. CDHZ6
   b. C6D6H6Z6
   c. CDHZ6666
   d. C6DHZ

► Civil Service Practice Exam 3 Answers

Section 1: Mathematics

1. a. To add mixed numbers with uncommon denominators, first convert all mixed numbers to improper fractions. First, convert $3\frac{1}{2}$ to $\frac{7}{2}$, $4\frac{3}{4}$ to $\frac{19}{4}$, $3\frac{2}{3}$ to $\frac{11}{3}$, and $3\frac{1}{2}$ to $\frac{7}{2}$. Next, rewrite $\frac{7}{2}$, $\frac{19}{4}$, $\frac{11}{3}$, and $\frac{7}{2}$ over a common denominator. Use 12 because it is evenly divisibly by 2, 3, and 4; $\frac{7}{2} \times \frac{6}{6} = \frac{42}{12}$, $\frac{19}{4} \times \frac{3}{3} = \frac{57}{12}$, $\frac{11}{3} \times \frac{4}{4} = \frac{44}{12}$, and $\frac{7}{2} \times \frac{6}{6} = \frac{42}{12}$. Now, add the fractions: $\frac{42 + 57 + 44 + 42}{12} = \frac{185}{12}$. Finally, divide 185 by 12 to produce the result, $15\frac{5}{12}$.

2. b. The question asks you to rewrite the improper fraction $\frac{28}{15}$ as a mixed number. To do this, divide the numerator 28 by the denominator 15. The result is $1\frac{13}{15}$.

3. a. To add and subtract fractions, first rewrite the fractions over a common denominator. Rewrite this problem as $\frac{9}{10} - \frac{4}{10}$, then subtract to get $\frac{5}{10}$, which reduces to $\frac{1}{2}$.

4. c. To solve rate problems, apply the equation $rt = d$, where r equals rate, t equals time, and d equals distance. This problem provides the rate (55 miles per hour) and the time (3 hours 24 minutes). Before plugging numbers into the formula, rewrite 3 hours 24 minutes as a decimal. $\frac{24}{60}$ equals $\frac{2}{5}$, so 3 hours 24 minutes equals $3\frac{2}{5}$ hours, which equals 3.4 hours. Now plug values into the formula: $55(3.4) = d$. Multiply 55 and 3.4 to get 187.

5. d. To reduce $\frac{18}{24}$ to lowest terms, divide both the numerator and denominator by 6. The result, $\frac{3}{4}$, is the correct answer. Choice **c** equals $\frac{18}{24}$, but it is not reduced to lowest terms because both 9 and 12 are divisible by 3.

6. b. The x-axis is the horizontal axis of a graph, which in this graph shows the names of the counties.

7. a. The y-axis is the vertical axis of a graph, which in this graph shows the amount of recycling collected.

8. c. According to the graph, Dunn County produces less than half as much recycling as does Earvin County. Therefore, the data in the graph supports the conclusion that Dunn County does not need to collect its recycling as frequently as does Earvin County. Choice **a** relies on faulty reasoning; just because Berkeley County produces more recycling than does Floyd County does not mean that the former has a larger population. It is possible that Berkeley residents simply produce more recycling per capita. Because the graph includes no information about citizens' attitudes toward recycling, choice **b** cannot be correct. Because the graph does not break out the different types of items that are recycled, it is impossible to draw any conclusions about the amount of newspaper recycled, and therefore, choice **d** cannot be correct.

9. d. Joanne takes 45 minutes to complete *each* of two tasks; therefore, the two tasks take a total of 90 minutes, or 1 hour 30 minutes to complete. The third task takes 2 hours 10 minutes, meaning all 30 tasks take a total of 3 hours 40 minutes to complete.

10. c. $\frac{4}{5} \times 60$ equals $\frac{4}{5} \times \frac{60}{1}$, which equals $\frac{240}{5}$. Divide 240 by 5 to get the answer, 48.

11. a. To add fractions, rewrite them over a common denominator. The least common multiple of 5 and 6 is 30, so rewrite each fraction over the denominator 30; $\frac{4}{5} \times \frac{6}{6} = \frac{24}{30}$; $\frac{1}{6} \times \frac{5}{5} = \frac{5}{30}$. $\frac{24 + 5}{30} = \frac{29}{30}$. If you selected choice **b**, you probably added numerator to numerator and denominator to denominator; you should review the rules for adding fractions.

12. b. Both 33 and 121 are divisible by 11. Divide each by 11 to reduce $\frac{33}{121}$ to $\frac{3}{11}$.

13. d. Mary's overtime pay is $1\frac{1}{2}$ times her regular pay of $8.50. Half of $8.50 is $4.25, so Mary's overtime pay is $8.50 + $4.25 per hour, or $12.75 per hour. Mary works 6 hours of overtime, so she earns $12.75 × 6, which equals $76.50, in overtime pay.

14. d. Divide 72 by 10 to get 7 remainder 2, or $7\frac{2}{10}$. Reduce $\frac{2}{10}$ to $\frac{1}{5}$ to reach the final choice of $7\frac{1}{5}$.

15. a. Study the relationship between cost and gas mileage shown in the table. The data show neither an increase nor a decrease in gas mileage of an automobile as its cost increases. Therefore, the data show no relationship between cost and gas mileage. Choice **b** is contradicted by the data, as explained previously. Choice **c** cannot be correct because the table provides no data on the size and weight of the different automobiles listed. Because no data on actual sale price is provided, choice **d** also cannot be correct.

16. d. The range of a data set is the difference between the greatest and least values in the set. The greatest value in this set is 38 and the least value is 20, so the range of the data is 38 − 20, which equals 18. Note that the question asks about highway mileage, so you must use only the second of the two numbers provided in the right-hand column of the table. Using the first number, which represents city mileage, produces an incorrect answer.

17. a. To find the mean price of the automobiles shown in the table, add all the prices together and divide by the number of automobiles shown. The sum of the four prices is $98,000. $98,000 divided by 4, the number of automo-

biles shown, is $24,500. So $24,500 is the average price.

18. b. To answer this question, you must calculate 5% of $8.5 million. One way to do this quickly and efficiently is to calculate 10% of $8.5 million by moving the decimal one place to the left. Thus, 10% of $8.5 million is $0.85 million; 5% is half of 10%, so 5% of $8.5 million is half of $0.85 million, which is $0.425 million, or $425,000.

19. a. To subtract mixed numbers, convert them to improper fractions. Rewrite $7\frac{1}{5}$ as $\frac{36}{5}$ and $4\frac{4}{5}$ as $\frac{24}{5}$. Now subtract: $\frac{36-24}{5} = \frac{12}{5}$, which equals $2\frac{2}{5}$.

20. b. The decimal 0.7 is equal to the fraction $\frac{7}{10}$, which can be rewritten as $\frac{70}{100}$. Because a percent is the numerator of a fraction with a denominator of 100, 0.7 equals 70%.

21. b. Mr. Wallace wants to spend $80 on SDRAM, $700 on software (two programs costing $350 each), $65 on flash memory, and $165 on a scanner; $80 + $700 + $65 + $165 equals $1,010. If you selected choice **a**, you probably forgot to double $350 to account for the fact that Mr. Wallace plans to buy two software programs that cost $350 each.

22. b. To solve rate problems, apply the equation $rt = d$, where r equals rate, t equals time, and d equals distance. The problem provides time (12 hours) and rate (20 miles per hour). Plug these values into the formula and solve; 12 × 20 = d, so $d = 240$.

23. d. To divide fractions, multiply the dividend (the first fraction in the equation) by the reciprocal of the divisor (the second fraction in the equation). Thus, $\frac{2}{5} \div \frac{4}{7}$ should be rewritten as $\frac{2}{5} \times \frac{7}{4}$, which equals $\frac{14}{20}$. Divide numerator and denominator by 2 to reduce $\frac{14}{20}$ to $\frac{7}{10}$.

24. c. The question requires you to find 60% of 140. There are many ways to solve this problem. One way is to multiply 140 by the decimal equivalent of 60%, which is 0.6; $140 \times 0.6 = 84$.

25. b. This question asks you to rewrite the mixed number $2\frac{3}{8}$ as an improper fraction. To do this, multiply the whole number 2 by the denominator 8 to get the product 16. Add 16 to the numerator 3. The correct answer is $\frac{19}{8}$.

26. c. To rewrite a decimal as a fraction, count the number of places in the decimal. The denominator of the fraction will be the digit 1 with as many zeros as the number of places you counted following it. In this case, the decimal 0.0034 has four places, so the denominator of the fraction will be a 1 and 4 zeros, i.e., 10,000. The numerator of the fraction is the decimal itself, less the decimal point and all consecutive zeros to the immediate right of the decimal point. Thus, the numerator of this fraction is 34, and the fraction is $\frac{34}{10,000}$.

27. a. The graph shows that 32% of household fires are caused by matches, more than any other single cause.

28. c. The question asks you to find 3% of 500; 3% of 100 is 3, so 3% of 500 is 5×3 (because 500 is 5×100). Thus, the answer to the question is 15.

29. d. The question asks you to determine what percentage of 40 is represented by 6. Use the translation technique to write an equation that asks "6 is what % of 40" as follows: $6 = \frac{x}{100} \times 40$. Next, divide both sides of the equation by 40 to get $\frac{6}{40} = \frac{x}{100}$. Now you can cross multiply to get $40x = 6,000$ and divide both sides by 40 to get $x = 15$.

30. a. Mr. Anderson plans to give 40% of his $180,000 estate to his daughter Melissa; 40% of $180,000 is $\frac{40}{100} \times \$180,000$, which equals

$72,000, leaving $108,000 to be divided evenly between Richard and Arlene. Thus, Arlene will receive half of $108,000, or $54,000, from Mr. Anderson's estate.

31. b. To solve rate problems, apply the equation $rt = d$, where r equals rate, t equals time, and d equals distance. This problem is a little tricky because it provides two rates, Bill's (110 yards per minute) and Melissa's (95 yards per minute). However, because Bill and Melissa are walking directly toward each other, they approach each other at a rate equal to the sum of their two rates. That is, for every minute they walk, Bill and Melissa get $100 + 95$, or 205, yards closer to each other. They approach each other at a rate of 205 yards per minute. Now, plug the rate and the distance (2,870 yards) into the formula and solve. $205t = 2,870$; to solve, divide both sides by 205. The result is 14.

32. d. The question tells you that 160 women work for the Raleigh postal service, constituting 40% of the workforce. This is enough information to formulate the question "160 is 40% of what," which can be written as the equation $160 = \frac{40}{100}x$. Now solve the equation by multiplying both sides by 100 to get $16,000 = 40x$. Divide both sides by 40 to get $400 = x$, the total number of employees. Because the question asks you how many men work for the postal service, you must subtract 160, the number of women working there, from 400, the total number of employees. $400 - 160$ equals 240, the correct answer.

33. b. To add and subtract fractions, first rewrite the fractions over a common denominator. The parentheses in the problem tell you that you must first subtract $\frac{1}{6}$ from $\frac{2}{3}$, so rewrite them over the common denominator 12 to get $\frac{8}{12} - \frac{2}{12}$, which equals $\frac{6}{12}$, which reduces to $\frac{1}{2}$. Next, rewrite $\frac{7}{9}$ and $\frac{1}{2}$ over the common denominator 18 to get $\frac{14}{18} + \frac{9}{18} = \frac{23}{18}$. Rewrite $\frac{23}{18}$ as a mixed number to get $1\frac{5}{18}$.

34. **a.** To divide mixed numbers, first rewrite the mixed numbers as fractions. Rewrite $5\frac{1}{3}$ as $\frac{16}{3}$ and $1\frac{5}{9}$ as $\frac{14}{9}$. Next, multiply the dividend (the first fraction in the equation) by the reciprocal of the divisor (the second fraction in the equation). Thus, $\frac{16}{3} \div \frac{14}{9}$ should be rewritten as $\frac{16}{3} \times \frac{9}{14}$, which equals $\frac{144}{42}$. Rewrite $\frac{144}{42}$ as $3\frac{18}{42}$, and then reduce $\frac{18}{42}$ to $\frac{3}{7}$ by dividing numerator and denominator by 6. The correct answer is $3\frac{3}{7}$.

35. **c.** When both pipes are used to fill the pool, they fill the pool at a rate of $\frac{1}{10} + \frac{1}{8}$ per hour; $\frac{1}{10} + \frac{1}{8}$ equals $\frac{4}{40} + \frac{5}{40}$, or $\frac{9}{40}$, per hour. That means that the pipes fill slightly less than one-quarter of the pool each hour; therefore, the job takes a little more than four hours to complete. Use process of elimination to determine that choice **c** is the only possible answer.

36. **d.** The problem tells us that 1.5 grams equals 5% of the weight of a granola bar. This is enough information to write the equation $1.5 = \frac{5}{100}x$, where x equals the weight of the granola bar. Multiply both sides of the equation by 100 to get $150 = 5x$, and then divide both sides of the equation by 5 to get $x = 30$. The granola bar weighs 30 grams.

37. **c.** First, rewrite $6\frac{1}{5}$ as an improper fraction by multiplying the whole number 6 by the denominator 5 and adding the product to the numerator 1 to get $\frac{31}{5}$. Next, multiply $\frac{31}{5}$ and $\frac{75}{1}$ to get $\frac{2,325}{5}$. Finally, divide 2,325 by 5 to get 465.

38. **b.** The range of a data set is the difference between the greatest and least values in the set. The greatest value in this set is 11 and the least value is 3, so the range of the data is $11 - 3$, which equals 8.

39. **d.** To find the mean number of accidents per time period, add the different data points, and then divide by the number of time periods shown. The data is 11, 3, 5, 7, 9, 6, 5, and 3. The sum of the data is 49. Divide 49 by 8, the number of time periods shown, to get $6\frac{1}{8}$. Thus, the mean number of accidents per time period is between 6 and 7.

40. **c.** The y-axis is the vertical scale of the graph.

Section 2: Written Communication

41. **c.** The purpose of this passage is to explain the clerk of the court's job. The passage is informational, not persuasive, so choice **a** cannot be correct. Choices **b** and **d** refer to details of one paragraph of the passage; the correct answer to a main idea question must describe the entire passage, not just one small part of it.

42. **b.** The final paragraph states, "Although demanding, work in a clerk's office brings with it the satisfaction of knowing that one has performed an essential role in allowing our court system to function properly." This sentence suggests that the clerk of the court's office is a satisfying place to work. Choice **a** draws too strong a conclusion; although working in the clerk of the court's office requires special skills, that does not mean that "very few people are qualified" to work there. Choice **c** is contradicted by the statement "Organizational skill is obviously required of anyone working for the clerk." The court's seal is not even mentioned in the final paragraph, so choice **d** cannot be correct.

43. **a.** *Domain* means "area under control of a particular government, court, etc." It is the best choice. The clerk of the court works for federal, state, or local courts whose jurisdiction is local or regional, not national; therefore, choice **b** cannot be correct. The clerk of the court functions in a system governed by the rule of law, not by an individual or a political party, so choices **c** and **d** cannot be correct.

44. d. In the second paragraph, the passages states, "First and foremost, the clerk maintains the court's clerical records."

45. d. Use process of elimination to find the answer to this question. Choices **a** and **b** refer to specific details of the passage. They do not summarize the entire passage and, therefore, cannot sum up the author's main idea. Choice **c** is contradicted by the example of Texas's outsourcing of welfare benefits, which the author tells us has *not* improved services.

46. a. This is a tricky question, because choices **b** and **c** make sense in context; the state's computer system may indeed have been *broken* or *slow*. However, the word *antiquated* means *old* or *obsolete*. The word shares a root with the word *antique*, which should have helped you figure out that the word *antiquated* has something to do with age.

47. c. The passage states, "Unfortunately, the quality of service was initially poor, with many clients complaining that the call centers were difficult to reach *and that the information they provided was often inaccurate*." This statement supports choice **c**. None of the other choices are supported by information in the passage.

48. b. The passage states, "Since contracting out operations, the city has reversed that $2 million loss, instead realizing an annual profit of $2 million; best of all, they've done it without significantly increasing course income." This statement supports the conclusion that the contractors who took control of New York

City's golf courses used course income more efficiently than did the city, because they have increased profits and improved services without increasing income.

49. c. The word *mandatory* means *required*; therefore, choice **c** is the best answer.

50. d. The passage describes an available position with the state Department of Transportation. Its purpose is to advertise the opening. Each of the incorrect choices refers to only one detail from one part of the passage. The correct answer to a main idea question must describe the entire passage, not just one small part of it.

51. a. Paragraph 3 of the passage provides the prerequisites for the job and explains which candidates will receive preferred treatment. Because preference is given to candidates with master's degrees and because "extensive related field experience will also enhance the application of any candidate," the individual described in choice **a** would be considered most qualified of the four applicants described in the choices.

52. d. The passage states this in paragraph 4: "Candidates should be aware that this job requires much work in the field and may be considered physically demanding by some."

53. c. *Commemorative* means *preserving or honoring the memory of*. Thus, *celebratory* is closest in meaning to *commemorative*. *Funereal* (choice **a**) means *sad* or *somber*; *mnemonic* means *promoting memory*; and *exclusive* means *available to a select group only*.

54. a. The passage explains the process by which subjects for U.S. stamps are selected.

55. b. In paragraph 3, the passage states that the committee meets four times each year. The passage does not say how the rules for selecting a stamp were established, so choice **a** cannot be correct. The committee is appointed by the Postmaster General, but the passage does not say whether it is made up of former Postmasters General, so choice **c** cannot be correct. Choice **d** is contradicted in the first sentence of the final paragraph.

56. d. The final sentence of paragraph 2 states, "Prohibited subjects include individual towns, cities, elementary and secondary schools, hospitals, and libraries; fraternal, political, sectarian, and service organizations; and religious groups." Chicago (choice **a**) is an individual city, so it cannot be honored in a stamp. Likewise, the Republican Party (choice **c**) is a political organization, and so it cannot be honored on a stamp. The passage also points out that stamps may not depict living human beings; therefore, choice **b** cannot be correct.

57. a. The passage states, "Tap water temperatures are measured to determine whether they are hot enough to sterilize dining ware and cookware adequately during washing." Choice **a** is a paraphrase of this statement.

58. b. Each of the incorrect answers refers to a single detail in one paragraph of the passage. Only choice **b** summarizes the entire passage. The correct answer to a main idea question must describe the entire passage, not just one small part of it.

59. d. Reread the sentence, substituting each choice for the word *implicit*. In context, *thorough* makes the most sense.

60. c. The passage states, "All food service establishments must at all times display their current sanitation grade in a place clearly visible to patrons." Choices **a**, **b**, and **d** describe locations that are clearly visible to patrons. Because

patrons are typically not allowed in restaurant kitchens, choice **c** is the best answer.

61. c. The correct spelling is *granulated*.

62. a. The correct spelling is *embarrassment*.

63. b. The correct spelling is *feasible*.

64. a. The correct spelling is *rectify*.

65. c. The correct spelling is *deteriorating*.

66. a. *Susceptible* means *vulnerable* or *at risk*.

67. c. *Inevitable* means *unavoidable*, so *avoidable* is its opposite.

68. b. *Pompous* means *stuck up* and *snobbish*, so *humble* is its opposite.

69. b. *Reciprocate* means *to repay*. The speaker in the sentence offers to repay a favor with a similar favor, so *reciprocate* is the best word for the blank. *Renege* (choice **a**) means *to go back on your work*. *Rejuvenate* (choice **c**) means *to modernize*.

70. a. *Incriminating* means *suggesting guilt*. Fingerprints on a murder weapon are definitely *incriminating* evidence. *Exonerating* (choice **b**) means *suggesting innocence*, which is the opposite of *incriminating*. *Dubious* (choice **c**) means *doubtful*.

71. b. Choices **a** and **c** consist of dependent clauses only, so they are not complete sentences.

72. a. Because the statement *Would you prefer sugar or artificial sweetener in your coffee* is a direct quote, it must be in quotation marks. Thus, choice **b** is incorrect. Because this statement is a question, it must end in a question mark. The entire sentence, however, is not a question; it is a statement of fact reporting what Humphrey asked. Thus, the sentence should not end in a question mark. Choice **c** ends in a question mark and is, therefore, incorrect.

73. c. The phrase *located along the railroad tracks* is a modifier describing *the community theater*. Choice **a** incorrectly states that it is *the noise of* *passing trains* rather than *the community theater* that is located along the tracks. Choice **b** is awkwardly and confusingly constructed; choice **c**, the correct answer, demonstrates how to express the same ideas much more clearly.

74. a. Choices **b** and **c** contain capitalization errors. In both, the word *Day* should be capitalized. In choice **b**, the word *Mrs.* should be capitalized. In choice **c**, the word *picnic* should not be capitalized.

75. a. The subject of the sentence is *each member*, which takes a singular verb. Therefore, choices **b** and **c**, in which the subject takes the plural verb *hold*, are incorrect.

76. b. Choices **a** and **c** include punctuation errors. In choice **a**, the words *boys* and *girls* should not take apostrophes because they are not used in the plural possessive form. In both choices **a** and **c**, the word *it's* should take an apostrophe because it is a contraction (meaning *it is*).

77. c. Each of the incorrect answers is written in the passive voice; the correct answer is written in the active voice, which is preferred.

78. c. *Committee* is a collective noun that takes a singular pronoun. Both incorrect choices use the plural pronoun *their* to refer to the committee.

79. a. The pronoun *their*, which appears in all three choices, tells you that the word *athletes* is plural rather than singular; therefore, the possessive form should be *athletes'* and choice **b** must be incorrect. There should be no apostrophe in the words *tests* and *performers*, so choice **c** is incorrect.

80. c. The phrase *consensus of opinion* is redundant; the word *consensus* means *unity of opinion*. Therefore, choices **a** and **b** are redundant. The term *free gift* in choice **a** is also redundant, because all gifts are free.

Section 3: Civil Service Skills

81. b. The correct term for this principle is *first contact resolution*.

82. c. The primary governing principle of customer service is to make things as easy and pleasant for the customer as possible. Choice **c** best articulates this principle. Each of the incorrect answers would result in an unnecessary delay in delivering service to the customer.

83. d. Once again, the correct answer reflects the need to place primary importance on the needs of citizens, the users of government services.

84. a. Choices **b** and **c** will almost certainly antagonize the customer, never a good idea when satisfying customer service is the goal. Choice **d** adds an unnecessary inconvenience and, therefore, will also probably annoy the customer. Only choice **a** reflects a "customer service first" attitude.

85. b. In general, the more accurate information you provide a customer, the better the customer's assessment of service will be. By informing customers of the approximate wait to speak with a representative, you allay their fears that they have been forgotten, that the call has been routed to a dead end, etc. Of course, some customers will be annoyed if the estimate turns out to be inaccurate, but not as annoyed as customers become when left on hold indefinitely with no idea of when they will ultimately be served.

86. a. Only one woman—the woman on the left—is holding a cell phone.

87. c. Both women have shoulder-length hair.

88. b. The vehicle is a cable car.

89. c. The notice states that "you should never attempt to extinguish a fire when . . . you cannot keep a clear path between yourself and the fire exit."

90. d. The notice simply states that people should not use the elevators; it does not explain the reasoning for this advice.

91. c. The first pair of digits in the code represent the employee's last name; the second pair represent the employee's first name. Marlene Romanoff's identification number should begin 54 (for the RO in Romanoff) 40 (for the MA in Marlene). Only choices **c** and **d** begin 5440; eliminate choices **a** and **b**. Job codes are a single letter; therefore, the two-letter job code AB that appears in choice **d** is incorrect. Choice **c** must be the correct answer by process of elimination.

92. a. Abdul Qoph's identification number should begin 54 (QO in Qoph) 00 (AB in Abdul). Eliminate choices **c** and **d**, which begin 0054. The code uses four digits to represent birthdays; therefore, choice **b** is incorrect. Choice **a** must be the correct answer by process of elimination.

93. d. This identification belongs to someone whose last name begins with the letter S, T, or U; the second letter in his last name is P, Q, or R. Only choices **c** and **d** meet this requirement; eliminate choices **a** and **b**. The employee's first name begins with the letter G, H, or I; this information allows you to eliminate choice **c**. The correct answer must be choice **d**.

94. b. The final four digits of the identification code represent the holder's birthday. The figures 1102 tell you that this employee's birthday is November 2.

95. c. The RO in Rodriguez is coded 54; the AL in Alexis is coded 03; the job grade 8 is coded H, because H is the eighth letter in the alphabet; the birthday September 22 is coded 0922. The correct identification number for Alexis Rodriguez is 5403H0922.

96. a. The rules of the code state, "The nature of complaint or complaints directly follows the code for the animal that is the subject of the complaint." Therefore, the code for a barking dog is D0 and the code for an improperly restrained horse is H1. The correct code for the incident described in the question is D0H1.

97. c. The code for a dog that is improperly fed and is not licensed is D23; the code for a cat that is not licensed is C3. The correct code for this incident is D23C3.

98. d. The code for a horse is H. The code for an abandoned animal is 5, and the code for improper food and water is 2. The code for this incident is H25.

99. c. The code Z refers to any animal other than a cat, dog, horse, or reptile. The code 5 refers to an abandoned animal. Thus, Z5 could refer to an abandoned pig.

100. b. The rules of the code state, "The nature of complaint or complaints directly follows the code for the animal that is the subject of the complaint." Therefore, the code for improper breeding of cats is C6; the code for improper breeding of dogs is D6, etc. The correct code for this incident is C6D6H6Z6.

Special FREE Offer from LearningExpress

LearningExpress will help you succeed on the civil service exam

 Go to the LearningExpress Practice Center at www.LearningExpressFreeOffer.com, an interactive online resource exclusively for LearningExpress customers.

Now that you've purchased LearningExpress's *Civil Service Exams*, you have **FREE** access to:

- **A full-length civil service practice test** that mirrors official civil service exams
- **Multiple-choice questions covering** memory, customer service, coding, math, reading comprehension, spelling, vocabulary, and grammar skills!
- **Immediate scoring** and **detailed answer explanations**
- Benchmark your skills and focus your study with our **customized diagnostic report**

Follow the simple instructions on the scratch card in your copy of *Civil Service Exams*. Use your individualized access code found on the scratch card and go to www.LearningExpressFreeOffer.com to sign in. Start practicing online for the civil service exam right away!

Once you've logged on, use the spaces below to write in your access code and newly created password for easy reference:

Access Code: _____   Password: _____